GLOBAL CHANGE

KEITH SUTER

GLOBAL CHANGE

ARMAGEDDON AND THE NEW WORLD ORDER

AN ALBATROSS BOOK

Published in Australia and New Zealand by
Albatross Books Pty Ltd
PO Box 320, Sutherland
NSW 2232, Australia
in the United States of America by
Albatross Books
PO Box 131, Claremont
CA 91711, USA
and in the United Kingdom by
Lion Publishing plc
Peter's Way, Sandy Lane West
Littlemore, Oxford OX4 5HG, England

First edition 1992

National Library of Australia
Cataloguing-in-Publication data

Suter, Keith D.
Global Change

ISBN 0 86760 135 3 (Albatross)
ISBN 0 7459 2191 4 (Lion)

1. United Nations. 2. International relations. 3. Progress
International Corporation. 4. Human rights. I. Title

327.17

Cover and interior illustrations: Michael Mucci
Printed and bound by The Book Printer, Victoria

Contents

PART C: *The new global warfare*

Acknowledgements

This work has its origins in two books I wrote in the mid-1980s around the time of the fortieth anniversary of the United Nations in 1985. In 1986, the International Year of the Peace (IYP), I went to Perth, Western Australia to work in the Trinity Peace Research Institute, Australia's first privately-funded peace research centre, set up by the Trinity Parish of the Uniting Church as its contribution to IYP.

Trinity enabled me to carry out the further research and overseas travel required for this book. I am most grateful to them for that opportunity. I am also grateful to Myrilla Radnedge, Lynda Langton-Smith, Jeanette Beer and Sue Willgoss for their secretarial assistance, and to John Waterhouse for his encouragement in this project. Ken Goodlet has been a fine and persistent editor — I am pleased to acknowledge all his work.

PART A:

The new global reality

1

THE NEW WORLD ORDER

Where do we go from here?

IT IS OUR GREAT GOOD FORTUNE to be living at this remarkable time. We have been destined to live in an age of momentous change. We are people about whom the history books will be written in a century's time.

THE HINGE OF HISTORY
We are living on the hinge of history. One era is ending and another is swinging into existence.

But what form will the new era take? It will have both global and individual lifestyle characteristics.

Some books provide hints and techniques which can be offered by Christians or environmentalists or feminists or 'peaceful' parents for individual action on these lifestyle issues — writing to newspapers, keeping files for information, forming pressure groups, lobbying politicians, running for parliament, sitting in front of bulldozers.

This book, by contrast, deals with the other end of modern problems: global changes in technology, law, economics and warfare. It provides the backdrop against which individuals need to make decisions about their own lifestyles. In particular, it is concerned about the phrase 'new world order' which is becoming a part — albeit a vague one — of the international political vocabulary.

By way of introduction in this chapter we'll explore the term 'new world order' and ways of thinking about the future. We shall then explore the Armageddon debate and suggest a new way of thinking about it in chapter 2. Chapter 3 focuses on Alvin Toffler's book, *The Third Wave*. He argues that the world, having gone through the agricultural and industrial revolutions, is undergoing a third one: technological. Although I have some doubts about Toffler's interpretation of history, I regard his book as one of the best ways of trying to understand the change we see all around us.

Chapters 4 to 9 deal with changes in government, the United Nations, international economics, and people power and warfare. Chapter 10 draws these threads together and provides a set of ideas for establishing values that we can carry with us into a new world order.

We shall begin our painting on the broad canvas of this big picture by looking first, then, at the term 'the new world order'.

THE NEW WORLD ORDER

The first important consideration is the relative economic decline of the US. In July 1988, an editorial in the *Australian* commented on the then current speculation of the decline of the US compared with the emerging economic powers:

> The US is not suffering from imperial overstretch. Rather by its
> idealistic assumption of a limited global role after World War II, it

has created a stable world order in which unprecedented prosperity among the trading nations has developed. The success of Japan, West Germany and the dragon economies of South-East Asia is a tribute to that stability.

The essence of the new world order should be that newly rich trading nations must shoulder what might appear to them to be more than their share of contributing to world stability, relieving the costs to those who are from a military point of view trying to keep the world at peace.[1]

The US may not be overcommitted — I happen to believe it is — but it is certainly no longer the economic giant it was only forty-five years ago.

The second important consideration is the end of Soviet control over Eastern Europe that took place in 1989. Mikhail Gorbachev, who came to power in 1985, began a process that, within only four years, was running well beyond his control. *Perestroika* (restructuring) and *glasnost* (openness) became catchcries around the world. Veteran European journalist Edward Mortimer found 1989 one of the most memorable years of his life — the ending of Soviet control over Eastern Europe:

Mikhail Gorbachev may have started his revolution from above with the idea of renovating communism, but in 1989 it has turned into an anti-communist revolution from below. The 'universal human values', whose paramountcy Gorbachev has acknowledged since 1987, turn out to be essentially the ideals long proclaimed by the West in the teeth of Soviet contempt: human rights and liberties, pluralism, tolerance of dissent. Even the free market and private property are now admitted to be indispensable components of economic salvation. The Cold War is ending not through the emergence of a 'third way' or synthesis between the rival systems, but with a hands-down ideological victory for the West.[2]

November 1990 saw the official end of the Cold War. Thirty-four nations from Europe and North America had their key meeting of the Conference on Security and Co-operation in Europe (CSCE). Ironically, the CSCE came into being at the agitation of the Soviet Union in 1972, chiefly as a means of ensuring the international recognition of East Germany. When the representatives of the two German states sat down together in Helsinki, they were joined by thirty-three other nations who had become involved in the negotiations. In 1975, these thirty-five leaders signed the Helsinki declaration or 'final act', which included key provisions on human rights. This document had a vital impact. Although it was not a treaty, it committed the nations of the communist bloc to recognise the rights of opposition groups, and inspired dissident groups in Eastern Europe.

The steady emergence of a culture of human rights in Eastern Europe was the essential condition for the political revolution that burst upon the continent in 1989. In this strange way, the formal proceedings of an international conference were transmuted into a potent moral force.

The 1990 sequel to the 1975 conference agreed on military reductions throughout Europe. After all, since the USSR was out of Eastern Europe, there was also far less need for military forces in Western Europe. Indeed, Western Europe's new worry was not an invasion of military forces, but a tide of refugees fleeing the USSR as it continued its descent into chaos and famine. What had begun in 1972, then, as a Soviet push for international recognition of the separate nation of East Germany ended in 1990 with both East Germany absorbed into West Germany and the USSR pushed out of the rest of Eastern Europe.

1991 continued the pace of change. The USSR itself dissolved and was replaced by the fragile Commonwealth of Independent States (CIS). President Gorbachev found himself without a nation to govern. But during his brief six years in power, he proved himself to be one of the most important world leaders of this century.

The ending of the Cold War is one of the twentieth century's main developments. Most of the world's population, by being born since 1945, have known only a Cold War world.

The Cold War was the central defining event of international politics between 1945 and 1990. Even the language of politics reflects the Cold War: the First World are nations loyal to the USA, the Second World were nations loyal to Moscow and the Third World — mainly in Africa and Asia — tried to avoid becoming entangled in the struggles between Washington and Moscow. The Second World has gone; it wants to join the First World — how, then, can there be a 'Third' world?

We will look back to the 1945 to 1990 period with a sense of nostalgia — everything seemed clear then. A nation knew where it stood. The post-Cold War world is one of shifting alliances, internal conflicts, regional disputes and the growing importance of economic power over military power.

But these political changes — dramatic in themselves — are only the tip of the iceberg. In a similar way, big changes are also taking place in technology, international law, public administration and economics.

This book tries to make sense of all the changes taking place. They may *seem* chaotic — but there is a pattern behind them. Forecasting helps us to perceive these patterns.

THE FASCINATING ART OF FORECASTING

Everyone is interested in forecasting. Purchasing a new house, arranging annual holidays, superannuation and pension systems are all examples of personal forecasting which each person is obliged to do. Movies such as *Star Wars* and *The Alien* involve viewers in forecasting in so far as they suggest future ways of living. Some writers, such as H.G. Wells (*The World Set Free*, *The Shape of Things to Come* and *The New World Order*) and George Orwell (*1984*), encouraged readers to look into the future. Indeed, both writers have had a better success rate on forecasting than 'professional' forecasters.

In *The World Set Free*, for example, H.G. Wells predicted the use of atomic bombs at a time when scientists thought atomic bombs impossible; he was about thirty years ahead of the scientists.[3] George Orwell also has, in a macabre sense, done well, scoring by 1978 over a hundred predictions that had come true — lotteries run by government, books written by computer, the construction of helicopter gunships, three-dimensional effects in art, machines that translate voice into print, and the merging of gender identities.[4]

Professional forecasters — 'futurologists' — have long figured in history. For example, Amos, an eighth century BC shepherd, is recorded in the Old Testament as correctly warning the newly enriched ruling elite that, despite their apparent wealth and national security, hard times were on the way. He predicted the destruction of Israel at a time when everything seemed to be going well.

Western social scientists — a status we give them, not necessarily one they would have claimed for themselves — have for several centuries mixed their visions for the future with optimistic forecasts, so that it is always impossible to distinguish what they actually foresaw from what they hoped for. Saint-Simon, Adam Smith, Karl Marx and Auguste Comte are examples.[5]

During the 1960s and 1970s, forecasting was put on a more scientific — though not necessarily more efficacious — level. The extension of Western governmental control into the economic and social life of their nations prompted governments to devise national plans, a policy started in the Soviet Union soon after the 1917 Revolution. The development of computers enabled social scientists to devise, as never before, complicated 'scenarios' and alternative models. Concern for the future was heightened by the environmental, energy and economic crises of the 1970s. Between 1965 and 1976 a wide variety of forecasts were made, ranging from predictions of eco-catastrophe to near-utopia around the corner.[6] It is not our purpose here, however, to review those predictions. Instead, let us look at the limits to forecasting.

THE LIMITS OF FORECASTING

The limits are identified not so much to dismiss or discourage forecasting entirely, but simply to throw additional light on forecasting itself and why caution is needed in heeding forecasters' advice.

1. *There is a lack of data.*

Within the Australian context, for example, there is no agreement on the total number of people unemployed. Even the Australian government publishes two sets of official figures. Social workers believe that the true number is much higher, since the official figures often exclude persons who have given up hope of finding jobs. A global example of a similar type is the varying estimates of how much fossil fuel the world has left and how many fish live in the ocean. If we do not know where we have been, how are we to know where we are going?

A more general problem is that there remains a lack of agreement on how the world does in fact change. Social scientists are still not agreed over what laws — if any — govern economic, political and social changes. Only a handful of social scientists will attempt to devise overarching theories; the rest are researching more and more into smaller and smaller aspects of human affairs. Added to this, natural and physical scientists, who once felt so secure with their explanations, are also developing methodological problems. They now have many of their accepted explanations challenged by new data.

2. *Trends are not necessarily destiny.*

There is a tendency to rely on linear extrapolation so that the future is assumed to follow in the same direction as contemporary situations. Forecasters know that their children's height does not continue in this way after a certain age, but they often assume that society will:

> Thus, for example, the visionaries who put together the 1939 World Fair in New York made grand predictions of the advent of picture phones — telephones that enable callers to see each other. They were right about the technology, but wrong in the assumption that once the invention was available, people would automatically want it.
>
> Some students of American leisure at the end of the 1950s predicted that a new vacation thrill of the '60s would be safaris through Vietnam — a forecast that could be greeted with only the blackest humour just a few war-torn years later. Similarly, most prognosticators at the end of the 1960s failed dismally to foresee the quadrupling of crude oil prices and the advent of the energy crisis — arguably the most significant events of the past decade. Year after year, economists have misread the inflationary state of the US economy. And the weatherman continues to be a national joke.[7]

Someone looking into the future from, say, 1910 would probably not have seen in only eighty years the following developments: two world wars (even H.G. Wells predicted only one), the collapse of all

European empires, access to radio receivers by almost every human in the world, the deterioration of most of the world's major currencies, the revival of Islam, the establishment and then collapse of communism for over half the world's population, nuclear energy, the abolition of most monarchies, and the enhanced status of women.

On the contrary, the world of 1910 looked very comfortable for the world's ruling elite. The risk of war between France and the UK had declined, though imperial rivalries remained in Africa and German militarism was causing worries. However, the world from a European point of view looked good and people expected it to get better. Even communist revolutionaries saw no immediate chance of assuming power in any country.

3. *It is difficult to predict major pattern shifts.*

A forecaster would have been inaccurate if he or she had thought that the two world wars were such pattern, or paradigm shifts. However highly significant for political and social purposes, they have left no trace in the economic statistics for the period 1913 to 1968. As American management expert Peter Drucker says, 'The tremendous economic expansion throughout the industrial world in the last two decades [to 1968] has by and large only made up for the three decades of stagnation between the two world wars. And the expansion has in the main been confined to nations that were at least rapidly advancing.'[8]

Further, the dissolution of European empires partly as a result of the world wars has given rise to neocolonialism so that developing countries are still tied economically to their former colonial masters. But looked at in terms of social and political consequences, the two wars were among the most significant events of this century.

What of the paradigm effect of the energy crisis of the 1970s? The OPEC price increases were seen as a major development in the UN's

New International Economic Order (NIEO) work, as first laid down in the 1974 UN General Assembly Special Session. The OPEC increases were not predicted by forecasters in the 1960s, who seemed to regard cheap energy as a common assumption, so their forecasts were wrong. The situation is being ignored by many drivers who reluctantly pay the extra costs and do nothing to decrease their reliance upon cars, so forecasts of a drop in reliance on oil have also proved faulty.

Life is changed as much by paradigm shifts as by gradual improvements or deteriorations. But paradigm shifts are difficult to forecast and people are often reluctant to believe them anyway because they could represent major changes to their way of living.

There are others who do accept the predicted paradigm shift, but disagree over its significance. In the case of the 1973 OPEC oil crisis, it could be argued that the increases, though traumatic, have at least forced the world into realising that cheap oil is not here forever and that the world should use the crisis constructively by treating it as an inducement to develop better energy sources.[9]

It is ironical that now, when we are living in such a difficult time to produce accurate predictions, we are so interested in forecasting. It would have been much easier in the century prior to 1970 when change was taking place on a more regular basis. We are interested in forecasting at the worst possible time. Indeed, the world is changing so quickly that it is hard enough to describe even the present situation in general terms. If we do not know where we are, how are we to know where we are going?

4. *Being right once is no guarantee of further success.*
The crucial factor here is not correct prediction but correct method. A prediction can be correct simply by guesswork. It is much more difficult to ascertain whether a person's technique is a suitable basis for forecasting. This in part explains the controversy in the early 1970s

over *The Limits to Growth* study[10] since some commentators were concerned less by the team's pessimistic findings than by its methods.

In order to illustrate both this problem and the way in which it is not limited to social scientists armed with expensive computers, it is useful to look at the example of Winston Churchill. Churchill has come down in history as one of the first people to warn the UK about Hitler and the need for a massive rearmament program. But throughout the 1920s and 1930s he was seen by his contemporaries as a brilliant man who lacked judgment. He was wrong over the Duke of Windsor and Mrs Simpson (he opposed the abdication), opposed limited self-government for India in the 1930s and helped damage the British economy by returning the UK to the Gold Standard when he was Chancellor of the Exchequer (1925). By the late 1930s, most people were sceptical of his statements.[11]

There are always leaders within the community who warn us about various problems. It is easy to see in retrospect who was right. But, like the British in the late 1930s, we can never be sure of who will, in fact, be correct in their predictions.

The success rate of all futurologists is dismal. I have already mentioned the way in which the 1973 OPEC oil price increases surprised everyone, as did the Vietnam War and the US's defeat. Among other surprises have been the entry of women into the US workforce; the combination of industrial stagnation and inflation – 'stagflation' (which apparently should not exist according to economic theory); the improvement of US-China relations in 1972; the rise of the Third World power bloc in international relations; the collapse of the Shah of Iran's regime in 1979; and the Islamic revival. And no-one predicted the rapid growth of futurology. Few are willing to predict its future!

To conclude this observation, two decades ago Patrick Moynihan, a US sociologist, public servant and senator, made a prediction which few accepted at the time (partly because it seemed so odd and, anyway, Moynihan was not among the elite band of professional futurologists). Events have not only proved him correct, but have thereby shown that amateur futurologists may have as good a batting record as the professionals:

> I'd like to state that most of the events that tore American society almost apart, or so it seemed in the 1960s, arose from conditions unique to the decade in which they occurred. They had not ever existed before. They will not ever exist again. . .
>
> I'm going to say to you that the 1960s saw a profound demographic change occur in American society which was a onetime change, a growth in population vaster than any that had ever occurred before or any that will ever occur again, with respect to a particular subgroup in the population, namely, those persons fourteen to twenty-four years of age. This sudden increase in population interacted in a synergistic sense with a whole series of other events which originate, if you will, in the world of ideas, as distinct from the physical world in which populations increase or decrease.
>
> In the best known example of the 1960s, people changed their minds about the requirements of justice and decent public policy concerning minority groups in American society at just the moment when the size and location of those groups were dramatically changing. But this was not the only change. People changed their minds about this, they changed their minds about that, and they changed their minds at just the point when the physical conditions of life, the ecological facts of how many people are around and where they are were also changing. These changes interacted in such a way as to produce extraordinary differences — discontinuities — with the period immediately preceding and which I think will now be seen to be discontinuous with the period that now follows. . .

I think I would predict a more 'conservative' society simply on the ground that a society whose population is barely growing tends to be curiously straightened and strict in its behaviour. I make no claim to any 'scientific' evidence on this point (although I don't know why we can't study the question). I speak more from literary sources. If I had been asked ten years ago whom to read to find out what American life was like, or was going to be like, I would unhesitatingly have said 'Read Mark Twain'. Mark Twain mostly tells the truth, as Huck Finn said in the opening lines of that book. He had a great sense of the ebullience, the growth, the prospects, the limitless energy and potential of this great and endless country.

I don't think I would say 'Read Mark Twain' today. I think I would advise a young person to read Balzac. Find out what it's like to live in a society where if you want to be a professor, you wait until the man who is professor dies. Then the fifteen of you who want the job compete in various ways. One of you gets it. The rest hope for the best for their sons. And you won't have had many sons; you'll only have two, as it were. This doesn't mean you have a less turbulent society or a society sated with social conservatism. Ideological radicalism is just likely. The French indeed have a phrase for it: 'Think left, live right.' I am inclined to think we're going to see a lot of both.[12]

5. *A great deal still depends upon each forecaster's stance.*
While a forecaster may have recourse to extensive data, computers and governments, there are still opportunities for the gaps or conflicting data to be decided by that person's own values. Herman Kahn's Hudson Institute, responsible for much recent pioneering work in forecasting, customarily takes an optimistic view of the future. A Hudson Institute study[13] of the period of 1775 to 2175 sees 1950 to 1990

as four decades of rapid worldwide economic and population growth, initial emergence of super-industrial economies, with technological crises and many historic transitions. 1990 to 2025 will see the emergence of post-industrial economies in most Western and some Asian countries and the (former) Soviet Union, and first signs of a worldwide maturing economy. 2025 to 2175 will see a worldwide slowing down in population and economic growth rates.

Another report, published at the same time by the Organization for Economic Co-operation and Development (OECD)[14] — the club of Western rich nations — took a more sombre view of the future. Kahn advised rich Western governments and so was biased in their favour. The OECD, while composed of these governments and so hardly at variance with them, does focus more attention on the needs of poorer countries and the importance of helping the less well-off nations. But the fact that it remains a document advising Western governments on how best to look after their interests means it is not likely to be all that pessimistic. A group of Western ecologists, however, with no governmental ties, took a more alarmist view of the future and urged a drastic alteration to lifestyle.[15] You pay your money and you take your choice.

6. *People often ignore warnings.*

People's concerns are largely based on the next twenty-four hours. Logic would suggest that world dependence on oil prior to 1973 would have encouraged plans for alternative measures. Oil had suddenly become the West's number one fuel around 1950 or even later. For the period prior to 1973, the West had control over oil and kept it at an artificially low price — the US with only six per cent of the world's population consumed about thirty per cent of the world's total energy output at a cost of only four per cent of US GNP. The West (including Japan) went on an energy binge which resulted in highly inefficient cars and architecture, the virtual destruction of public transport systems, and a downgrading of coal production.

All good things have to come to an end. The hangover commenced in October 1973 when the Organisation of Petroleum Exporting Countries (OPEC) could exploit the West's over-dependence on oil and the new shortage of oil. Overnight, OPEC stopped the Arabian and Iranian 'development aid' to the West by both taking control of their own resources and by, in true Western style, charging what the market would bear.

For this reason alone, then, the world can never return to the affluence of the 1950/60s; there simply is not the oil for it. But cheap oil did more than turn the West into oiloholics; it discouraged the development of alternative energy for when the oil suddenly increased in price. Some people could see the need to develop alternative energy sources but, like eighth century BC Amos, they were not taken seriously because the present situation was apparently so good. Such failure to follow the logic of preparing for a crisis is difficult to predict and this makes forecasting tricky.

7. *People do at times heed the warnings and*
   so they take evasive action.

This is clearly now the case with the renewed attempt at ending the arms race. Various forces — the peace movement worldwide, the growing awareness of the fragile preciousness of our earth, a growing awareness of the indecisiveness of modern warfare — have seen to that.

THE VALUE OF FORECASTING

If forecasting is so unreliable, why worry about it?

1. *The future is all that is left so we should make of it what we can.*

It is not my task to predict exactly what people will do in the future, but rather to help people to understand the possibilities of the future so that a better world can be created. In other words, there is a need to move away from the tendency to wait upon events — to do something when the situation arises — and to promote actively the circumstances favourable to the success of one's visions.

2. *By focussing on the future we can see the 'big picture' changes taking place.*

There is a tendency in human affairs to become so focussed on today's events that we fail to see these changes. Winston Churchill, for example, in World War II, focussed his attention not only on the current enemy (Germany), but also on the risk of a new enemy (the USSR) — but his US allies were too focussed on only beating Germany. Harold Macmillan, one of Churchill's wartime colleagues, recalled a November 1943 conversation with Churchill:

> In an after-dinner conversation, Churchill remarked to Macmillan that Cromwell was a great man, but 'he made one fatal error. Born and bred in fear of Spain — Spain was claiming and holding the hegemony of the world — he failed to see in the decline of Spain the rise of France — Richelieu, Mazarin: hence Louis XIV, hence the Marlborough wars, hence the long struggle for Europe. Will that be said of me?'
>
> With this appeal to his sense of history, Macmillan knew exactly what Churchill meant. Hitler was already beaten; but what sort of threat would the victorious Russians — with whom 'our American friends' were at that moment rather obsessed — present in the post-war world? The problem at the end of 1943 was how

far the Soviet imperialism would stretch, and how to keep it as far away as possible to the east.[16]

Ironically, for the period from 1945 to well into the 1980s, the US was so focussed on the threat from the USSR, that it failed to pay enough attention to the rise of Japan!

3. *A focus on the future encourages prudence.*

That focus — rather than prediction — should be the aim.

As noted earlier, humans are prudent — when planning holidays and pension schemes, for example. Since our planning encourages prudence in our personal lives, it is likely to do so if we plan the future of the planet's life.

4. *Statements about the future are staple items in politics and the mass media and need to be scrutinised.*

This scrutiny should be aimed at separating statements that will bring an immediate return from those that have our long-term interests in mind. Indeed, the difference between a 'politician' and a 'statesperson' is that a politician is concerned about scoring small points today, while a statesperson sees their main constituency as the next generation.

There is much talk in Australia and many other nations about the 'troubled future'. But what visions — or goals — do the leaders actually have of the future? Too much debate is focussed on daily practicalities — interest rates, balances of payments, levels of government expenditure and schemes for combating crime. Leaders are not challenged nearly enough to provide the 'big picture' of where they are taking — or would like to take — the nation.

5. *We are made wise, not by the recollections of our past, but by our responsibility for the future.*

This does not mean that we should ignore history — on the contrary, part of Winston Churchill's genius was derived from his ability to think through his memory. Consequently we need to study history not so much as a guide to the future (to learn the 'lessons of history'), but to understand the present. For example, ethnic groups have their own histories and a study of these histories would help explain some of the turbulence in Eastern Europe today and the continued instability in most African nations.

6. *Those with a values-related agenda have the potential to shape a better world.*

The Christian church, for example, could do much. Its record however, is not good. The church (especially in Europe) largely allowed the Industrial Revolution to pass it by. The ethical teaching of the eighteenth century church was based on over fifteen centuries of service to rural communities. In many ways that teaching is still unchanged, although the needs of people working in industry's many repetitive jobs and living in today's competitive society are very different. As crises arose, the church made attempts to cope with some of the major issues, the early years of trade unionism being a notable example. But there was no understanding of how the Christian faith might be worked out in practice to address the Industrial Revolution.

The church is in danger of 'missing the boat' again, in the face of the new revolution which is taking place. If the Christian mission in the year 2000 and beyond is to encompass justice for the whole creation, the churches, which have generally found it easier to address injustice on an individual and personal level, will need to give increasing attention to the underlying causes of injustice. A shift towards this approach will require education on a wide range of complex matters involving economics, science, law and public policy. The church has often found this kind of education to be difficult and divisive; nonetheless, it must be done, or the world will lose the benefit of the input of many who put values first.

7. There is a need to investigate the underlying causes of the new revolution — and not just its symptoms.

Various books have been published dealing with ideas for individual actions, such as how to live peaceful, ecologically sound and economically frugal lifestyles. But there is far less attention being given to the global backdrop against which individuals are being encouraged to adopt new lifestyles.

FAITH IN THE FUTURE

This book is one Christian's perspective on present global trends. It is not the only Christian view of these trends. Nor is it written only for a Christian audience. Since all writing is subjective — each author makes their own decisions about what is included or excluded from the books — it is necessary to share with readers my own perspective; to indicate 'where I am coming from'.

1. I believe the earth belongs to God.

The central conviction that runs right through the Bible is that 'the earth is the Lord's and all that is in it, the world, and those who live in it' (Psalm 24, verse 1) and that 'the Lord is the everlasting God, the Creator of the ends of the earth' (Isaiah 40, verse 28). The Bible affirms that God is the Creator of the whole universe.

God created the earth out of a formless void (Genesis 1, verse 2), separated the sea from the dry land, planted natural vegetation upon the land and gave the power of life to the natural environment. God created men and women and gave them life and 'dominion over the fish of the sea and the birds of the air and over every living thing', and also gave them 'every plant yielding seed which is upon the face of all the earth' (Genesis 1, verses 26 and 29).

2. *I believe in the Bible's teaching that God created humans to live within a moral order.*

Injustice, oppression, lies and deceit are all roundly condemned throughout scripture. They are seen as the kind of behavioural traits that act as corrupting forces in society. God reminds his people time and again that it is not possible to turn the moral code of the universe upside down without suffering the direst consequences. The human race is doing just that.

As journalist Philip Kay points out in dramatic journalese, humanity is destroying God's creation:

> Planet earth is 4 600 million years old.
>
> If we condense this inconceivable time-span into an understandable concept, we can liken earth to a person of forty-six years of age.
>
> Nothing is known about the first seven years of this person's life and, whilst only scattered information exists about the middle span, we know that only at the age of forty-two did the earth begin to flower.
>
> Dinosaurs and the great reptiles did not appear until one year ago, when the planet was forty-five. Mammals arrived only eight months ago; in the middle of last week man-like apes evolved into ape-like men; and at the weekend the last ice age enveloped the earth.
>
> Modern man has been around for four hours. During the last hour man discovered agriculture. The Industrial Revolution began a minute ago.

During those sixty seconds of biological time, modern man has made a rubbish tip of paradise.

He has multiplied his numbers to plague proportions, caused the extinction of 500 species of animals, ransacked the planet for fuels and now stands like a brutish infant, gloating over this meteoric rise to ascendancy, on the brink of a war to end all wars and of effectively destroying this oasis of life in the solar system.[17]

3. *I believe we should put our faith in God and not in machines, institutions or human beings.*

Human beings (and consequently their machines and institutions) are flawed by their fallen nature.

4. *I believe it is our responsibility to keep working for justice and peace.*

James Callaghan (British Prime Minister from 1976 to 1979) set out his philosophy in this way:

There will never be final answers so long as mortal man is fallible, but the satisfaction of a political life lies in searching for the solutions. Democratic politics is more than manipulation, and leadership more than the efficient management of affairs. In a civilised society both rest on ethics and on consent.[18]

5. *Christian witness is more than just individual moral rectitude.*

Such witness requires a forthright proclamation of religious values and their relevance to the political, social and economic conditions that shape our lives. Our faith requires us to exercise a commitment which addresses not only personal sin, but also the systemic ills of institutions and governments — 'to speak truth to power' as the prophet

Nathan did to King David. Christians need, therefore, to examine the structures of the society in which they live.

Australian 'bikie evangelist' John Smith made this point in the context of explaining the often-misunderstood remark by Jesus that there will always be poor people:

> In fact, Jesus was quoting from the Old Testament book of Deuteronomy, in a section on the social and economic laws to be observed by the people of Israel. The passage Jesus referred to starts by saying, 'Not one of your people will be poor if you obey [God] and carefully observe everything that I command you today.' Among the laws he alluded to was one which instructed, 'Do not charge interest on a loan to a poor person.' But later, in a very human understanding of the way things work out in reality, the Old Testament writer continued, 'There will always be some Israelites who are poor and in need, and so I command you to be generous to them.'
>
> In other words, if they obeyed God's commands, which demanded fairness and generosity, it was possible to eliminate poverty. The passage implies that poverty in Israel was a direct result of their failure to live by those principles. This puts what Jesus had to say in a new light and makes sense of Jesus' own total commitment to the sick, poor and rejected people of his own day. It warns that poverty is not simply personal in its cause. It is structural. Unjust social structures institutionalise poverty and powerlessness.[19]

6. *While all this good work is being done, there is a need for individual integrity and determination to follow principles of reason, justice and compassion.*

Sir Brian Urquhart, a senior United Nations official for four decades, has set out his views (which I endorse) in this way:

> Reason, justice and compassion are small cards to play in the
> world of politics, whether international, national or tribal, but some-
> one has to go on playing them. If you hold on to your belief in
> reason and compassion despite all political manoeuvering, your ef-
> forts may in the end produce results. A determined effort to do
> what seems objectively right may sometimes eventually transcend
> the vicissitudes of politics.[20]

7. *I believe humans are meant to live in a community —* *both locally and globally.*

Local society is not a box of marbles; it is a honeycomb, an intricate
net of relationships. The basis of society is not the individual; it is
relationships. For who is the individual? He is John and Mary's son,
Jane's husband, Richard's father and Eric's workmate. There is also
the global community, where all humans are sisters and brothers of the
one father, God.

Patricia Mische (of the New York-based Global Education Associates) has challenged fellow Christians to acknowledge that
underlying sense of human unity through Christ:

> Christ stood outside the structures of dominance and in doing so il-
> luminated the basis of a truly new world order: not power over
> the other, but standing in relationship with the other.
>
> He stood with the sinners, the crippled, the lepers, the 'foreigners',
> the poor, the hungry, the women, the humble fisherfolk. All these
> were in one way or another the 'untouchables' of society, those living
> on the underside of dominance. And he witnessed that all were im-
> portant, all were sacred. All were part of a Love and Power that had
> nothing to do with military, social or economic supremacy, but had

everything to do with reconciliation, forgiveness, doing justice, peacemaking and the love of God and each other.

What seemed logical and acceptable in the constructs of the power paradigm — that is, war, injustice, division, hatred of perceived enemies — became illogical in the new world paradigm exemplified in Christ. Were not all one in the Father, all branches of one vine, members of one body, sharing life in one Spirit?[21]

Thus we end where we began: thinking about the 'big picture' — a new world order. My commitment is to work for a Christian world order. But before I can make recommendations in the last chapter about how that work could be done, I need first to look at the speculation over Armageddon in the next chapter and the likely form that a world order is taking in chapters 3 onwards.

Endnotes:

1. 'The Post-Imperial New World Order', *Australian*, 16 July 1988
2. Edward Mortimer, 'A Turning Point in Europe's History', *Tablet*, 6 January 1990
3. William Irwin Thompson, *Passages about Earth*, Rider, 1975, pp.56–57
4. David Goodman, 'Countdown to 1984: Big Brother May Be Right on Schedule', *Futurist* (Washington DC), December 1978, pp.345–355
5. For a controversial examination of their views, see Krishan Kumar, *Prophecy and Progress: The Sociology of Industrial and Post-Industrial Society*, Penguin, 1978.
6. See Sam Cole, 'The Global Futures Debate 1965–1978', in *World Futures: The Great Debate*, Christopher Freeman and Marie Jahoda (eds), Martin Robertson, 1978, pp.9–49. Within the Australian context, there are also wide views, such as *Australia 2025*, Electrolux, 1975 and Patrick Tennison, *Heyday or Doomsday? Australia 2000*, Hill of Content, 1977
7. Merrill Sheils, 'The Cracked Crystal Ball', *Newsweek*, 19 November 1979
8. Peter F. Drucker, *The Age of Discontinuity*, Heinemann, 1969, p.3
9. For example, John Maddox, *Beyond the Energy Crisis*, Hutchinson, 1975
10. D. Meadows et al., *The Limits to Growth*, Universe, 1972
11. Robert Rhodes James, 'The Politician', in *Churchill: Four Faces and the Man*, Allen Lane, 1969, pp.93–108
12. Daniel P. Moynihan, 'Peace', in *Coping: Essays on the Practice of Government*, Random House, 1973, pp.422–429
13. Herman Kahn and John B. Phelps, 'The Economic Present and Future', *Futurist*, June 1979, pp.202–222
14. OECDE, *Interfutures, Final Report*, June 1979
15. 'A Blue print for Survival', *Ecologist*, January 1972
16. Alistair Horne, *Macmillan: 1884–1956*, Macmillan, 1988, p.205
17. Philip Kay, Editorial, *Adult Education News*, November 1989, p.3
18. James Callaghan, *Time and Chance*, Collins, 1987, p.566
19. John Smith, *On the Side of Angels*, Lion, 1987, p.140
20. Brian Urquhart, *A Life in Peace and War*, Weidenfeld and Nicholson, 1987, p.196
21. Patricia Mische, *Christian Voices on World Order*, Global Education Associates, 1978, pp.2–3

2

ARMAGEDDON

Are we at the end of time as we know it?

SPECULATION ABOUT ARMAGEDDON — the final cataclysmic battle between the forces of good and evil prophesied in the Bible — was a growth industry in the 1980s. This was based on the increased US-Soviet arms race and the chances of a World War III. This speculation declined in the late 1980s, thanks to progress on limiting the arms race.

However, just as we were about to relax, along came the 1990/1991 Gulf crisis. This was initiated by Iraq, whose capital of Baghdad is close to the old city of Babylon, the chief city of ancient Mesopotamia, the location of the hanging gardens, one of the ancient world's 'seven wonders' — a city which had an impact on Jews in Old Testament times, and notorious then for its luxury and corruption.

With the decline of the USSR, Iraq's sudden rise as the world's most sinister nation filled a gap in the world's thirst for demons. The world overlooked that for the past decade, the USSR, US, UK and smaller players like Australia had all supported Iraq in its war against Iran, a war which Iraq started. Iraq and Iran agreed on a truce, thereby enabling Iraq to feel secure on its eastern front, while it prepared for a war on its southern front.

The January/February 1991 war — billed by President Hussein as the 'mother of all wars' — turned out to be a showcase of US military might. However, the US won the war, but lost the peace. Iraq's future remains unclear — as does the US's long-term policy for the region. For example, if the US encourages or permits the fragmentation of Iraq, then a new power vacuum will be created — which will be filled by either Iran or Syria, neither of which is friendly to the US. What is clear, however, is that Iraq has been removed from the status of an Armageddon-initiating nation.

The new Armageddon industry is based on the destruction of the environment. 'Eco-catastrophe' speculations now include an enlarged hole in the ozone layer, the 'greenhouse effect', the melting of the polar icecaps, and a global population growing faster than global food production. In due course, this brand of alarmism will also disappear as progress is made in protecting the environment.

The tragedy in all these speculations about Armageddon is that there *is* a major change taking place in the world. It is not taking place in the way being predicted by all these doomsayers. Indeed, focussing on Armageddon is misleading: it encourages people to look for the wrong event — Armageddon — in the wrong place, usually the Middle East.

Chapters 3 to 9 deal with the emerging new world order. But before dealing with that subject, it is first necessary to look at the limitations of extracting from the Bible a strange way of interpreting the world: Armageddon theology. This is not a major strand in conventional Christian thinking. But unfortunately the mass media's love of doom and gloom stories has suggested that it is. This has been particularly so when linked to nuclear weapons and the Middle East.

I believe that Armageddon theology is not a satisfactory way of trying to understand the global changes currently under way, a point I shall argue in this chapter. Indeed, to follow Armageddon theology is to be diverted down side streets of conspiracy theories and alarmist fears.

Hal Lindsey is the best known advocate for Armageddon theology. I shall examine his two main books on this subject as well as a book by the Walvoords. All three are unsatisfactory. The decline of Armageddon theology is also examined, but since it taps into the feelings of insecurity that some people have, the decline is probably only temporary. The chapter ends with some suggestions for an alternative approach to Armageddon.

HAL LINDSEY AND ARMAGEDDON

Hal Lindsey is a best-selling author. He is in the vanguard of Christian authors seeking to compare certain biblical prophecies with contemporary events. One reason for his popularity is the strident tone with which he makes his predictions; he writes with great confidence and conviction.

His two main books, *The Late Great Planet Earth* and *The 1980s: Countdown to Armageddon*,[1] are very stimulating and a short summary cannot do them full justice. He takes as his starting point 14 May 1948, the date on which Israel was reborn as a nation-state. He sees that point as the beginning of the prophetic countdown. The other main actors are: the freshly reunited Arabs, the rise of the Soviet Union, the rise of China and the new European Economic Community (a revived Roman Empire).

In part of Matthew 24, verses 1 to 35, Jesus — in reply to questions about the end of the age — made not a specific prediction, but a general listing of events which would precede it. These events are taken up by Lindsey who identifies them as religious deception, international revolution, war, famines, earthquakes, plagues and strange events in the skies — unidentified flying objects. He arranges evidence to show how contemporary events conform to this pattern.

The reborn state of Israel is understood to be predicted, in parts of the Bible, as the centre of events that will lead to Armageddon. The Soviet Union, according to Lindsey, is moving south and communism is growing rapidly throughout the world. Meanwhile, according to Lindsey, the Chinese are moving west towards the Middle East. At the same time the new-found unity among the Arab states is making them stronger and more ambitious.

In Phase I, the Arabs attack Israel, which Lindsey claims is rich in key minerals. In Phase II the Soviet Union swoops through Israel and then in Phase III takes over some of the Arab states. The new Roman Empire will intervene to stop the aggression, as does China, thereby forcing the Soviet Union to regroup — this is Phase IV. The final battle takes place at Armageddon, Mount of Megiddo: Phase V. As the battle of Armageddon reaches its climax and it appears that all life on earth will be destroyed, at this very moment Jesus Christ will return and save humankind from self-extinction. This all makes gripping reading.

The two books are fascinating to read, the type publishers like to claim are impossible to put down until read. They no doubt appeal to readers who want a book which can somehow make sense of all the world's current confusing developments by putting them into a comprehensible pattern.

They are also evangelistic publications in that the main point is to argue the validity of the Bible as the key to understanding current events and to call upon readers to prepare themselves for Jesus' return. They appeal to readers who are troubled by contemporary events, and seek reassurance. They also, ironically, conform to the pattern, set by both the extreme Left and the extreme Right, of seeing many of the world's problems created by sinister US bankers, the United Nations and the Soviet Union all working together.

Lindsey in 1989 reaffirmed the points made in those two books:

In looking back over the nineteen years since *The Late Great Planet Earth* was written, virtually all the things that were anticipated in the book have emerged and fit into the prophetic scenario. The only major prophetic sign that is not yet visible is the appearance of the Antichrist and the False Prophet. But I do not believe they can be manifested until the church has been snatched out in the rapture.

With the European Economic Community's announcement that they will unify politically by 1992, the predicted revival of the old Roman Empire in the form of a ten-nation confederacy appears to be a possibility in the very near future. Once that is established, the Antichrist of Rome must appear and lead the confederacy to establish a world government. It is because of factors like these that I believe the rapture cannot be far off.[2]

Consequently, even though the original book is two decades old, the author himself still endorses his original views — and I am not therefore providing a critique of old material which has been subsequently rejected by its author.

However, I remain dissatisfied with the two books. There is no doubt at all that the earth is undergoing one of the most significant transformations ever seen. Agreeing that the earth is changing dramatically is not, however, the same as agreeing with Lindsey's books.

First, his scholarship is not always thorough. His errors vary from clear errors of fact, such as the rank of Neville Chamberlain and the date of his meeting with Hitler at Munich, to errors of interpretation, such as the use of erroneous figures to claim that the former Soviet Union was ahead in the arms race at the time he wrote. His strident views on Soviet aggression were not shared by all commentators even before the disintegration of the Soviet Union.

Second, there are some doubts as to Lindsey's five-phase scenario for World War III and the second coming. Despite Lindsey's claims about Israel's strategic importance, it has little military significance. It is one of the few Middle East nations with no oil reserves. It does not straddle a major line of communication (like the Suez Canal or Straits of Gibraltar). Israel is important politically to the United States because of the Jewish vote in US elections, though at the time of the 1956 United Kingdom/France/Israel invasion of the Suez Canal, President Eisenhower fought — and won — a presidential election supporting Egypt and so there is no guarantee that Israel is even politically important to the US. Economically, the US would be better off without supporting Israel, both because of the immense US foreign aid to Israel and because the oil exporting nations — especially Saudi Arabia — are far more important to the US.

Third, Lindsey provides a detailed forecast of military activities which is hard to believe. The Soviet Union, I agree, may have wanted to get into the Middle East. But I do not see how China will be able to deploy a large military force in the Middle East since it does not have the transportation. As for the new Roman Empire, the European Economic Community is not a military organisation. NATO is the western military organisation, but this includes two nations outside Europe — Canada and the United States — and France has a minimal military role in it. All these massive military manoeuvres may have made sense before 1945, but nuclear weapons have made these operations obsolete. The list could go on. But the main point is the lack of military sense in Lindsey's detailed predictions.

Fourth, Lindsey's interpretation of the 'rapture' (in which Christians on the eve of Armageddon will be swept up to heaven and so miss Armageddon) makes Christians vulnerable to satire. If the rapture were to take place in the way Lindsey envisages, then passengers in aircraft would find themselves without a pilot if the pilot is himself a Christian — so perhaps they should refuse to fly in an aircraft piloted by a Christian!

Fifth, Lindsey's argument is based on fatalism and the minimal role of human beings. It assumes that nuclear warfare is inevitable, and humans can do nothing to avoid it — indeed they should avoid hindering it. Nuclear warfare is to be welcomed — not prevented. This is contrary to Christ's command to be peacemakers. It also provokes the question: why should God bother to create human beings if they are going to destroy both themselves and the rest of his creation?

Finally, Lindsey's method of prophetic biblical interpretation is to convert, in effect, the Bible into a massive jigsaw puzzle from which the Christian has to pick pieces. Lindsey leaps back and forth between the Old and New Testaments, selecting the bits which fit his pattern and ignoring the majority which do not. The Bible, instead of being God's word for daily inspiration and guidance, is converted into a vast puzzle not unlike an Agatha Christie novel.

THE WALVOORDS AND ARMAGEDDON

Another contribution to the Armageddon industry comes from John F. Walvoord (a theologian) and John E. Walvoord (a business consultant), both of Dallas, Texas.[3]

According to the Walvoords, in Matthew 24, verses 4 to 14, Jesus gave nine indicators of the coming of the final age: many would claim to be Christ, but are impostors; 'wars and rumours of wars'; famines; 'pestilences'; earthquakes; many martyrs; many false prophets; increasing wickedness and decreasing love for God; and the gospel of the kingdom preached to all nations. The Walvoords argue that the last 1900 years have demonstrated the accuracy of this prophetic analysis of the present age.

The focal point for Christ's return is events in the Middle East, as it is with Hal Lindsey. The area will become the scene of the greatest war in history. Great armies from the south, representing the millions of Africa, will pour into the battle arena. Other great armies from the north, representing the USSR and Europe, will descend on Palestine. Climaxing the struggle will be millions of men from the Orient, led by China, who will cross the Euphrates River and join the fray. Locked in this deadly struggle, millions of people will perish in the greatest war of all history.

Before the war is finally resolved and the victor determined, Jesus Christ will come back in power and glory from heaven. His coming, accompanied by millions of angels and saints, is described in graphic terms in Revelation 19. Coming as the king of kings and judge of the world, he will destroy the contending armies and bring in his own kingdom of peace and righteousness on earth.

As with Lindsey, the Walvoords have written a stimulating book with a breathtaking taste for detail. For example, in the field of economics, they claim the scriptures predict that the world ruler will have absolute control of the economy, and no-one will buy or sell without his permission (Revelation 13, verse 17). Today, with the advent of modern computers, for the first time in history this would be possible. A world government could keep financial accounts of all the businesses in the world, controlling purchases and sales and compiling an infinite amount of information about every individual.

New computer technology has already been developed for what is called the electronic transfer of funds. This allows a person to buy and sell without using credit cards, cheques or money in the form of currency. In a government-controlled economy, the electronic transfer of funds approach would allow complete control of all transactions. Each person would have an account on a central computer and be assigned an approved number. When he was paid, his employer would credit his pay to his account by an electronic transfer of funds. When a person wanted to buy anything, the store would simply check his number on the computer and then subtract his purchases instantly by using a small computer terminal. If a world ruler chose to use such a system instead of money, no-one could buy or sell unless he gave them an approved number.

However, I have grave doubts about this book. Some of these have arisen in the context of my worries about Lindsey's books. For example, their assessment of the USSR's power is now — almost two decades after they wrote their book — highly inaccurate. On pages 109 and 110, for instance, they claim:

One of the phenomena of the twentieth century has been the rapid growth of communism which has swept more than one-third of the world into its clutches. Although the political idealism of communism does not seem to be perpetuated in the end time, the communist dedication to atheism, materialism and military power will prepare the way for the final form of world religion. . .

World communism today presents a similar atheistic, materialistic and religious system, which is an obvious preparation for this final form of world religion. According to Daniel 11, verses 36 to 38, the final world ruler will disregard all previous gods and will honour only 'a god of fortresses', referring to military and materialistic power personified. The final form of world religion, empowered by Satan himself, will be the worship of the world ruler who is Satan's substitute for Jesus Christ. In the world today there is already a world church movement preparing the world for a world church. And the communist movement is preparing the world for the final form of atheistic religion. This makes it clear that the stage for the end time is already set.

I have consistently argued that the USSR was not as strong as was being claimed by conservatives. The stunning collapse of the USSR's control in Eastern Europe and the current disintegration of the USSR itself have vindicated my (often unpopular) views. If the USSR could not control Eastern Europe, it certainly could not have moved large conventional troop formations into the Middle East.

The Walvoords are concerned about 'World Government'. On page 136, they write:

The prophets may never have realised the modern reasons for a world government, but they did predict that history would end in one central government that would embrace the entire world. The Bible not only predicted the rise and fall of the important world empires that have passed, but with prophetic accuracy has described the events that will lead to a final world government before the second coming of Christ.

On page 142, we read:

It is most significant that in our twentieth century not only does a need for a world government exist, but the tools for establishing such a government are now in our hands.

I disagree. There are certainly campaigns for some form of world government. But I believe we are heading into an era of fragmentation of power rather than concentration of power.

Finally, the book is misleading about Armageddon. I believe that Armageddon can occur at any time. But someone reading the Walvoord's book today and seeing the big difference between their timetable and today's reality could easily assume that Armageddon is a long way off.

As a prelude to the next section, here is a comparison by one writer of two approaches to Daniel and Revelation:

[To many,] Daniel was a prophet of the Babylonian captivity who, in the sixth century BC, predicted events that were to occur between 1948 and the end of the present century. [Others] contend that the book was completed between 166 and 164 BC and reflects the oppressive occupation of Palestine by the Syrian king Antiochus IV Epiphanes, who stopped the sacrifice in the temple in Jerusalem and set up a statue of Zeus on the altar of burnt offering, an act aptly described as 'the abomination of desolation'. The book is regarded as a standard example of apocalyptic literature. . . capable of inspiring faithfulness at a time of religious persecution. In similar fashion, the visions of Revelation are understood. . . to be symbolic descriptions of the persecutions anticipated and experienced at the hands of Rome near the close of the first century AD.[4]

CURRENT THEOLOGICAL TRENDS AND ARMAGEDDON

Eschatology is the study of last things or end-time itself and is derived from the Greek word *eschatos*, meaning 'last' or 'final'. Christian teaching on this subject remains largely unclear. It is interesting to note that Armageddon theology is not an old theology. It is only about a century or so old. Nor has it reached into the mainstream of theological teaching. But some of the present thinking on it, such as there is, can be seen in the writings of Gordon Dicker and Paul Barnett.

Australian theologian, the Rev. Gordon Dicker, has identified the main trends of thinking. First, he identifies *consistent eschatology*, linked particularly with Albert Schweitzer, who overturned traditional Christian thinking (which regarded this as a fringe issue) by claiming that eschatology was at the very centre of Jesus' teaching. He encouraged far more scholarly attention to the subject.

Second, Dicker mentions C.H. Dodd, who, in the 1930s, was among the scholars who opposed Schweitzer's views:

Dodd pointed to aspects of the teaching of Jesus and elements in the apostolic preaching which suggested that with the coming of Jesus a quite new age was inaugurated in which Old Testament expectations were fulfilled, and the kingdom was already present and accessible. The kingdom had already come. Dodd argued, in fact, that some of the prophecies attributed to Jesus concerning cataclysmic events yet to come were not a genuine part of this teaching. Dodd's view is known as *realised eschatology*, for according to it the expected end has already come.[5]

However, there are many sayings of Jesus in which the kingdom is still in the future; not least indicated by part of the Lord's Prayer, 'Your kingdom come'.

Third, Dicker identifies *inaugurated eschatology*, in which the new age has been inaugurated but the final consummation still lies ahead. T.W. Manson identified five points about this looked-for consummation:

1. It does not come as a peaceful reformation of the existing order as the social gospel movement imagined it would. It does not emerge as the end-point in an evolutionary process. It comes rather as a drastic breaking-in-upon the existing order, taking everyone by surprise.

2. One aspect of the event is a great judgment (Matthew 25, verses 31 to 46) in which all that is good is affirmed and all that is evil is condemned. The test of good is what he represents. Those who have not had the opportunity to take up any attitude to Jesus will be judged by their response to whatever

manifestation of God was available to them in their time and place (Matthew 12, verse 41f; Luke 11, verse 31f).

3. The final consummation marks the end of the present era, and all that is evil is eliminated. It is a victorious day for God the King. However, although it is represented as such in other parts of the New Testament, Jesus does not speak of it as a great battle; rather he presents it as a great moral victory.

4. A new era is inaugurated in which God is truly king in a universe cleansed of all evil, and life is lived in its truest and fullest sense (Luke 13, verses 28 and 29; Matthew 22, verses 1 to 14). Jesus was reticent to speak about conditions of life in the kingdom. Several times he used the analogy of a wedding feast to depict it, but life in the kingdom is not simply one of passive enjoyment. It is also a state of enlarged opportunities, as the parable of the talents suggests, but in the end all that can be said about it is that it is beyond our experience, and therefore beyond our imagination (1 Corinthians 2, verse 9).

5. No-one can predict the time of its coming. Even the Son does not know it, but only the Father (Mark 13, verse 32).[6]

Lindsey's views, therefore, represent only one trend out of several. Dicker deals with the Lindsey approach as follows:

There are, however, some people of adventist outlook, whether in a sect or in the church, who are not satisfied with such general conclusions as Manson's. They still believe that the time of the second coming can be calculated and the events surrounding it depicted in brilliant and graphic detail by means of deductions from enigmatic passages of scripture, despite the fact that people have been attempting to do just that for centuries with no success, and despite Jesus' warning that no-one knows the time, not even the Son.

This kind of speculation can very easily supplant all genuine concern about the gospel and all concern for actually following Christ. The world in all its need is abandoned for a life of apocalyptic excitement. Christians must be warned against this danger. Eschatology is meant to be the background against which we live as disciples, not the foreground which leaves not room for discipleship now.[7]

Sydney Anglican Bishop Paul Barnett has written a commentary on Revelation.[8] He believes that to read Revelation as a guide to the future is to miss the message of the book.

He notes that Armageddon is mentioned only once in passing with no more significance than other minor references scattered throughout Revelation. It is not the popularly conceived prelude to the millennium so much as just one of the symbols for the second coming of Jesus. It is true that on that occasion the kings of the world assemble for battle. Nonetheless, there is no actual battle, merely the language of battle which is used to provide the setting for so momentous an event as the return of Jesus.

Second, there is no actual description of the return of Christ in Revelation. The promise of the coming is there, but no detail is given concerning how or when it will happen.

Third, the great emphasis of Revelation is on the already completed victory of Jesus. Revelation leaves us in no doubt: the great end-time battle does not lie in the future, but in the past. The battle has been fought and won: Jesus is the victor. Christ has conquered the twin evils of guilt and death by his own death and resurrection. As a consequence, God's kingdom is now a present reality.

Much of the language of Revelation concerning Babylon, the beast and the mark of the beast refers to the Roman society of the time and its emperor. John was comparing the new community of the church with the society of pagan Rome, characterised by murder, fornication, sorcery and lies. This was a subversive and dangerous course at a time when Roman power was at its height. John veiled his attacks on Rome and what he regarded as the diabolical religion of emperor worship with the use of symbolism.

To conclude this section, then, it is necessary to note that the views of Lindsey and the Walvoords, though fascinating, do not represent the only Christian explanation of current events, nor indeed do they find favour among the more established Christian scholars.

THE DECLINE OF ARMAGEDDON THEOLOGY

Those who live by Armageddon theology shall perish by it. Hal Lindsey, it is true, still has his followers. But the people who tried to take Armageddon theology into the US political arena in the 1980s have all entered the 1990s with far less public support.

President Reagan (1981–1989) was the first president to endorse Armageddon theology explicitly. By embracing their agenda on such social issues as abortion and school prayer, Ronald Reagan won the support of the people who followed Armageddon theology. This was a crucial element in the coalition that twice elected him president. But while Reagan kept this social agenda in the background throughout his presidency, the Armageddon theologians played a vital role in both supporting and implementing US foreign policy. During the early 1980s, then, there was a marriage of convenience between the president and the politically-motivated Armageddon theologians.

But during the late 1980s, the tide turned against the Armageddon theologians. President Reagan changed sides and said that a nuclear war could never be won and should never be fought. The Soviet Union was led by a new dynamic leader who tried to reduce communism by, for example, trying to introduce an element of private enterprise into the Soviet system. During the late 1980s in opinion surveys, Americans evidently had higher opinions of Gorbachev than they did of any member of Reagan's cabinet. Various scandals took place concerning television evangelists (though no television evangelist identified in this book was involved in those scandals). The scandals have put all forms of television evangelism under a cloud. The mass media also became bored with speculation about nuclear doom.

In November 1987, the Rev. Jerry Falwell announced the ending of the Moral Majority organisation (created in 1979) and his return to parish work at Lynchberg, Virginia. The Rev. Pat Robertson, who ran as a Republican candidate for the presidential nomination, received very little support in early 1988 and did not figure at all in the mid-year Republican convention.

In retrospect, the influence of the politically-motivated Armageddon theologians may have been overstated. They constituted part of the New Christian Right (NCR) and a British sociologist, Steve Bruce, has claimed that the NCR was fatally flawed from the outset.[9]

Although they tried to make common cause with various other conservative groups on such issues as abortion, Protestant exclusiveness prevented them. Conservative Catholics could hardly combine with organisations which had been predominantly anti-Papist. The Ku-Klux-Klan, for example, were as much anti-Catholic as anti-black at one time. Although the NCR supports Israel, its support is based in part on eschatological views that imply the extermination of millions of Jews at Armageddon, salvation coming for 144 000 of them who will convert to evangelical Protestantism. So conservative Jews were alienated, as were black Baptist fundamentalists, by the traditional belief in one nation under God that is white and Protestant.

Hence, although the NCR may have helped Ronald Reagan in his election by politicising moral issues, it has been less successful on the federal stage than in local politics.

The fundamentalists suffered from a division: there were those who would like to impose the rule of saints and their standards on their fellow-citizens and those who see the individual's conscience under God as the arbiter of human behaviour. The latter have played a leading role in producing the pluralist society which is now in many ways repugnant to them; more than fifty per cent of the pastors of the Southern Baptists' convention reject political action and prefer to concentrate on the saving of souls.

Steve Bruce concludes that what troubles the supporters of the NCR is modernity, which pluralises choices and institutions and will not go away. Cultural fragmentation is a feature of modern society.

But Armageddon theologians will not disappear. They ebb and flow like waves. An earlier fashion occurred fifty years ago in the 1930s. No doubt in due course they will return. Instead of the possibility of World War III, the next focal point will probably be environmental, such as the end of the world arising out of the 'greenhouse effect' and the hole in the ozone layer.

HOW, THEN, SHOULD WE LIVE?
The following points are offered as a reply both to Lindsey's predictions in particular and Christian concern about World War III in general.

1. *Have faith in God.*
The earth is the Lord's and the fullness thereof. God alone has the authority to end this planet's life. By the same token we can be assured that if World War III is not on God's agenda, then it will be averted.

The military situation is certainly gloomy. But much the same could have been said two centuries ago when William Wilberforce and his colleagues decided to oppose the slave trade. That was supported by vested interests, it provided employment, some Christians claimed biblical support for it, the mass media supported it and the general public were largely apathetic — the list seems strangely familiar! But the slave trade and slavery were ended.

2. *Be aware that the end might be near.*

The second coming of Jesus may occur at any time. Even Jesus admitted that he did not know the date: 'No-one knows about that day or hour, not even the angels in heaven, nor the Son, but only the Father' (Matthew 24, verse 36).

During the past almost 2000 years, there have been various predictions of the second coming.[10] Indeed, this matter troubled the early church, some of whose members and critics were disappointed that it did not occur quickly (2 Peter 3, verses 3 to 18). 150 years ago, supporters of William Miller, in the north-east US, were convinced that the Second Coming would occur in 1843. Herbert W. Armstrong's organisation — the Worldwide Church of God — set 1972 as the date. A number of people took AD 1000 as the date and doubtless there will be similar claims for AD 2000. This is a constant feature of Christian life. Compared with the old oriental religions such as Hinduism, and Greek and Roman gods, all of which look back to a golden age, the religion of the Jews and Christians is forward-looking. It is natural, then, for Christians to be anxious for the second coming.

We should live as though we are going to die tomorrow, but study as though we are going to live forever. This is not just advice for people at school, but is a reflection of the need for lifelong education and the need to have an enquiring mind.

We should keep our affairs in order; we should live responsibly; we should not become prisoners of earthly possessions. We should recognise the value of learning, the arts and the importance of transcendent values.

3. *Have a sense of history.*

Christians should not assume that because the current era is one of doom, gloom and disaster, that it is automatically the period prior to the second coming. Unfortunately, life for most humans has always been harsh.[11] This is not necessarily the way it is taught in school and certainly the mass media glamorise certain historical eras (currently it is the pre-industrial era which is receiving favourable mention, as distinct from the damage allegedly done by industrialisation), so that there is a perpetual temptation to always assume in material terms that previous eras were better than our own (this is a secular form of the 'golden era' mythology of the Greeks and Romans). In short, many of the so-called indicators identified by Lindsey have been around for some time.

The US historian, the late Barbara Tuchman, was so worried about the prevailing doom of the late 1970s that she wrote a history of Europe in the fourteenth century specifically to inform readers that the twentieth century was not necessarily the worst century in history. The plagues, wars and riots of that century gave rise to forerunners of Lindsey and the Walvoords. The most celebrated of these was Jean de la Roquetaillade, a Franciscan friar incarcerated at Avignon because of his preaching against corrupt prelates and princes. He sympathised with the oppressed against the mighty, lay and clerical. Barbara Tuchman writes:

> From his cell in 1356, the year of Poitiers, he prophesied that France would be brought low and all Christendom be vexed by troubles: tyranny and robbers would prevail; the lowly would rise against the great, who 'shall be cruelly slain by the commons'; many women would be 'defiled and widowed' and their 'haughtiness and luxury shall wither'; Saracens and Tartars would invade the kingdoms of the Latins; rulers and peoples, outraged by the

luxury and pride of the clergy, would combine to strip the church of its property; nobles and princes would be cast down from their dignities and suffer unbelievable afflictions; Antichrist would appear to spread false doctrines; tempests, floods, and plagues would wipe out most of mankind and all hardened sinners, preparing the way for renewal.

These were the concerns and real currents of the time. Like most medieval doomsayers, however, Roquetaillade predicted debacle as the prelude to a better world. In his vision, the church, purified by suffering, chastisement and true poverty, would be restored, a great reformer would become Pope, the King of France against all custom would be elected Holy Roman Emperor and rule as the holiest monarch since the beginning of time. He and the Pope together would expel the Saracens and Tartars from Europe, convert all Moslems, Jews and other infidels, destroy heresy, conquer the world for the universal church and, before they died, establish a reign of peace that would last a thousand years until the day of judgment and the end.[12]

The sixteenth century also contained dire predictions. There was a conjunction of constellations in the heavens which was held to portend an imminent apocalypse. A century later, as the year 1666 approached, there was another wave of hysteria. Christians anticipated the imminent arrival of the Antichrist, who was presumed to measure time in strict accordance with the Gregorian calendar.

Very often, Armageddon thinking has gone hand in hand with political revolutions. In both the French and Russian revolutions, many people, on both sides, contrived to see an apocalypse of cosmic proportions. Upheaval in the social order was interpreted, depending on one's politics and caste, as either a blessing or a curse bearing God's signature.

Ironically, scholars continue to debate just how revolutionary in fact the French Revolution was — it seemed to replace one tyranny with another. The 1917 Russian Revolution certainly did replace one tyranny with another — with present leaders now trying to undo that damage with some form of parliamentary democracy (which the UK achieved — with little bloodshed — three centuries ago).

4. Keep working for peace and justice.

One by-product of the current interest in Armageddon has been the belief that since Armageddon is inevitable and imminent, it is not necessary to worry about today's violence and injustice.

Indeed, for many people, especially in the Third World, Armageddon is already here. As American social scientest Ruth Sivard said:

> In today's world of abundance of knowledge and resources, no-one need be hungry, or deprived of clean water, or of shelter; no-one need live out a life in the darkness of illiteracy; no-one need carry through life the mental and physical scars of extreme poverty. Yet hundreds of millions of individuals do, and they are in the richest countries as well as in the poorest.
>
> The numbers stand in low rows, like tombstones, monuments to lives lost to neglect:
>
> 100 000 000 people have no shelter whatsoever.
>
> 770 000 000 do not get enough food for an active working life.
>
> 500 000 000 suffer from iron-deficiency anemia.
>
> 1 300 000 000 do not have safe water to drink.
>
> 800 000 000 live in absolute poverty, unable to meet minimal needs.
>
> 880 000 000 adults cannot read and write.
>
> 10 000 000 babies are born malnourished every year.
>
> 14 000 000 children die of hunger-related causes every year.[13]

Even if various predictions about the future are unclear, the need to work for peace is clear. War and other forms of organised mass violence receive a great deal of attention in the Old Testament. Indeed, the history of the Jews is one of military victories, defeats and doubts about the value of warfare. Moses was one of the world's finest leaders of a national liberation movement. He opposed one of the world's first powers, which had advanced military technology, especially the chariot. The Jews escaped by the use of guerilla warfare. They had to use force both to obtain and maintain Israel.

By the time of David and Solomon, a close connection existed between religious personnel and the armed forces. Priests often accompanied Israel's armies into battle. Battles were preceded by sacrificial rites and advice was sought from priests. The Old Testament provides detailed accounts of how wars were fought, both in terms of weapons and numbers of combatants, thereby implying a close interest in military matters by the authors of the Old Testament's historical books. Solomon's nation was organised along military lines.

Indeed, Israel's decline offers advice for our contemporary reliance on weapons. Solomon's nation, which had itself by this time become a super power, placed too much reliance on military power both to deter enemies and to keep society together. The subsequent history showed that this reliance was fatal.

Meanwhile, the new-found wealth was turning the citizens' minds away from God's laws and onto materialism. Solomon and his immediate successors would have been better advised to negotiate, in our terms, some international systems for settling disputes and for easing economic and social tensions. This period reflects the wisdom of the statement that, when nations are strong, they are not necessarily wise and, when they are wise, they are not necessarily strong.

After Israel's downfall, there is a note of combat fatigue and more interest in peace. A few examples will illustrate this new attitude to war. Isaiah, who is writing at a time of war and rumours of wars, is the most famous author of this new mood.

It is notable that in foreshadowing the arrival of Jesus, he makes the following description: 'A child is born to us! A son is given to us! And he will be our ruler. He will be called, "Wonderful Counsellor", "Mighty God", "Eternal Father", "Prince of Peace"' (chapter 9, verse 6). There is no mention of his being a great general. On the contrary, 'His kingdom will always be at peace' (chapter 9, verse 7 and chapter 11, verses 1 to 9).

This new mood underpins the New Testament. Jesus nowhere appears as a military leader. He avoids the trappings of the military; for example, his final entry into Jerusalem is on a colt (Luke 19, verses 28 to 34), not a stallion. He travels in a land in which armed bandits are active, but he lacks an armed guard. Even during his most dangerous trip, his trip into Jerusalem, his disciples were only lightly armed (Luke 22, verse 49) and, when one of them injured an official, Jesus stopped the violence and healed the man (Luke 22, verse 51). Indeed, it may have been precisely Jesus' lack of military standing which turned the citizens against him and resulted in their call for his crucifixion (Luke 23, verse 21).

On the other hand, in keeping with his policy of meeting people in all strata of society, Jesus did not boycott military personnel. He considered them as eligible to receive his assistance as anyone else; for example, Jesus healed an officer's servant (Matthew 8, verses 5 to 13). Jesus was concerned to bring unity among all people: 'My commandment is this: love one another, just as I love you' (John 15, verse 12).

This is also reflected in the obligation for all Christians to become peacemakers. Peacemaking is the church's task because Jesus is the Prince of Peace: 'Happy are those who work for peace; God will call them his children!' (Matthew 5, verse 9). It is necessary not merely to be tranquil, but to work for peace.

Later on, in Matthew 10, verse 38, Jesus says, 'Whoever does not take up his cross and follow in my steps is not fit to be my disciple.' Jesus calls Christians to service in this world and this means taking on some difficult tasks. Working for peace is one of them. For as it is written in 1 John 3, verse 18, 'My children, our love should not be just words and talk; it must be true love, which shows itself in action.'

5. Do not be self-indulgent.

The popularity of Armageddon theologians is partly a reflection on how people perceive their position. There seems to be little interest in Armageddon theologians when life is comfortable. They are more popular, however, when difficulties arise. It is also an indication of how self-indulgent has been Armageddon theology that its supporters have come largely from the wealthier nations, concerned about the decline of their own standards of living, rather than the poorer world, where people have had a perpetual struggle simply to stay alive.

The popularity of Armageddon theology, ironically, was derived not from religious factors, but from current trends in society. First, it appealed to the widespread fear held by many citizens of an impending nuclear war.

Second, the Armageddon theologians were highly critical of the Soviet Union at a time when the Soviet Union was perceived as having aggressive foreign policies and interfering in the affairs of other nations. Third, it appealed to Americans who found themselves under threat by religious extremists such as the Ayatollah in Iran and Colonel Gadaffi in Libya.

Finally, Armageddon theology was endorsed by President Reagan. But as the secular trends changed, so support for Armageddon theology declined. People came to — and left — Armageddon theology as their sense of insecurity grew and faded. We need to guard against this self-indulgent approach to theology.

6. *Beware of conspiracy theories.*

An interesting link between the previous paragraph and this point is provided by Roy Livesy who has written about the 'preparations for the Antichrist's One World Government':

> In 1977 a chief computer analyst of the EEC (European Economic Community) announced that he was ready to begin assigning a number to every person in the world and that it would be a three six-digital unit with eighteen numbers.
>
> As well as the personal details (based on social security numbers, driving licence numbers, birth certificates, passport numbers, etc.) from the industrial nations, credit cards have made more information available. The capacity was set for two billion people.[14]

I will not comment upon the claim itself. I simply quote this as an example of Western self-indulgence. The alleged computer has the capacity to store information on two billion people — from industrial nations. In other words, over half of the world's population will not be counted — they live in poorer nations which do not have social security systems (let alone social security numbers); where people are too poor to travel in their own nations, let alone overseas (for which they would require passports); and where people are too poor even to have power points in their huts.

Livesy, a subscriber to Armageddon theology, has set out to demonstrate that we are on the verge of Armageddon because of the 'One World Government' being formed. Livesy seems to have little time for anyone or any organisation. He runs through a list of sinister organisations: the Catholic Church, the Society of Jesus (Jesuits), the World Council of Churches, the Council of Foreign Relations (the equivalent of the Australian Institute of International Affairs and the Royal Institute of International Affairs), freemasons, the Club of Rome, international banks and communism.

The book, incidentally, suffers from the same flaw as the rest of Armageddon theology. A person reading the chapter on communism (written in the mid-1980s) and seeing the abrupt decline of communism in the late 1980s may assume that Armageddon has been postponed. Alternatively, Armageddon could occur at any time — my view, in fact. But trying to predict its coming diverts attention away from how we are to live today.

Indeed, people with a sense of history will become blase about this type of conspiracy theory. Livesy's chapter on the Trilateral Commission is a good example of how such conspiracy theories become derailed.

This commission was established in 1973 by David Rockefeller, Chase Manhattan Bank chairman; Zbigniew Brzezinski, later President Carter's National Security Adviser; and other like-minded 'eminent private citizens'. Some 300 members are drawn from international business and banking, government, academia, media and conservative trade unions. The commission's purpose is to engineer an enduring partnership among the ruling classes of North America, Western Europe and Japan — hence the term *trilateral* — in order to safeguard the interests of Western capitalism in a turbulent world. The private Trilateral Commission is attempting to mould public policy and construct a framework for international stability in the coming decades.[15]

One obscure southern governor who was appointed to the commission was a Jimmy Carter. In 1976, this obscure politician was elected president. Many of his key colleagues (from Vice President Walter Mondale downwards) were members of the Trilateral Commission. During the late 1970s/early 1980s, there were dire predictions from the extreme Left and extreme Right about the commission's control over the US. But the US suffered no dramatic changes.

The dire warnings were for nothing. President Carter lost the 1980 presidential election and spent most of the 1980s home in Georgia rebuilding the family fortune from the chaos into which it descended after he had to leave his financial activities to become president. The Trilateral Commission still operates — publishing booklets, holding seminars and such like. But it has not as an organisation acquired the power that its left-wing and right-wing critics argued it would. Consequently, reading Livesy recycling the old material about the Trilateral Commission makes the reader sceptical about all his other claims.

I am sceptical of all conspiracy theories. I find it hard to believe that a small group of people — Jews or communists or freemasons or the UN or CIA or KGB — can run the world when I see in everyday life how foolish, ignorant or inefficient humans can be. Cars break down, trains run late, lifts get stuck, letters get lost, water pipes get blocked — and yet a small group of individuals (we are told) can somehow be held responsible for running — or ruining — the world.

Anyone familiar with how large organisations *really* operate knows that the organisations are chaotic! Dean Rusk (one of the longest-serving US Secretaries of State this century) had various forms of government experience from World War II to the Vietnam War. A sympathetic biography brings out some of the chaos in US foreign-policy making.[16] Posted to the US War Department in 1941, Rusk was put in charge of an intelligence section dealing with the British colonies in Asia — on the basis of three years' residence at Oxford University. The principal file was a tourist handbook on India and Ceylon — it was stamped 'confidential'!

Similarly, in 1945, Rusk and a colleague on the State-War-Navy Coordinating Committee — a predecessor of the National Security Council — were charged with selecting a boundary between Soviet and American occupation forces in Korea. Using a National

Geographical Society map that just happened to show the 38th parallel of latitude, they fixed on it as the boundary. They did not know that in 1896 the Russians and the Japanese had signed a formal compact dividing Korea into two spheres of influence along this line. Nor did they know that the 38th Parallel had been an administrative line for Japan. Unwittingly, the Americans had selected a boundary that the Soviets would look upon as a deliberate division into two geographic spheres of influence, one Soviet and the other American. Thus, Dean Rusk and his colleagues unintentionally fixed the boundary which still divides South Korea from North Korea.

Conspiracy theories say more about their subscribers than about the world. People who subscribe to conspiracy theories like to see the world in clear contrasts — 'goodies' or 'baddies'. The theories also put the blame for an individual's misfortune on someone or something else. The problem is 'out there' — never in oneself. The theories create scapegoats — Jews, communists, CIA, KGB — so that there is the belief that if the scapegoats can be removed in some final solution, then all will be well.

Life is not that simple. Even if the scapegoats were removed, the flaws in humankind would mean that other problems — even in one's own relatives, colleagues or leaders — would emerge. Life's complexity has to be confronted and understood rather than evaded by blaming scapegoats.

7. *Chaos should be seen as a prelude to something new.*
Chaos around the globe should be viewed not as the automatic prelude to Armageddon, but as the components of a new stage in humankind's continuing history.

Human history can be viewed as a tapestry. Certain themes can be found in all parts of the tapestry; human nature does not change much from one generation to the next. But over the thousands of years the themes are incorporated into new patterns.

Instead of viewing the current global trends as the onset of Armageddon, we should see the rich tapestry of humankind as undergoing a change in its pattern.

Of course, Armageddon can occur at any time — even today. But until the time that it does, we should be examining the new pattern in the human tapestry. The new pattern may not necessarily be the last pattern before Armageddon — God may have humankind contributing many new patterns before Armageddon.

It is this new pattern that is now emerging, rather than any specific future one, that most of the rest of this book will examine. This should enable us to understand something of the likely shape of the new world order, the one that is likely to shape our future.

Endnotes:

1. Hal Lindsey, *The Late Great Planet Earth*, Bantam, 1970; *The 1980s: Countdown to Armageddon*, Bantam, 1980
2. Hal Lindsey, *The Road to Holocaust*, Bantam, 1989, p.282
3. John F. Walvoord and John E. Walvoord, *Armageddon: Oil and the Middle East Crisis*, Zondervan, 1974
4. William Martin, 'Waiting for the End: The Growing Interest in Apocalyptic Prophecy', *Atlantic Monthly* (US), June 1982, p.37
5. Gordon S. Dicker, *Faith with Understanding*, Unichurch Publishing, 1981, p.194
6. *Ibid*, pp.195–196
7. *Ibid*, pp.196–197
8. Paul Barnett, *Apocalypse Now and Then: Reading Revelation Today*, Anglican Information Office, 1989
9. Steve Bruce, *The Rise and Fall of the New Christian Right: Conservative Protestant Politics in America, 1978–1988*, Oxford University Press, 1988
10. See *End-time, the Doomsday Catalogue*, William Griffin (ed.), Collier, 1979, pp.42–71.
11. For a survey of opinions predicting war, see I.F. Clarke, *Voices Prophesying War 1763–1984*, Oxford University Press, 1966.
12. Barbara Tuchman, *A Distant Mirror*, Macmillan, 1979, pp.196–197
13. Ruth Leger Sivard, *World Military and Social Expenditures 1987–1988*, World Priorities, 1987, p.25
14. Roy Livesy, *Understanding the New Age: Preparation for Antichrist's One World Government*, New Wine Press, 1986, p.200
15. For a detailed study by an equally hostile left-wing critic, see *Trilateralism: The Trilateral Commission and Elite Planning for World Management*, Holly Sklar (ed.), South End Press, 1981.
16. Thomas J. Schoenbaum, *Waging Peace and War: Dean Rusk in the Truman, Kennedy and Johnson Years*, Simon and Schuster, 1988

3

THE THIRD WAVE

Is there a clear pattern to the changes all around us?

I BELIEVE IT IS POSSIBLE TO MAKE SENSE of the changes taking place around the world. The most stimulating way of trying to understand these changes is found in the writings of Alvin Toffler. His writings include *Future Shock*, *The Third Wave*, *Previews and Premises* and *Powershift*.

Although Marxist as a young adult, Toffler has since parted company with the political left and now mixes more comfortably with industrial concerns. Toffler does not apply the term 'futurist' to himself. He regards himself primarily as a writer and author and a social critic. He does not believe that anyone can predict the future.

ALVIN TOFFLER AND THE ACCELERATION OF CHANGE
Alvin Toffler made his name with the book *Future Shock*[1] which has sold over seven million copies around the world. Its key theme is that the acceleration of social and technological change has made it increasingly difficult for individuals and organisations to cope. It is not

merely change to which we must in some way adapt, but acceleration itself.

Toffler not only set out the problem, but he also made intriguing proposals. For example, he suggested that people suffering from future shock could retreat to enclaves of the past similar to colonial Williamsburg in Virginia, Mystic Seaport in Connecticut, and Old Tucson in Arizona — in Australia, I suppose the example would be Tasmania! — where they could live for periods ranging from a few days to several years.

Living and working in one of the enclaves could also be a valuable educational experience for students. Such living education would give them an historical perspective no book could provide. Toffler speculated that computer experts, roboteers, designers, historians and museum specialists could join to create experimental enclaves that reproduce, as skilfully as sophisticated technology will permit, the splendour of ancient Rome, the pomp of Queen Elizabeth I's court, or whatever. By this means, they would give themselves space to escape from the rapid pace of modern change.

ALVIN TOFFLER AND THE DEMISE OF
THE SECOND WAVE

In 1980, Toffler published *The Third Wave*.[2] In this book (also a best seller), Toffler argued that the future is beginning to take shape. The First Wave occurred soon after the last Ice Age, in which civilisations in the eastern Mediterranean developed the plough and cultivated the land, rather than remain as nomadic hunters. This wave was largely initiated about 10 000 years ago.

The Second Wave, which took only about 300 years to run its course, was the industrial revolution, with its energy based on non-replaceable fossil fuels, such as coal and oil. Its basic family was the nuclear family: father, mother and a few children, but with no encumbering relatives. Its organisations — schools, churches, governments, community groups — were all of hierarchical structure. Its standard method of communication was via paper and, later, the telephone. Its standard economic feature (both capitalist and communist) was the separation of individuals into either producers or consumers (depending on the goods and services they made or bought).

Its basic framework consisted of six standard operational procedures: standardisation, specialisation, synchronisation (as in school and factory timetables), concentration (such as economic power), maximisation (the concern for economic growth and bigness) and centralisation. Prevailing ideas of the Second Wave were such notions as the need for humans to conquer nature, the belief that humans were the highest forms of earthly life and the concern for economic progress irrespective of social cost.

It is unclear why the Second Wave was initiated. Its origins were varied and colourful. For example, the exhaustion of the UK's forests prompted the use of coal. This in turn forced the mine shafts to go deeper and deeper until the old horse-drawn pumps could no longer clear them of water. The steam engine was perfected to solve this problem and in turn it created a new set of uses for the steam engine. But this is only one element in the Second Wave's emergence; the total picture remains unclear.

There is also no difficulty in seeing why the Second Wave is faltering. The era of cheap energy has gone, the environment is in danger, governments are collapsing under their responsibilities and nothing seems to work any more.

The Second Wave economy is certainly under stress. The centralised system of economic management is no longer effective. Every attempt to offset inflation or unemployment through nationwide tax rebates or tax increases, or through credit control, merely aggravates the problem. The Second Wave mass media are ceasing to be a mass media. Large circulation daily newspapers are declining, while there is an increase in the number and circulation of local newspapers and newsletters. A handful of television and radio stations are being replaced by a growing mixture of television (including cable television) and radio stations (such as those on the FM wave band).

ALVIN TOFFLER AND THE CURRENT ECONOMIC UPHEAVAL

Toffler claims that the previous economic depressions resulted in crises in the basic industries. But during those depressions, there were rarely powerful new industries rising up at the very same time — something which is different now. We are now seeing the rise of electronic, computer information, genetic, aerospace and environmental recycling industries. It follows, then, that this is not a recession through which the industrial world is passing, but a restructuring of the entire economic base of society. The crisis is not capitalist or communist — it is industrial. *Both* capitalist and communist economies are crumbling. It is all part of the decline of the Second Wave.

The factory system of production was notable for its centralisation of power, synchronisation of production and uniformity of produce. Those qualities are now passing. For example, we now have the de-massification of society. The more the economy becomes varied, the more information must be exchanged to maintain integration in the system. All of this leads to 'social diversity' (some people would call it 'chaos').

ALVIN TOFFLER AND THE THIRD WAVE

'The Third Wave' is the name Toffler gives the emerging order. It will, he says, have a number of key features:

1. *The home will be the central unit in the Third Wave society.*
While at home, the workers will be able to carry out some or all of
their jobs, the student will be able to learn via the television (as
adapted), and people will make many of their own clothes and furniture, mend their own domestic appliances and grow their own food.
That is, they'll become 'prosumers', both producing and consuming.
But he warns that it is unlikely that any institution — not even the
home — will be able to play the central role as the factory did in the
past. Society is likely to be built around a network of institutions and
relationships, rather than a hierarchy of new institutions.

The changes in information technology have refocussed attention
on the home. In 1956, because of the increased demand for telephone
services and the cost of employing operators, the American Telephone
and Telegraphic Company (ITT) introduced a new electronic technology that made it possible for callers to direct-dial many overseas calls.
In the US, some manufacturers now provide a telephone consultation
facility in which a mechanic avoids a costly service visit by giving
blow-by-blow advice over the telephone to the consumer with a
machine in need of repair.

In the next few years, we will have some form of viewdata
technology — the UK has been experimenting with Prestel for some
years. This new technology uses existing telephone lines and
television sets (with alterations) as visual display units. By means of
a control panel, a viewer will be able to call up data on the television
set which will come from a mainframe computer and travel along the
telephone line. Both the telephone and television will retain their
original uses. But when used in this new way, the viewer will be able
to see, for example, what films are showing in town, what the weather
will be like and stock market fluctuations.

Eventually it will be possible for the viewer to order items of
purchase via viewdata; the person will see an advertisement and be

able to place the order immediately. A child doing homework will have no need of encyclopaedias, since the necessary information can be accessed via the viewdata system. Newspapers can be replaced by viewdata. The big obstacle to educational television has been the way in which each child learns at a different pace but the program moves at a uniform pace. With viewdata, the child can be taught at home and each child can move at his or her own pace.

He recommends the breaking up of the mass education system, with more education in the home — or smaller and more local schools — with more parental involvement, more creativity and less learning by rote. Such views are likely to run up against the dead hand of bureaucracy and teacher unions.

2. *The emphasis will be on working smarter, not working harder.* Second Wave industries made profits partly by forcing their workers to work harder. The Third Wave companies will be unsuccessful in this method since the emphasis will not be so much upon labour but upon intelligence. About eighty-five per cent of all the scientists who have ever lived are alive today. This in itself creates new challenges. The head of a factory can instruct workers to arrive at 7.00 am sharp and produce. But that same person cannot tell a researcher or an engineer to show up at 7.00 am and have a creative idea.

This new emphasis on smart work does not mean that manufacturing will disappear any more than the advent of the industrial age meant that First Wave agriculture disappeared. Like agriculture today, manufacturing will produce more goods for more people with less labour. But a significant change will be that the relative importance of 'intellectual capital' invested in software and systems will increase in relation to the 'financial' capital invested in physical plants and equipment. Traditional accounting systems designed for an earlier age no longer reflect what is really happening, either in business or national economies.

3. *The traditional power structures will go.*

According to Toffler, the terms 'right' and 'left' are relics of the industrial period now passing into history. 'Right' and 'left' had to do with those who got what — how the wealth and power of the industrial system were divided. But today the situation is much more complicated. For a start, the configuration on issues has changed and the political community has become de-massified. A voter may be left on some issues, while right on others. So this change has already started.

Power resides in 'property', whatever that might mean. In the First Wave societies, the only property that meant much was land. In Second Wave societies, the essential property was no longer land, but ownership of such 'means of production' as factories. In Third Wave societies, the essential property becomes information — this is the first form of property that is non-material, non-tangible and potentially infinite.

As Toffler says of persons owning shares in IBM today: 'What do I really care about? What do I own? I don't care about the land upon which IBM has some buildings. I don't care about its plant in California or Colombia. I don't care about the buildings or even the machines. What I really care about is the organised information it can control. My property is now doubly abstracted from reality. A share of IBM is a piece of paper — a symbol. And beyond that it is a symbol, not of hardware or of real estate, but a symbol of other symbols inside people's heads.'

Power in the Third Wave is likely to be delegated. Within institutions today there are problems of deterioration in decision-making. This is not because the people in charge are stupid, but because they are all running too fast, making too many decisions about too many things they know too little about. In the Third Wave, decision-making will need to be delegated. Instead of the centralisation of power — a quality of the Second Wave — there will need to be the devolution of decision-making.

ALVIN TOFFLER AND THE SOURCES
OF POWER IN THE NINETIES

Toffler's most recent book is *Powershift*: *Knowledge, Wealth and Violence at the Edge of the 21st Century* published in 1990. It is amazing how he produces a best-seller every decade! This builds upon his earlier books.

This time he focusses on the distribution of power. Power is derived from three sources: knowledge, wealth and violence. Of the three, knowledge has now become the most important. Toffler claims that some of the components of the new era are the following:

The number and variety of organisational units multiply. The more such units, the more transactions among them, and the more information must be generated and communicated.

Workers become less and less interchangeable. Industrial workers owned few of the tools of production. Today the most powerful wealth-amplifying tools are the symbols inside workers' heads. Workers, therefore, own a critical, often irreplaceable, share of the 'means of production'.

The new hero is no longer a blue-collar worker, a financier or a manager, but the innovator (whether inside or outside a large organisation) who combines imaginative knowledge with action.

Wealth creation is increasingly recognised to be a circular process, with wastes recycled into inputs for the next cycle of production. This method presupposes computerised monitoring and ever-deeper levels of scientific and environmental knowledge.

Producer and consumer, divorced by the industrial revolution, are reunited in the cycle of wealth creation, with the customer contributing not just money but market and design information vital for the production process. Buyer and supplier share data, information and knowledge. Some day, customers may also push buttons that activate remote production processes. Consumer and producer fuse into a 'prosumer'.

The new wealth creation system is both local and global. Powerful microtechnologies make it possible to do locally what previously could be done economically only on a national scale.

Simultaneously, many functions spill over national boundaries, integrating activities in many nations into a single productive effort.[3]

THE LIMITATIONS OF ALVIN TOFFLER'S IDEAS

While there is much to commend Toffler's thinking, there are some major omissions:

1. *Toffler does not acknowledge sufficiently his dependence on technology for the changes he envisages.*

For a person who says he is not a technological determinist, there is the irony that the world will only last long enough to move into the Third Wave if the current technology governing the arms race does not break down. Toffler does not deal very much with the arms race in his book. But the arms race is the most expensive manifestation of Second Wave technology.

The good news is that this form of Second Wave technology may go the way of all such technology and be replaced by some other way of resolving disputes — perhaps we are in for a new era in conflict resolution? My application of the Third Wave model to the warfare State is set out in chapter 9 below.

2. *Toffler is vague about the four new clusters of economic growth.*

These clusters are electronics and computer, the exploitation of outer space, the exploitation of the seas and the genetics industry. Indeed, it is notable that almost all of them are high technology activities which cannot be carried out in Toffler's electronic cottage.

3. *Toffler only makes a passing reference to most of humanity.*

Most of the world — the less developed world — is not yet covered by the Third Wave's development. They are still moving from under-developed societies into the Second Wave. The gap between the rich and the poor on the global scene looks certain to widen as in-dustrialised societies reap greater benefits from the new industrial revolution.

To complicate matters for the less developed world, the Third Wave is likely to be even more revolutionary than the Second Wave industrial revolution. The industrial revolution was spread over time. Its passage could be viewed. One could see in what ways it was developing. It did not turn on just one technology as its fulcrum. It started in a few nations like England and Germany, and took almost two centuries before it reached the less developed world. Even now it has not reached most of it. So it was possible for nations to learn from the experiences of those who went before. But the communica-tion revolution is occurring around the world simultaneously. So there is little opportunity for a society to learn from the experiences of another.

Radios have been introduced into almost every village in the world. Television is being developed in many poor countries, and films are shown widely. This explosion in communications is having a radicalising effect. The poor are becoming painfully aware of the discrepancy in lifestyles among rich and poor nations. A cottage does not seem small until a great castle is built beside it. The peasant comes home day after day and rejoices in his cottage. When a castle arises, the peasant says, 'Why should I live badly when it is possible to live so much better?'

Thus, one of the new elements in the world — an element which differentiates it from the relatively stable world of the past — is the awareness that the poor now have of their poverty. Contributing to this new consciousness is the direct exposure to rich foreign tourists which has been brought about by the technological advances in transportation. Jets have permitted tourists to visit every corner of the globe, demonstrating how incredibly rich they are.

An example of the less developed world's dismal future arises from the debt crisis. The causes of the debt crisis are complex. One cause lies in the legacy of colonialism, which enriched colonising nations and exploited the land, resources and people of the colonies. They were exploited and robbed of the land, mineral resources and agricultural products for the benefit of the colonisers. In the post-colonial era, the nations of Africa, Asia, the Pacific, Latin America and the Caribbean struggled to gain full control of their land and resources. But the trading system gave former colonial powers an advantage by controlling international markets.

Most colonies have become independent since 1945. They received some loans to assist the development of their economies. These came from developed nations, private banks and international financial institutions, notably the World Bank and the International Monetary Fund.

There are two types of debtor nations. The relatively better-off 'middle income' debtors (mostly in Latin America and South East Asia) have the largest debts and owe most of them to Western commercial banks. The world's poorest nations (mainly in Africa and South Asia) were not considered 'creditworthy' enough for commercial loans from banks. They borrowed mostly from governments of the developed nations or from international financial institutions like the International Monetary Fund (IMF) and World Bank which are controlled by governments.

The debt crisis started as trade imbalances began to escalate in the early 1970s. The oil-producing nations deposited billions of dollars in Western commercial banks. In turn, many banks aggressively marketed their loans to developing countries which were short on cash, facing high oil costs and eager to borrow. Banks' normal loan review procedures were often abandoned in the rush to lend large amounts of money quickly.

Some of the loans to developing countries went to such productive uses as water purification and sewerage systems, education and health programs and subsidies for basic food staples. Many, however, went for purposes that had little to do with the needs of the majority, such as loans that went towards such large projects as nuclear power plants and dams. Other sums disappeared into the private bank accounts of corrupt rulers.

Some funds (like those to the Marcos government) simply did not appear in the nation's ledgers. Incidentally, to illustrate the extent of the debt problem for Marcos' successors, if they were to drop a 100 peso bill (almost US$5) into a pit every second, it would take them 182 years to deposit funds sufficient to pay the current foreign debt of the Philippines.

When debtor nations run into serious trouble paying either their debt or at least the interest on their debt, they have few options but to turn to the International Monetary Fund (IMF), the lender of last resort. In return for emergency loans, the IMF has required debtor governments to adopt certain policies often referred to as 'austerity packages'. In such packages, debtor governments are usually required to cut wages, increase exports and cut imports, cut subsidies for farmers, eliminate low prices for vital foodstuffs and reduce government spending on items such as health and education.

While such measures are designed to restore a nation's credit worthiness in the future, the immediate impact is to hurt the poor disproportionately. The burden of repayment has forced debtor nations to gear their economies further towards exports since the debt has to be repaid in hard currencies such as the US dollar. This tends to divert resources away from production to meet local needs.

The economic adjustments taking place, particularly in Africa and Latin America, have led not only to more people living in absolute poverty, but also to increasing inequality among social groups. There is the prospect of a lost generation of children due to deteriorating nutritional status, increasing infant mortality rates in some nations and declining access to and quality of health and educational services.

More than 11 000 African children are dying every day because of the failure to put Africa's economy on track. Natural and human-made disasters combined with unprecedented economic crises have resulted in a critical situation which kills eight African children every minute. Africa is the only continent where infant mortality is increasing. In many African nations, decline in social spending has resulted in a reduction of health services and lack of essential drugs. Africa has the lowest rate of access to clean water in rural areas in the world.

It is in everyone's interest that the Third World debt problem be eased. The benefits for the less developed are clear: a major cause of social unrest in Third World nations arises out of governments having to cut back on social welfare expenditure so as to service debts. Also, if the less developed nations can pay less money in interest, they will be able to import more goods from developed nations. In other words, money which could be used to purchase Australian goods and services is currently going only to Australian and other banks.

In placing so little emphasis on the Third World, Toffler denies what he calls 'the world web' — the interdependence of the globe — as a key characteristic of the Third Wave. His examples are derived mainly from the developed world, but the need to solve the Third World debt crisis has to find a place in his framework.

* * *

Despite these reservations about Toffler's three wave model, there is much to commend it. For this reason, some themes from his work will be reflected throughout the rest of this book. According to Toffler, the following themes were present in the Second Wave:

* centralisation of power
* standardisation of production
* uniformity of produce
* synchronisation of time

In the Third Wave, by contrast, the following themes stand out:

* decentralisation of power
* flexibility of production
* variety of produce
* complexity
* interdependence
* networking

These themes will recur throughout this book as I set out the three waves in the contexts of law, administration, politics ('governance') and warfare:

DATE	TOFFLER	GOVERNANCE	WARFARE
Since last Ice Age	Agriculture	Tribe	Guerilla
17th century	Factory	Nation-state	Conventional/ Nuclear
Late 20th century	Third Wave	New international order	Guerilla/ Economic pressure/ Conflict resolution

Much of the rest of this book is given over to explaining the two right-hand columns.

Endnotes:

1. Alvin Toffler, *Future Shock*, Random House, 1970
2. Alvin Toffler, *The Third Wave*, Collins, 1980
3. Alvin Toffler, *Powershift: Knowledge, Wealth and Violence at the Edge of the 21st Century*, Bantam, 1990, pp.239–240

PART B:

The new global governance

4

GOVERNMENTS

*Can nation-states cope with
the new world order?*

GEORGE ORWELL GOT IT WRONG. In his brilliant novel *1984*, he warned about the concentration of power in the hands of 'Big Brother'. That was Second Wave thinking. Third Wave thinking is based on the fragmentation of power.

As a consequence of this fragmentation, governments are in crisis. This crisis is not necessarily or only due to the low quality of people entering politics. It is, instead, a reflection of the collapse of the Second Wave institution: the nation-state. The following diagram indicates the fragmentation that is occurring in the new international order:

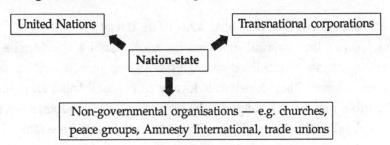

Power is leaving the nation-state and being dispersed among international institutions (notably the UN), transnational corporations and grassroots organisations.

The Second Wave nation-state will continue to exist. After all, factories (Second Wave manufacturing units) still exist. But the importance of the nation-state will decline as its power is dispersed in those three directions.

Heads of government have become managers rather than leaders. They are trying to stabilise a sinking ship. Japan, Germany and the four Asian tigers (Singapore, Taiwan, Malaysia and South Korea) might protest that their ships of state are not sinking. But their ships are simply sailing in a different 'ocean' from that of the old imperial nations like the Netherlands, Portugal, Spain, France and the UK. There is now far less room in which to manoeuvre. Today's power comes far more from finance than military hardware, national economies are now far more interdependent than ever before and far more subject to international influences, and periods of international dominance are now shorter.

The next four chapters deal with this new international order. This chapter deals briefly with the First Wave of governance (the tribe) and then the rise and fall of the Second Wave (the nation-state). Chapters 5, 6 and 7 deal respectively with the components of the new era: international institutions (especially the UN), transnational corporations and non-governmental organisations.

THE FIRST WAVE: POLITICAL ORGANISATION

The world's first political unit was the tribe. Until a few hundred years ago, most people lived in small groups and were settled on set pieces of land. They owed their loyalty to the local tribal chieftain. The tribes may have belonged to larger geographical groupings (such as England) but national rulers with centralised power were rare.

Territory and food-gathering were key components of the First Wave. All tribes had a set piece of territory. Even nomadic tribes were not aimless wanderers, but followed a specific pattern in such a way as to avoid overusing the food resources of a particular location. By the time the tribe returned to that location, the land would have regenerated, providing such resources as fresh fruit.

Most people, however, were not nomadic. They had set territory and stayed on it. The plough and other components of the agricultural revolution enabled them to grow food not just for a day at a time but for a surplus. This meant that some people could be deployed on other tasks such as calculating the rise and fall of the Nile, creating irrigation canals and protecting the tribe from other tribes.

First Wave government had limited responsibilities: maintaining law and order at home and protecting the tribe from external attack. Education, social services and health were not seen as matters for tribal leaders. People were expected to look after themselves — or perish through neglect.

In Europe during the Middle Ages, the church was a guardian of the interests of the disadvantaged. Sister Joan Chittister OSB (prioress of the Mount Saint Benedict priory in Erie, Pennsylvania) has explained the role of the church in this way:

> The church punctuated the calendar year with feasts. The whole notion was to lift moments of time out of the humdrum for special consideration.
>
> Feast days were very important in early Europe, in an agrarian society that worked so hard from dawn to dark. The peasants and the serfs carried the entire economy on their backs. The feast day was one of the ways that the church, like the Jews in the observance of the Sabbath, brought equality to the society.
>
> It was a long time before the forty-hour week. But the church

said this great feast is like a Sunday, and therefore you cannot force these serfs to work. So it was free time. It was the first contribution to the labour movement, the first contribution to equality, and it was a profound theological contribution to the notion of hope. It was a sign that the victory had come for some, that life was a great gift.[1]

The church also provided social services. Sr Chittister has explained how her order developed its tradition over a thousand years ago:

Nothing was more dangerous than crossing Europe. Benedictine monasteries were the first Holiday Inns of the Western world. [The monastery] was one of the few places where people could come and sleep well and not have to worry about being mugged, rolled or knifed in their sleep.
It was a tremendous contribution to the western Europe of the time. You could cross Europe and stay in a monastery of your own tradition every single night, because they were spaced a day's journey apart. So for a Benedictine not to practise hospitality is for a Benedictine not to practice Benedictinism.

It's a very special gift, and I think it has an awful lot to say to our own time. The Benedictine monasteries were among the first to take the sick and the dying into their own infirmaries. Because death in a pagan world was a punishment, there were all sorts of taboos surrounding death. Barbarian peoples left the dying on the sides of the roads. And the monasteries were very, very quick to begin the first hospices, so that these people could die in clean beds in a Christian environment.[2]

People had limited contact with the world beyond their tribal boundaries. Even seafarers could take only limited journeys because of their small craft and reliance upon wind patterns. Individuals were certainly conscious of a world beyond their tribal boundaries. But most had limited opportunities for learning about that world — they had little time for vacation travel and they could not read. Patriotism — the love of one's nation — was slow to emerge. After all, the nation itself was only slow to emerge! The medieval peasantry had no concept of 'nation' in the modern sense. Their affections were directed at their immediate surroundings: the countryside, people and customs with which they were familiar.

THE SECOND WAVE: POLITICAL ORGANISATION

The growth of strong centralised government was impeded by many obstacles, such as difficulties of communication, sparsity of population and primitive economic conditions. Additionally, in the European context, tribes and national rulers were overshadowed by the power of the Christian church, based in Rome.

Not until after the Reformation was the civil authority in any country regarded as supreme. Governmental authority was always divided; the church claimed and received the obedience of the citizens and its claims were not always limited to the purely spiritual sphere. The extent of the church's power varied from one geographical area to another. But prior to the Reformation, few challenged the principle that the church had some powers.

The turning point came with the Peace of Westphalia, which brought to an end in 1648 the great Thirty Years' War of religion and marked the acceptance of a new political order in Europe. This is usually taken as the beginning of a new era in international law.

However, historians tend to see the beginning of that new era as being far less distinct. For example, the first explicit formulation of the doctrine of sovereignty was written in 1576 by Jean Bodin (*De Republica*). France in Bodin's time had been rent by faction and civil war. Bodin was convinced that the cause of its miseries was the lack of a government strong enough to curb the subversive influences of feudal rivalries and religious intolerance, and that the best way to combat these evils was to strengthen the French monarchy. Whatever the debate on the precise date of the beginning of the nation-state era, it is clear that approximately 300 years ago a major change took place in the evolution of international law and political organisation.

Nearly all modern governments of a European type have developed from a common origin. The original models were characterised by an attempt to create a balance between political authority and the powerful representative institutions of the day. There was a monarchy; and it was usually balanced by a chamber of landowning barons, a chamber of lesser landowners and merchants and the international church.

The monarchy has now either disappeared or, where it still exists, has lost its governing powers. The church now has far less influence. The long and painful retreat from power of both monarchy and church has been accompanied by the acquisition of power by political parties.

Power is now exercised by the people, who either elect a legislature from which the government is derived, as in most of Western Europe, or alternatively elect both a legislature and an administration, as in the US. The US constitution still attempts a 'balance of power' between the different facets of political authority — executive, legislative and judicial.

The rise of the nation-state benefited from the Second Wave technological revolution. Communications were improved; communities were far less isolated; there was an increase in national wealth; and it was possible to develop more of a sense of national identity. The rapidly increasing international intercourse also meant that there had to be a rapid expansion in international law and diplomacy. In a more static era of isolated communities there was far less interchange. Now there was far more international trade, for example; and there had to be rules governing that trade.

TOWARDS THE THIRD WAVE: THE WAYS THE NATION–STATE'S ROLE IS DECLINING

The nation-state era is now drawing to a close. While it is too soon to predict precisely what form the new international order will take, it is far easier to identify the symptoms of collapse of the Second Wave of international law and political organisation.

The rest of this chapter, then, looks at the ways in which the nation-state's role is being eroded: first, the changing perceptions of government; second, the fragmentation of political power; third, the triumph of form over content; fourth, the complexity of modern diplomacy; fifth, the creation of a post-imperial world; and sixth, the increase in transnational problems which cannot be solved only by national action.

☐ First, changing perceptions of government

The common law of England (which is also the basis of the Australian legal system) stretches back for at least 800 years. But during the first 700 years at least, the role of government was circumscribed. The legal remedies that were developed for the citizen reflected this limited conception of the functions of government. It is only in this century that the public sector has come to assume such a significant role in the daily life of citizens.

British historian, the late A.J.P. Taylor, wrote: 'Until August 1914, a sensible law-abiding Englishman could pass through life and hardly notice the existence of the State beyond the post office and the policeman.'[3] In the course of this century, however, there has been an expansion of State activity. More and more of the life of the community is now the subject of State control. In particular, the development of the welfare state — with all its undeniable merits — has meant that the State has impinged ever more closely on the life of people.

The growth of government intervention began partly as a way of coping with German military activities in the two world wars and as a reaction to the Great Depression:

> The vast increase of state intervention in the First World War owed more to German submarines than to Keir Hardie; when the blockade began to throttle Britain's food supplies, even Churchill told the House of Commons he preferred 'War Socialism' to a negotiated peace. It was much the same in the Second World War, and national planning and national ownership, which in the period 1945-1951 seemed the result of a Labour government putting socialist principles into effect, were to a great degree the legacy of a state which had been organised to fight a total war.
>
> Owing to the number of and influence of active socialists in the government or in the upper ranks of the temporary civil service, and to the strong socialist commitment of the trade union leaders in some of the basic industries, the solution to the nation's wartime planning problems was frequently coloured, if not fashioned, by socialist attitudes or objectives. Yet many of the wartime currents which flowed in the direction of a welfare state came from Liberal, Conservative and non-political sources, and emanated much less from theories about social organisation than from a feeling that the poverty, ill health and injustice of the twenties and thirties could, and should, be eliminated, if not during the war, at least after the war was over.[4]

Is the State a 'mother' or 'big brother'? For the survivors of the Great Depression and World War II, the State was a 'mother'. The trend now, however, is to perceive the State as a maligned 'big brother' or (at least) the costly inefficient bumbler portrayed in *Yes Minister* and *Yes Prime Minister*.

Here are some examples of the changing perceptions of government from 'mother' to 'big brother':

1. ***There has been the gradual acceptance of the views of the 'New Right' critics of big government.***

The most important are Hayek and the Friedmans. The Friedmans have described their struggles as follows:

> Friedrich Hayek's *Road to Serfdom*, a surprise best-seller in Britain and in the United States in 1944, was probably the first real inroad in the dominant intellectual view. Yet the impact of the free market countercurrent was at first minute. Even for those of us who were actively promoting free markets in the 1950s and 1960s, it is difficult to recall how strong and pervasive was the intellectual climate of the times.
>
> The tale of two books by the present authors, both directed at the general public and both promoting the same policies, provides striking evidence of the change in the climate of opinion. The first, *Capitalism and Freedom*, published in 1962 and destined to sell more than 400 000 copies in the next eighteen years, was not reviewed at the time in a single popular American periodical. The second, *Free to Choose*, published in 1980, was reviewed by every major publication, became the year's best-selling non-fiction book in the United States, and received worldwide attention.[5]

2. ***Public administration scholars have questioned the efficacy of 'big government'.***

Political analyst Glyn Davis has this to say of one such scholar:

Aaron Wildavsky began as a sympathetic observer, but soon
professed disappointment in the effects of state intervention.
Everywhere he discovered the small achievements of public policy
overwhelmed by their unintended consequences. It was easier to
find an honest person than an effective program.

Public policies so often fail, Wildavsky argued, because minds
are small while the world is huge, complex and disorderly. Political volatility and theoretical poverty limit guesses about the future.
Existing economic and social models of causation are too simplistic
or underdeveloped to sustain viable attempts at controlled change.
Life is larger than our categories.[6]

An example of Wildavsky's thinking is his book *Implementation*[7]—
which has a very descriptive sub-title: 'How Great Expectations in
Washington are Dashed in Oakland; Or, Why It's Amazing that
Federal Programs Work at All, This Being a Saga of the Economic
Development Administration as Told by Two Sympathetic Observers
Who Seek to Build Morals on a Foundation of Ruined Hopes'.

The book describes the federal US Economic Development
Administration's attempt to create employment for US minorities in
the Californian city of Oakland during the period 1966-1970 — an
attempt characterised by a gap between promise and performance
even greater than that normally experienced in public administration.
This was a program which had an auspicious beginning: finance
(US$23 000 000) had been appropriated; city officials and employers
were in accord with the project; and federal officials were enthusiastic.
But possibly less than one hundred jobs were created permanently.

What went wrong? Implementing a policy requires clearance from
a multiplicity of agencies at various levels of government, each of
which has its own priorities and perspectives; unforeseen technical
problems arise in the most mundane of projects; key personnel resign;

costs escalate; governments (and priorities) change; set routines necessitate delays; and so on.

In the Oakland case there were no villains. The conflict which did occur was prosaic rather than dramatic. The apparently simple and straightforward was in reality complex and convoluted.

The authors' analysis of the process of implementation stresses that, in the complexity of joint action, it is often easier to agree about the ends of a project than the means to achieve them. This may be due, for instance, to incompatability with other commitments; a preference for other programs; simultaneous commitments to other projects; dependence on others who lack a sense of urgency in the project; differences of opinion on leadership and proper organisational roles; legal and procedural differences; or lack of resources.

Michael James (a visiting Fellow at the Sydney New Right think-tank, Centre for Independent Studies) has examined the question of why it is so difficult for politicians to keep promises to make government smaller. Proponents of fiscal responsibility and smaller government have vowed to prune government size and spending. Yet, despite the political rhetoric, there is a realisation that governments seem to grow of their own accord.

James argues that as government grows, it becomes increasingly difficult to trace its total impact on the original income distribution. Consequently, it is difficult to sustain the claim that big government promotes any particular pattern of income distribution, just or otherwise. The phenomenon of big government is the unintended consequence of established political commitments and the interaction between political actors. The incentives facing politicians make it difficult for them to act in the long-term interest of society when so many special interest groups are pressing for short-term favours for themselves.[8]

US New Right activist Robert Poole has argued that privatisation is being forced on governments because they are trying to do too much:

> Privatisation is a global phenomenon because governments everywhere have become overextended. Shrinking big government is far less a matter of ideology than it is a fiscal necessity. State-owned enterprises are money sinks. Insulated from marketplace discipline, they operate inefficiently (often requiring taxpayer subsidy). Moreover, they pay neither corporate income taxes nor local property taxes, thus draining the economy and the national treasury. Selling such enterprises produces both one-shot revenues and ongoing annual operating savings, as well as new tax revenues.[9]

3. *The pendulum of state intervention is perceived as having swung much further than could ever have been imagined back in the 1930s and 1940s.*

Here are three illustrations of this. The first is 'tort liability' — liability that is not criminal. David Blundy writes:

> The idea that consuming things can be a health hazard began with that American 'whistle-blower' of the 60s, Ralph Nader. Having killed off General Motors' Corvair motor car with a devastating book *Unsafe at any Speed: The designed-in dangers of the American automobile*, he quickly became the guru of the burgeoning green movement and a prophet of the anti-establishment, middle-class soft Left. But it seems the consumer watchdogs have succeeded in scaring to death the consumers themselves.
>
> Mary Douglas and Aaron Wildavsky, the US authors of *Risk and Culture*, ask: 'Are the dangers really increasing or are we more afraid?' The answer, they say, is the latter.

They ask: 'What are Americans afraid of?' Nothing much except the food they eat, the water they drink, the air they breathe, the land they live on, the energy they use. In only fifteen to twenty years, confidence in the physical world has turned to doubt, they say.

Writer Peter Huber argues that Americans pay an enormous 'safety tax', levied on virtually everything they buy, sell and use. It accounts for thirty per cent of the cost of a stepladder and more than ninety-five per cent of the cost of childhood vaccines.

Its legal name is 'tort liability' and Americans pay more than $80 billion a year in insurance against the risk of being sued. Those billions are passed on to the consumer. . .

The risk of litigation means you cannot use the diving-board in New York city schools or a sled in city parks in Denver and fireworks displays are banned across the US. The famous rollercoaster, the Cyclone on Coney Island, has been shut because of the fear of an accident and the litigation that would ensue.

A litigious lunacy has gripped the US. A family won $1 000 for 'emotional distress' after their dog died in the municipal pound.

A man in a telephone booth which was demolished by a drunk driver successfully sued the manufacturer of the booth.[10]

The second illustration is the growth of 'red tape'. Australian science affairs commentator Robin Williams writes:

The Ten Commandments is made up of 216 [words]. Even the Gettysburg Address is only 256. Yet the US regulations on Cabbage Imports require 36 217 words![11]

The third illustration is the foolish behaviour of bureaucrats. Australian political scientiest Allan Peachment writes:

[Some] individuals almost had their livelihood taken away by ministerial mismanagement. For example, a Geraldton [West Australian] farmer was prevented from farming his property for five years due to the discovery of a rare plant species. He was obliged to threaten and attempt a hunger strike to the death in order to speed compensation of about $400 000, and had not eaten for twelve days when the issue was reconsidered on election day.

In similar style, the state's only cooper, who had been producing barrels for twenty-five years and selling them seven days a week, was informed that his products were classed as furniture and could not be sold outside normal trading hours. Nor was he allowed to employ apprentices as he had no trade papers — but then, no-one could test him. A departmental spokesman claimed that the cooper had been told that, because his products were unique, an application for weekend trading would probably be approved, a claim that the cooper denied. There should be a prize for people who survive this kind of 'how not to do it' administration.[12]

So the 'big brother' perception of government is well established.

❑ Second, the fragmentation of political power

Politicians have become the 'after dinner mints' of society. They are a pleasant addition to a meal, but not an essential one. Most politicians are to be assessed, at most, by their entertainment value, rather than by what they achieve.

I do not disparage those people who work for social change through political parties. If people think that is where their efforts are best directed, fine. All I wish to emphasise is that political power does not necessarily reside in politicians or political parties.

One hundred and twenty years ago, the English economist and

journalist Walter Bagehot distinguished between the *decorative* and the *executive* parts of politics. Queen Victoria, contrary to current views, did not run the UK; the Crown was the decorative part of politics. The Crown's task was to be colourful, honourable and inspirational. The sordid part of politics, with its horse-trading, was the parliament and the cabinet. The Queen had three rights as the monarch: the rights to be consulted, to encourage and to warn.

Since about World War II, I believe, parliament has joined the Crown in the decorative part of politics. However, the media focus on elections, foibles, finances and factions of politicians implies that the parliament is running the nation.

This trend is further bolstered by the involvement of movie stars, pop singers and sports people in running for office. The general public's attention is thus being further diverted from the real issues affecting their daily lives. Glitz and glamour have replaced substantive debate.

There is no media conspiracy involved. The media controllers have assumed that the public has little appetite for complicated issues and that superficial reporting — if not downright fiction — will suffice. A whole generation has come along which knows no better than the current low levels of journalism and so has nothing with which to compare it. Thus, sex and sport sell newspapers; the royals are always good copy; and the politicians can also provide some entertainment. Politicians have become people who are entrusted with speech but not authority.

Who then now forms the executive? Who has the power? I believe — contrary to the view of people who like a conspiracy theory of life — that there is no single source of power. We are now in an era of the fragmentation of power. For about three centuries the core of politics has been the national government. That era is now ending. Some power is going to international entities such as the transnational corporations and the UN, and some is going to grassroots non-governmental organisations. National governments will linger on for years but will no longer be the sole focus of political interest.

Whichever political party comes to office in Canberra or London or Washington, it does not come to power. In the economic sphere, for example, the government has to struggle with business, including transnational corporations, and trade unions. There are also restraints imposed by legal, conciliation and arbitration procedures.

There is also the civil service, immortalised in the television series *Yes Minister* and *Yes Prime Minister.* In *Yes Prime Minister,* Sir Humphrey Appleby is the Cabinet Secretary. An anonymous verse describes the crucial role of the Cabinet Secretary:

Now that the Cabinet's gone to dinner
The Secretary stays and gets thinner and thinner
Racking his brains to record and report
What he thinks they think they ought to have thought.[13]

Backbench government MPs and the opposition are out in the cold. But surely cabinet ministers have real power? No: they will only have a narrow range of options because of each government's declining power.

It is difficult to find anyone nowadays who has a good word to say for the civil service. This is very different from the 'mother' days of the 1930s. For example, a famous movie made in 1935, *Sanders of the River* (starring Paul Robeson and Leslie Banks), portrayed an imperial civil servant in British West Africa who tracks down a group of white crooks encouraging rebellion among Africans by exploiting tribal differences.

Its UK image then changed to that of the 1950s of tea-sipping lethargic bumblers in the BBC's radio comedy, *The Men from the*

Ministry. Now the image is one of all-powerful manipulators who control their political masters as portrayed in the award-winning BBC television comedy series, *Yes Minister,* first broadcast on 25 February 1980.

Yes Minister contains a great deal of truth. Quotations are used extensively in this section. Since most readers will not have direct work experience in the civil service, some of the main points may be hard to accept. Watching them in a television comedy is one thing: being told that they are true is another. Consequently, to avoid the risk of readers accusing me of summarising the extracts incorrectly, the full extracts are given. Readers who still remained stunned by these revelations are urged to read the books cited.

There are, for example, the *Diaries* of the late Richard Crossman (a minister in Harold Wilson's UK government between 1964 and 1970). A later UK government tried to get the *Diaries* banned (largely because of pressure from civil servants). The *Diaries* are all the more amazing since Crossman used to lecture on politics and had a long parliamentary career before becoming a minister. But, despite his background, he still remained surprised by the way in which his civil servants misled him, were occasionally uncooperative and combined together to block his schemes. If such an experienced person had difficulty with his civil servants, then one can only speculate on how much more difficult it is for someone far less experienced to cope with them.

Harold Evans was the Editor of the *Sunday Times* when it decided to publish extracts from the *Diaries*. Evans later recalled:

> His diaries were not exciting because of scoops and stories, though they were 'a good read', but because they realised his ambition to show how the British system of government really works in practice, for good and for ill. The mass of detail of Prime Ministerial

and Cabinet manoeuvres and Ministers' arguments with civil servants showed the extent to which the doctrine of collective responsibility is a mask for Cabinet ignorance and impotence.

Such is the power of the permanent officials that a Minister without the backing of the Prime Minister or Chancellor cannot hope to appeal against an interdepartmental paper produced by civil servants. And a much-debated constitutional change of significance had indeed taken place. The Prime Minister is not first among equals. He (or she) has become all-powerful. Or, as Crossman put it in conversation: 'He can now snuff out an opponent in his own party more easily than any Soviet leader can demote or dismiss anyone opposed to him.'[14]

The candid memoirs of some politicians, then, contain graphic accounts of how little power they had in office. Here is one such example — from UK Labour MP George Thomas, who was for a time a Home Office Minister:

[A] case that caused me anxiety concerned one of my own constituents. A lady had been fined two pounds for a motoring offence in Cowbridge, in the Vale of Glamorgan. She maintained that she had been to Cowbridge to pay the fine, but two years later police had come to her home and arrested her for non-payment. The neighbours had watched her being taken away and in the police station she had been treated as a common criminal.

The registrar's book at Cowbridge had an entry in pencil indicating that she had indeed paid the fine as she claimed. However, since it was not written in ink, it was not valid. Unfortunately the man in charge of the book had died at about the date of the pencilled entry, so we could only guess why it had not been inked over.

Before the election, I had had great publicity when I unsuccessfully raised this case in a Commons adjournment debate. Now my constituent wrote and asked if I could reopen it as I was a Home Office minister. It was a humiliation for me finally to have to write to her and report that red tape had defeated us. I was convinced that an injustice had been done, but without more proof I could do nothing. That case will always rankle with me.[15]

Why, therefore — from a civil service point of view — bother to have ministers? Richard Crossman says they have four main uses in the UK (and, it may be assumed, elsewhere):

1. We have to win the battle in the cabinet. The cabinet minister goes to the cabinet as the champion of his department and, therefore, goes supplied with a departmental brief. Where expenditure is concerned, a department is usually well enough briefed to give him the arguments which the Chancellor is going to use, and the reply to them. (And, no doubt, the Chancellor has been briefed in the same way against him!) He is there to fight the battle of the department in the absence of the department. . .

2. The minister is there to present the departmental case to parliament. Civil servants don't pretend to be expert on handling parliament. They sit there in their little box, ready to brief us as we answer questions and handle debates. They really rely on the minister to look after them in parliament.

3. Our job is to look after them in the country, to go around opening new buildings and attending banquets — performing in a minor way the jobs which endear our monarchy to the public. This is a minister's representational role, to represent the Queen on official occasions. And that is very useful to the ministry — as well as to the party.

4. Lastly, there is decision-making. There's a whole mass of

routine decisions, departmental decisions, decisions which are
not to do with politics, and which have to be taken regularly
and quickly. Therefore, a minister who is available to give a
decision in twenty-four hours is essential to a ministry.[16]

Gerald Kaufman, a minister in the UK Labour government (1974–
1979) has recalled the efficiency with which each department operates.
Prior to each cabinet meeting, the civil servants hand their respective
ministers a briefing document for the meeting:

Your departmental briefing documents are works of art. They will
analyse the issue in question and the papers concerned, not only from
the standpoint of the government as a whole but purely from the
departmental point of view. They will advise you on the 'Line to
Take' (a heading all on its own), the sentences beginning with master-
ly injunctions such as, 'The minister will wish to say. . .' (This form of
words was, in fact, banished from all briefing documents submitted to
me but officials, nothing abashed, simply submitted alternative for-
mulations which amounted to the same thing.)

They will even include speaking notes, which the minister can
read out without having taken the trouble to study the actual
cabinet papers at all. This did indeed happen from time to time at
meetings I attended, the minister in question giving himself away
by unusual fluency and cogency of argument, coupled with
stumbles over faulty punctuation. Other ministers would hide
smiles of amused superiority, but at one meeting, dealing with an
exceptionally complicated subject, all of those gathered together
simply read out their briefs to each other; it seemed the most sensible thing to do.[17]

In all this, civil servants are out to protect their territory. Former presidential adviser William Safire, in writing of the situation in the US, says:

> While newspaper exposes of pettiness or corruption sometimes result in bureaucratic embarrassment or even prosecution, the press has been frequently used by the bureaucracy to build its protective shell. An adept bureaucrat, his domain threatened by a cutoff of funds, is able to alert those interest groups about to be adversely affected and to zero them in on the appropriate newsmen. A judicious leak, a horrendous prediction of the homelessness, starvation or pestilence the cutback would cause, a follow-up reaction story about the interest group, a letter campaign by them to interested congressmen, a severe editorial or two, and the public interest gives way to the bureaucracy's focussed interest.[18]

US political commentator Charles Peters has written:

> 'No activity in a government agency is given as high a priority as securing and enlarging its budget,' Leonard Reed, a writer and former bureaucrat, has said. 'Bureaucrats almost invariably believe in the function their agency exists to perform, whether it is providing information to farmers or preserving the national forests. A new bureaucracy, the darling of the administration that establishes it, has a missionary zeal about its function. As a bureaucracy ages, it loses glamour and finds itself expending an increasing share of its energy on obtaining funds. . .
>
> 'Gradually a hierarchy of administrative officers, executive officers, budget officers, congressional liaison officers and public information officers grows up, almost the sole purpose of which is fund-wheedling. Since there is a certain logic to the proposition that without money an agency can't function, the bureaucrat. . . finds nothing wrong with spending more and more of its time and

attention aiding the quest for more money, much of which is now needed to support the large money-raising apparatus that has grown up in the agency.'[19]

William Safire has an amusing account of President Nixon's attempt to abolish the Board of Tea-Tasters, established in 1897. While this may have done good work in the nineteenth century, its work had been taken over by the Food and Drug Administration. But when the White House tried to abolish the Board, President Nixon could not get his legislation through Congress — the key committee reviewing the legislation contained friends of the Board. At the time Nixon left office, the Board still existed, costing $125 000 per year and still with no work to do.[20]

The civil service is difficult to change. Safire records President Nixon's personal campaign to have some old Navy huts, built alongside the Mall in Washington, demolished. In contrast to his clash with the Board of Tea-Tasters, the president eventually won:

Because the President of the United States took a continuing interest, because at least two of his aides were made to feel that its success was a crucial test of their ability, and because the president kept prodding, issuing orders, refusing to be 'reasonable', a few miserable buildings were finally knocked down and their occupants reassigned. An elephant gun should not be used to kill a rabbit, the saying goes, but on some matters affecting entrenched bureaucratic elephants, only elephant guns will do. Combining pride, relief and wonderment, the president called Ehrlichman and then Hughes to say, 'We have finally gotten something done.'[21]

Almost all politicians find government a frustrating experience. They come to power expecting to bring about changes, but usually leave office with comparatively little achieved. The system itself thwarts major changes. Indeed, a leader's supporters may be disappointed that the leader, once in office, goes in an entirely different direction. Instead of changing policies, the leader's own policies get changed.

The only politician who now counts is the Prime Minister. Of course, Mr Hawke as Prime Minister of Australia did have different policies from Mr Fraser as Prime Minister. But there is an even larger difference between Mr Hawke before he came to office and while in office. Mr Hawke in the 1979 ABC Radio Boyer Lectures, entitled 'The Resolution of Conflict', made various proposals for reform such as abolishing state governments, strengthening local governments and filling a quarter of the positions in the federal ministry with appointments from outside the parliament. None of these major reforms was introduced during the eight years he was Prime Minister.

I do not believe that politicians are today any more stupid, corrupt or ignorant than they have been over the past two or three centuries. It is simply that we are using a Second Wave institution in a Third Wave era.

Politicians are being required to make too many decisions, too quickly, with too little information. Until about a century ago, life was easier for politicians. Governments were expected to defend the nation from foreign attack and to maintain law and order at home. They had little or no responsibility for the poor, education, unemployed, the homeless, the disabled, under-production in factories, transportation, disease or the environment.

In London in the mid-nineteenth century, eighty-five people worked in the foreign departments (the UK was controlling about a quarter of the globe at this time), eighty-five at the Home Office and 103 at the Board of Trade. A minister knew all his members of staff. There were only eight government departments.

During the past century, governments have been expected to take a more direct role in virtually all issues confronting their citizens. The welfare state has been created. A vast civil service has been created providing care for the community, regulating industry, protecting workers, educating children. Unfortunately, every time a new service is provided, a new responsibility is given to a minister. No cabinet minister knows for sure what is being done in his or her department, let alone what is happening in other departments.

The 'overloaded agenda' is also manifested in just how long it now takes to do something. The world is drowning in paperwork. It has been estimated that paperwork in organisations doubles every three years. The advent of computers has not helped ease the overloaded agenda. In the pen and ink era, reports were provided on a monthly basis; now they can be spewed out on an hourly basis. We are getting more information, but time is taken up absorbing it rather than acting constructively.

Sir James Callaghan, who rose from being a tax clerk to become the UK Prime Minister, was asked on a BBC radio program what was his greatest achievement. He was, incidentally, the first Prime Minister this century to hold the three great offices of state: Chancellor of the Exchequer, Home Secretary and Foreign Secretary (1964–1970 and 1974–1976). His greatest achievement, he said, was to get 'cats' eyes' (reflector discs) put in the centre of British roads. That was when he was in Attlee's government in the late 1940s! The rest of his career was an anti-climax.

What do politicians (even as prime ministers) manage to achieve? What achievements last? The achievements of most politicians are no more permanent than perfume on a lace handkerchief.

In November 1990, Mrs Thatcher ended her eleven years as UK Prime Minister — one of the longest in UK history. But what did she actually achieve? Privatisation, deregulation and reducing trade union power were all key policies. But did they bring about economic progress? Her economic failures outweigh her economic successes:

FAILURES	1979	1990
Inflation:	10.3%	10.9%
Trade balance:	–£549m	–£19.1bn
Mortgage payments:		
(People 6-12 months in arrears)	8,420	76,280
Mortgage interest rate:	11.75%	14.5%
Growth in GDP:	2.8%	2.1%
Share of GDP invested		
in manufacturing	3.35%	2.4%
People on less than half		
average income:	4.4m	7.7m

SUCCESSES		
Strike days:	29.4m	4.13m
Company shareholders:	3m	11m
Home owners:	11.35m	15.05m[22]

Despite Mrs Thatcher's undoubted energy and political courage, she was drowned by the oncoming Third Wave of governance. The emphasis in public affairs has shifted from politics to economics; it has shifted from things which politicians *can* control to things which they *barely* control. Politics have remained largely national, whereas economies have become increasingly international and, thus, manageable by national governments only within narrow limits.

Since politicians speak of the 'national economy', it is assumed that there exists a nationally manageable economy — which ignores how far all national economies *have* become mere slices of an international economy. This has lowered the reputation of politicians who cannot cope with economic problems, but talk as if they can.

❑ Third, the triumph of form over content

Unfortunately, fame remains a powerful attraction for politicians. David Stockman (a disenchanted member of President Reagan's cabinet) complained that for Reagan and his staff 'reality happened once a day on the evening news'. All presidential activities were geared to their presentation on television. If something was too complicated for television, it was not on his agenda. President Reagan's ship of state was staffed by a public relations crew.

Since politicians are now a decorative part of politics, a large amount of their time has to be given over to creating and maintaining the right image. This reduces the amount of time available to running a government department. It also means that, with rare exceptions, the best and the brightest are not likely to be attracted to a career in politics. People with a concern about substantive issues, rather than being exposed to media intrusions, will have careers elsewhere.

Sir James Callaghan has recalled the impact of the mass media on the regular meetings, begun in the 1970s, of the seven major non-communist industrial nations:

> Bonn [1978] was the last summit I attended, and with the passage of time their character has changed. The participants of the 1970s have now left the scene, and their successors seem to regard summits as media events or as opportunities to enhance their election prospects, with thousands of photographers and journalists jostling for the best angle. The leaders make speeches to each other which are intended for public consumption back home. All this is a far cry from our original intention.[23]

However, all these high level visits and summit conferences are great fun for the participants. John Kenneth Galbraith (an economist and former US Ambassador to India) has explained the significance of these events:

> Since World War II, the visit by a head of state to his counterpart
> in another capital has become our most relished form of interna-
> tional intercourse. It wins an impressive if depressingly repetitive
> press coverage, but its purpose is only slightly understood.
>
> Such visits are not to do business; the principals are rarely in
> command of the detail that any genuine negotiation requires. Also
> — a further handicap to any achievement — both disagreement
> and agreement must be avoided. Disagreement signifies failure
> and reflects badly on the participants; agreement, as distinct from
> mere ratification, is too dangerous. As noted, one or both of the
> principals are certain to be insufficiently informed; a contract
> agreed to at their level cannot easily be undone.
>
> State visits are almost entirely a pleasurable requisite of high of-
> fice. They are greatly enjoyed by those making them and, on
> frequent occasions, evoke a display of enthusiasm and affection in
> the country visited that the visitor knows he will never achieve
> or deserve at home.
>
> New Delhi, next only to Washington, London and perhaps
> Paris, was the best place to observe these ceremonials. The Indian
> scene and tradition lend themselves well to pageantry; having no
> alternative occupation, thousands of Indians can be counted upon
> to turn out for a visitor, although on occasion for the head of a
> very minor principality a small subsidy had to be paid to those
> bringing bullock carts to line the route. In my years, the state
> visits averaged around one every fortnight in the season of
> tolerable weather.[24]

❏ Fourth, the complexity of modern diplomacy

The scale of modern diplomacy is underlined in this comparison with
a past age from the US:

The [US State] Department has come a long way since September 15, 1789, when it began with a staff of six, a budget of $7 961, and two diplomatic missions. Today, the Department employs more than 24 000 American and foreign citizens, has a budget of almost $4 billion, and operates more than 250 posts overseas.

Two centuries ago, the first Secretary of State, Thomas Jefferson, walked only a few feet to reach his office. He lived across the street from a modest three-storey building in Philadelphia that was the Department of State. Its current home, occupied since 1961, contains more than 1.3 million square feet of space.[25]

Diplomacy is now a lot more complicated than it used to be. For example, an international conference a century ago could be conducted by less than twenty persons (always men) negotiating on behalf of most of the world's population. The Briton would speak on behalf of one-third of the globe (including Australia, New Zealand, Canada, India and parts of Africa), while the Frenchman would speak also on behalf of a large number of colonials. All negotiations were conducted in French.

There was a common system of values; these white men were drawn from the upper classes of their society and knew that they were destined to govern the world. There were disputes as to who should be governing what, but none of them challenged the overall idea that they were meant to govern the world.

Contemporary negotiations, by contrast, are much more complicated. The UN has two working languages (English and French) and all key documents and statements have to be provided in an additional four other languages (Chinese, Arabic, Russian and Spanish). There is obviously a breakdown in shared values; negotiators are no longer drawn from one class or one sex or one skin colour.

Similarly, there are many more nation-states. They vary in population size from China (of well over a billion persons) to small Pacific island communities. There are similar disparities in terms of economic and military power.

An indication of the complexity of modern negotiation is the Law of the Sea Conference which involved 4 000 delegates working for well over a decade to produce the new treaty. This complexity should be contrasted with the swift action taken in the 1940s during which the International Monetary Fund, the World Bank and the General Agreement on Tariffs and Trade were set up.

A good example of this is the Marshall Plan. In 1947, US Secretary of State, George C. Marshall, proposed a plan to help put Europe back on its feet. He outlined a basic proposal at the Harvard University graduation on 5 June 1947. The Europeans should plan their own reconstruction, while the US supplied the credits and loans to help them buy needed material.

It took only five weeks from General Marshall's announcement that the US would pay for the reconstruction of Europe to the creation of the Organisation of European Economic Cooperation and Congress's vote to spend initially US$4 000 million on rebuilding Europe. By the end of 1952 — at its conclusion — the Marshall Plan had sent some US$13.3 billion (an estimated US $100 billion in today's dollars) to aid Europe. In return, Europe was transformed from a site of ruin to become a political, economic and military partner to the US.

Even the labels in diplomacy are now more complicated. One example is the labels 'First World', 'Second World' and 'Third World' discussed in chapter 1. But the Second World is rejecting Stalinist centralised planning and trying to develop free market economies. If the Second World wants to merge into the First World, what number should be accorded the so-called Third World? Moreover, First World nations are now trying to stabilise their regions by absorbing poorer (Second or Third World) nations: the US is focussing on Latin America,

Japan on China and the EEC on Eastern Europe.

A second example of this increasing complexity is the definition of a 'less developed nation'. Singapore was certainly a less developed nation when Mr Lee Kuan Yew became president in 1960. The *Australian* newspaper has written:

> By all material measures it is a successful society. For the past twenty-five years its economy has grown at an average of nine per cent a year.
>
> When Mr Lee took over, twenty per cent of all households were living in poverty; today there are none. Instead, there is full employment among Singapore's 2.7 million people. And there is a gross national product per capita of $13 420 — higher than that of Ireland and Spain, not far short of Australia's $15 700.
>
> Thirty years ago Singapore was a Third World mini-state with few resources beyond the unemployed potential of its people. It was threatened by communist subversion. Today it is one of Asia's leading financial and manufacturing centres — a 'tiger' with per capita reserves second only to Taiwan's.[26]

What category is Singapore now in? The old categories obviously don't work.

Why should foreign policies be left to national governments? Why cannot local and state governments have their own foreign policies? Given the fragmentation of modern authority, this is now occurring. American international lawyer Richard Bilder indicates how this is happening in the US:

> Over 830 cities and other municipal governments have established official 'sister city' relationships with over 1 270 cities and communities in ninety other countries. Almost every state has sent

trade missions to other countries to encourage exports and foreign direct investment, and over forty states have established trade or investment offices in foreign countries. Over twenty-eight cities and communities have declared themselves 'sanctuaries' for refugees from Central America. Some twenty-three states, fourteen counties, eighty cities and the Virgin Islands have enacted various kinds of divestment or procurement legislation or ordinances directed at South Africa's apartheid policies. And states and municipalities have taken a variety of other specific actions to express or implement their foreign policy views.[27]

Australia is also moving in this direction. One example of local governments expanding their international networks has been town-twinning. This is the standard way of enhancing friendship with cities of close allies or trading partners. A second example has been the declaration of municipal 'nuclear free zones'. Australian local councils were, in fact, among the international pioneers in this work.

A third example comes from the periodic attempts of capital cities to host the Olympics. To help its 1986 attempt to host the next Olympics, the Lord Mayor of Brisbane said that her city was a 'zone of international friendship'.

Why is local government more involved in the foreign policy process?

1. *Because of the greater pluralistic nature of modern society, a national government does not necessarily speak on behalf of all of its people.*

Americans certainly supported Roosevelt in World War II, but not all of them have supported recent policies on the arms race, Central America or South Africa — hence their policies on these matters are at variance from that of the US government.

In 1988, with mounting concern about the erosion of the ozone layer, some US councils acted independently to pass legislation banning food packaging and plastic foam products containing chloroflurocarbons (CFCs). With the depletion of rainforests, I expect similar laws on rainforest products entering municipal areas from nations like Malaysia.

2. *International affairs have become too complicated for top-down oversight.*

Before World War II, national governments had a limited range of foreign responsibilities — mainly the maintenance of diplomatic relations and securing national defence. Diplomats were not expected, for example, to drum up foreign trade for their citizens.

Since 1945, however, the globe has become more interdependent. There are few issues which are solely 'national' in character. Problems do not recognise national boundaries, thereby obliging national governments to cooperate on such matters as telecommunications, pollution and AIDS.

Furthermore, national governments have become more involved in the daily affairs of their citizens and corporations. Diplomats are now expected to operate as public relations officials for their citizens' activities and to drum up foreign trade. But national governments cannot hope to control all the non-governmental activities.

The Clearing House Interbank Payments System (CHIPS), for example, which is operated by 140 US banks specialising in international finance, conducts several billion international transactions daily. Attempts by the national government to control these transactions tightly, will not only inevitably fail, but will also inadvertently scare off international trade and stifle domestic economic growth.

Allied to this is the networking impact of modern technology. The impact of technology on transportation and communication is making it possible for cities and regions formerly isolated to establish direct links beyond their national boundaries. For example, in the US, before the jet aeroplane, air travel to Europe and Asia originated from a few cities on the east and west coasts of the United States. Now it originates from Houston, Atlanta, Pittsburgh, Cleveland, St Louis and Chicago.

If charter flights were included, the list would comprise at least thirty US cities.

Additionally, cities are linked directly abroad by satellite, telex and other forms of electronic communication. Inland cities in Africa, Asia, Europe and Latin America are being increasingly linked directly to cities in other nations. Since cities are linked directly to each other, there is far less need to centralise contacts through capital cities.

3. *In many countries there is greater public debate of foreign policy than there once was, and centralised control tends to restrict this.*

Prior to World War I, the US and British tradition, which was followed in Australia, was that public debate was largely limited to domestic policies; it was assumed that national governments were better informed on foreign matters and so were left to make the decisions. World War I shattered that confidence.

Organisations like the Royal Institute of International Affairs, the Australian Institute of International Affairs and the League of Nations Union (forerunner of the United Nations Association) all date from the World War I period of disillusionment with leaving foreign policy to national governments. Policies devised in secret, out of the public eye, are not necessarily adequate ones. Closed doors create closed thinking.

Foreign Service officials have no monopoly of wisdom when it comes to foreign policy.

4. There has been an increasing desire to take responsibility for our own affairs across the political spectrum.
There has been the amalgam of New Right thinking of limited government intervention in the economy and the 'think globally/act locally' activism from the so-called left wing. People want to take more responsibility for their own affairs — including seeing themselves as global citizens.

5. There has been greater regional government interest in foreign policy.
In Australia, state governments are devising their own foreign policies, especially on trade and tourism. For example, the June 1988 edition of the Australian government's *Australian Foreign Affairs Record* contained a long article on South Australia's overseas links.

All Australian states, of course, have retained their pre-federation 'colonial high commissioner' posts in London, the agents-general (each in separate buildings). The South Australian agent-general operates primarily as a trade development and promotion post and its roles include the investigation of market opportunities in Britain and Europe for South Australian manufacturers and primary producers, and assistance to exporters in the key markets of Britain, France, the Netherlands, Sweden and Germany.

If state governments are seeing themselves as actors on the international scene — especially now that Australia itself is more active on that scene — it is appropriate to see local governments also doing so. It would be in itself an educational experience for local government office-holders to be obliged to think about the international dimensions of their decisions.

❑ Fifth, the creation of a post-imperial world

We will look back on the Cold War era (1945–1990) with a sense of nostalgia. Life seemed far more straightforward then. With the ending of the Cold War, political attention is, among other things, back on old ethnic rivalries.

1. *The collapse of the Eastern European Soviet empire*

Moscow used brute force and the secret police to maintain order and stifle ethnic unrest. With Moscow no longer maintaining order in Eastern Europe, old rivalries are once again coming to the fore. A November 1990 survey of Eastern Europe flashpoints contained this list:

Germany and Poland. Issues include ownership of property in Poland once held by German citizens and the two states' conflicting claims about rights in the Baltic. Disagreements are likely to recur, notwithstanding the German parliament's reassurances and the September 12 treaty officially recognising the Oder-Neisse frontier.

Poland and Byelorussia, the Ukraine, and/or Lithuania. Since the end of World War II, the Bug River has been Poland's eastern border, but nationalists on all sides still debate the issue fiercely.

Hungary and Romania. The treatment of the Hungarian minority in Transylvania has been a source of conflict. In addition, both countries have at times claimed the region — a territorial dispute that goes back to the 1920 Treaty of Trianon and before.

Albania and Yugoslavia. At issue is the Serbian treatment of Albanians living in Kosovo. Serbian leader Slobodan Milosevic has relied on anti-Albanian sentiment as a key component of his popular appeal.

Bulgaria and Yugoslavia. At issue is Macedonia, with Bulgarians suspicious of Serbian sponsorship of a nationalist movement among Bulgarians who identify themselves as Macedonians. This nationalist movement has re-emerged in 1990 in an organisation called 'Ilenden'.

Greece and Yugoslavia. Greece denies the existence of a Macedonian identity, and border tensions run high due to an influx of people from Yugoslavia's 'Macedonian' republic, whose political intentions may include the eventual recreation of a greater Macedonia.

The [former] Soviet Union and Romania. The ethnic Romanian population of the Moldavian Soviet Socialist Republic wants cultural and political autonomy; nationalist advocates on both sides of the border want a unified Moldavian-Romanian state. Moscow denies that any abrupt reunification can take place.

Bulgaria and Turkey. Here the problem is the treatment of the Turkish minority in Bulgaria, and the Bulgarian perception of Turkish interference and threats.

Bulgaria and Romania. Dobrudja, a territory on the Black Sea, is divided between Romania and Bulgaria, but Bulgaria claims it entirely for itself. These countries are also in conflict over cross-Danube pollution and ancillary issues.[28]

Even this list is now dated. The very term 'Yugoslavia' has been dated by the 1991–1992 creation of the independent states of Slovenia, Croatia with its mix of Serbs and Croats, and Bosnia-Herzegovina with its volatile and warring mix of Muslims, Serbs and Croats, and Macedonia.

2. The collapse of the empire of the Soviet Union

But Moscow now also has problems closer to home. The USSR was, for example, one of the world's major Islamic nations. The fifth largest

Muslim population in the world is to be found in six former Soviet republics: Kirghizia, Tajikistan, Turkmenistan, Uzbekistan and Kazakhstan in central Asia and Azerbaijan in the Caucasian mountains to the west of the Caspian Sea. The Soviet Muslims are basically of Turkic and Iranian stock, with some admixtures from the Mongol hordes of the twelfth and thirteenth centuries. Linguistically and ethnically, they are related to the indigenous populations of Afghanistan, Iraq, Iran, Turkey and Sinkiang in China. Their Muslim heritage derives from Turkic, Persian and Arabic sources and consequently their written languages used Arabic script prior to the Soviet period.

The central Asians were amongst the earliest converts to Islam, adopting it around AD 622. The Arab conquest next carried it to the Caucasian mountains. Islam in the Caucasus was reinforced by the Ottoman campaigns of the sixteenth and seventeenth centuries; the Tartars of the Golden Horde embraced Islam between AD 1260 and 1340. The Kazakh and Kirghis tribes became Muslims under the Tartar influence in the nineteenth century while already under the Russian (Czarist) rule.

The Russian domination of central Asia began under the Czars' eastward and southward expansion of the sixteenth century. By the time of the 1917 Revolution, Czarist imperialism had established domination over the entire region from the Caucasian mountains to the Pamirs, eventually colliding with British interests in Afghanistan and Chinese interests in Sinkiang. While the USSR had established domination over entire central Asia and the Red Army hastened to absorb the nominally independent republics of Khiva and Bukhara in 1926, the armed conflict did not end till the crushing of the Basmachi independence movement led by traditional Muslim leadership in 1930.

Six decades later, the Islamic revival is well under way. Communism did not destroy Islam — its resistance to communism strengthened it and made it resilient. Mr Gorbachev was, in retrospect, very naive: he tried to abolish repression and tyranny in the USSR; what he did, in fact, was destroy the USSR because it was only held together by repression and tyranny. Both Islam and Christianity are flourishing in the former USSR.

Meanwhile, the European part of the former USSR continues to fragment. The Russian/Soviet empire kept the lid on the ethnic saucepan while the pressures built up. It is not yet clear if the new nations will become Switzerlands (with each one being composed of different but co-existing nationalities and languages) or Lebanons (falling apart in ethnic rivalries).

The first republics to leave — and the last to be absorbed into the USSR — were the three Baltic states (Latvia, Lithuania and Estonia), which Stalin took over at the beginning of World War II. Moscow rulers knew that if they were ever to permit those to go, this would create a precedent for the rest of the USSR. They left in August 1991 as the USSR was falling apart. The Baltic trickle became a flood and the USSR perished during the rest of 1991.

Empires rarely die peacefully. The break up is preceded by violence and there is often violence after independence as the new entities settle down. The Soviet pattern was a little different. Moscow could always mobilise sufficient repressive force to put down rebellions — often at great cost. But then, suddenly, the 1991 break up occurred quickly and with little bloodshed.

Russians are scattered throughout the old republics — they were often sent there to help run them because the locals were not sufficiently loyal to Moscow. They settled in the republics. Now there is no clear home for them. The 1990s will see the empire strike back.

3. The pressures on empires throughout the world
Most of the world's nations today are not homogeneous from an eth-

nic viewpoint. Most African nations had their borders drawn by colonial powers without regard to linguistic, ethnic or natural boundaries. Many other nations are composed of different ethnic groups which migrated from other places. Some nations are the current embodiment of old empires or the result of the conquest of many diverse groups. Nationalism takes a variety of forms: it can exclude ethnic diversity and be zenophobic; it can be a defence against the imposition of external domination; it can be a weapon to stop separatist movements.

While we still have a basic grid system of nation-states, there are other unifying factors spilling across this neat patchwork quilt. One is the different types of religion, notably Christianity, Islam and Buddhism.

A second is derived ethnic and language qualities. For example, there are 'German' communities in Czechoslovakia, Hungary, Rumania, Switzerland, France, Belgium and the former Soviet Union, and an entire sovereign state, Austria, belongs to the 'German nation'. Also Indians — as distinct communities — are to be found in the UK, Fiji, East Africa and the US. Further, Europeans of many ethnic backgrounds are also scattered around the world.

Here is another way of putting it: these two factors are continuations of the First Wave which have not been accommodated fully by the Second Wave nation-state: transnational religions and population groupings whose tribal boundaries do not match nation-state boundaries. The nation-state did not — and could not — resolve these problems in its heyday and now they are contributing to the erosion of the status of the nation-state.

❑ Sixth, the increase in transnational problems

There are no domestic markets any more: finance, trade and investment are global issues; debt and financial instability have become transnational. Migration does not stop at borders. AIDS and pollution of the environment are worldwide crises.

This globalisation creates two major problems. One is how to create an international framework enabling us to manage interdependence. A strengthened but restructured UN system should be the basis of such a framework. The other is how to manage interdependence, not only in an efficient, but also in an equitable way. Worldwide integration of markets does not have the same effect on all nations. For some nations, the process of increased interdependence results in marginalisation. The necessary framework for managing interdependence will have to be built around the notion of international social justice.

These challenges will be examined in more detail in the rest of the book in the context of the Third Wave. This chapter ends with a case study which demonstrates the current collision between Second Wave national attitudes on money and the emerging Third Wave global finance system.

In response to chaos in international monetary affairs during the Great Depression of the 1930s, the industrial world sought a system that would prevent such disorder after World War II when all the international economic institutions were created afresh. At the end of World War II, the Bretton Woods Conference was held. A new international monetary system was established (called the Bretton Woods system) and this system was to dominate the global political economy for some twenty-five years. Fixed exchange rates were established between national currencies under the Bretton Woods system; the International Monetary Fund (IMF) was created to ensure the stabilisation of these exchange rates.

The IMF was given the authority to lend monies to nations in balance of payments difficulties so those could both reduce their balance of payments deficits and stabilise their foreign exchange rates through sales and purchases of their own currency in other hard currencies. The US dollar became the preeminent world currency, supplanting the faltering British pound sterling.

But by the mid-1960s stresses began to appear. The US began to run larger balance of payments deficits and West Germany and Japan began to challenge the US domination of world trade. The first signs of the crack in the power of the dollar appeared in the mid-1960s and some nations (notably France) changed their dollars in exchange for gold. The US over-extended itself militarily and economically during the entire post-war period, culminating in its defeat in Indochina.

Finally by the late 1960s and early 1970s, it was apparent that the old Bretton Woods system could not last. President Nixon took the US out of the fixed exchange rate system in 1971 when he permitted the dollar to 'float' against other currencies, abandoning the obligation to enter into foreign exchange markets to stabilise the value of the dollar around a narrow band of fluctuations. Other nations followed suit and in 1973 the system of flexible exchange rates was formally adopted in the Smithsonian Agreement. The collapse of the Bretton Woods system had begun.

Another development was the holding of US dollars 'off shore' — beyond the control of the US government. The Eurodollar market began in the early Cold War years when the USSR wanted dollar deposits because the dollar was the most useful currency in financing its international transactions. But it was reluctant to hold these deposits in New York because of the threat that the US authorities might freeze the deposits.

The USSR believed that the political risk of dollar deposits was lower in London than in New York. After all, London was then the world's banking centre and, even though the UK was the US's political ally, no UK government would jeopardise London's banking reputation by caving in to any ally.

Global economic integration has outpaced political integration.

The Bretton Woods institutions established at the end of World War II — the IMF, the World Bank, and the General Agreement on Tariffs and Trade — are clearly inadequate to the task of managing a US$20 trillion world economy in which capital and trade flows have reached such volume and speed that they can wreak havoc with individual nations' economic policies.

In the immediate future, adjustments in the IMF's and World Bank's power structures will have to be made to give Japan, Germany and many nations outside the traditional developed world a greater say and to accommodate the former Soviet Union's and China's eventual integration into the world economy. Over the medium term, though, nothing less than a major overhaul of the Bretton Woods institutions will suffice. The US is no longer the world's sole economic giant. National politicians may not want to admit it, but financial factors are often largely beyond their control.

John Langmore, an Australian MP, has provided an example of the global economic integration:

> There is only one global financial market. Computers, combined with global telecommunication systems, have created the global financial market. Not only are the major currencies, including Australia's (which is the fifth or sixth most traded currency) traded throughout the whole twenty-four hours, but trends on Wall Street, Tokyo, London and Frankfurt strongly influence all other stock exchanges. There is one international currency market, one bond market, one market for credits and one stock exchange. International trade, too, continues to rise faster than national incomes, showing the growing interrelationships between national economies.[29]

Eventually, Third Wave global economic integration will be aided by a truly international currency (and not just a national currency like the US dollar being the basis of international transactions). But that is a long way off. Second Wave political considerations are obstacles. Having a national currency is like having a steel mill, a national flag and a national airline. Only with a national currency can a nation have its 'own' monetary policy. Governments want their constituents to be proud of their heritage — the prouder they are, the less reluctant they will be to pay taxes.

International monetary reform would be easier if nations were homogeneous. But most national borders are arbitrary — they tend to segregate economies with different industrial and institutional structures and electorates with different values. Conflicts in interest are inevitable, and complicate the process of monetary reform.

Two facts of national political life explain why efforts to reform the international system have not proved very successful. One is that the residents *within* nations frequently have conflicting interests. The second is that foreigners do not vote in domestic elections. Nations compete for markets. Whenever payments imbalances occur, there is conflict over whether the nations with a deficit or the nations with a surplus should take the initiative in making the necessary adjustments.

Political leaders talk about the virtues of international cooperation — but domestic factors frequently merit priority, especially when the next election may be only months away. As populations have become industrial and urban, governments have become increasingly concerned with economic welfare issues. Full employment, never a problem in an agricultural economy, has become a matter of importance for the urban wage worker.

The financial role of governments has increased to the point where in some nations taxes may amount to thirty per cent of national incomes. As expectations of higher living standards have become more widespread, raising the annual economic growth rate has loomed increasingly important as a national objective.

A final example of how Second Wave national policies lag behind Third Wave global finance is the problem of curtailing the 'laundering' of drug trafficking proceeds — estimated to involve about US$85 billion per year.[30] Drug funds enter the financial system either through the domestic financial system or by being sent abroad to be integrated into the financial systems of tax havens and then repatriated in the form of apparently legitimate transfers. Once within the banking system, these funds can easily be moved around and reinvested in drug production.

There is a UN treaty on this matter adopted at the end of 1988 as a global attack on drug trafficking. The convention put forward the principle that banking secrecy, which banks have often cited as their unassailable right, should not be allowed to interfere with criminal investigations. But only four of the eighty nations which signed the convention have yet ratified it — indicating how slow international cooperation on money-laundering has been.

The Bretton Woods Agreement provides some inspiration. That was a visionary concept. True, it has been superseded by events — some of which it helped create. But it was derived from imagination and hope. These are precisely the qualities needed on drug-money laundering. A new approach is required for this new era.

Part of the drug funds come from the trafficking in Colombia's cocaine (the world's biggest cocaine exporter). Why not provide financial incentives to Colombia to grow something else?

Colombian president Virgilio Barco says the failure of the United States to support renewal of an international coffee agreement has triggered a fifty per cent fall in world coffee prices that could cost Colombia US$400 million a year. That, reports the Washington Post, 'is six times greater than the $65 million in emergency aid. . .

that the Bush administration is sending Colombia to help it fight the drug barons there'. The price cut, Colombian officials warn, makes it harder to prevent farmers from diverting to coca, whose dried leaves are made into cocaine. Barco wrote to President Bush that the best way to help Colombia is through increased access for Colombian products, especially coffee, to the United States.[31]

In other words, international cooperation (a Third Wave characteristic) would be more successful than reliance upon national police action (a Second Wave characteristic).

This chapter demonstrates, I believe, that governments cannot cope. There is a great reluctance by politicians to admit this. But the reality is that political power is being fragmented. Additionally, the new political crises are more intangible than the old ones. The nuclear arms race, for example, was essentially between the US and USSR. By contrast, no one nation (or small group thereof) can be held responsible for global warming or the greenhouse effect. Similarly, no one nation, acting on its own, can solve these crises.

Consequently, it is necessary to look for a new form of global governance. An international perspective (dealing with affairs between nations) is now not enough: there has to be a planetary perspective.

Endnotes:

1. Joan Chittister, 'A Sign and A Choice', *Sojourners* (Washington DC) June 1987, p.19
2. *Ibid*, p.17
3. 'The Irish Ombudsman', *Bulletin of the Department of Foreign Affairs* (Dublin) May 1987, p.4
4. Kenneth Harris, *Attlee*, Weidenfeld & Nicholson, 1982, pp.216–217
5. Milton Friedman and Rose Friedman, 'The Tide in the Affairs of Men', *Economic Impact* (Washington DC), No.1 1989, p.78
6. Glyn Davis, 'Aaron Wildavsky, Public Policy and the Problem of State Action', *Canberra Bulletin of Public Administration*, October 1987, p.90
7. Aaron B. Wildavsky and Jeffrey L. Pressman, *Implementation*, University of California Press, 1973
8. Michael James, *How Much Government?*, Centre for Independent Studies (Sydney), 1987
9. Robert W. Poole Jr, 'Stocks Populi: Privatization Can Win Bipartisan Support', *Policy Review* (Washington DC), Fall 1988, p.24
10. David Blundy, 'America the Pathetic, Land of the Wimp', *West Australian*, 11 March 1989
11. Robin Williams, 'Beyond Babel', *National Times* (Sydney), 6 January 1984
12. Allan Peachment, 'Administrative Chronicle — West Australia', *Journal of the Royal Australian Institute of Public Administration* (Sydney), 1986, p.162
13. Anthony Adamthwaite, 'Overstretched and Overstrung: Eden, the Foreign Office and the Making of Policy, 1951–55', *Foreign Affairs* (London), Spring 1985, p.242
14. Harold Evans, *Good Times, Bad Times*, Coronet, 1984, p.37
15. George Thomas, *Mr Speaker*, Arrow, 1985, p.93
16. Richard Crossman, *Inside View*, Jonathan Cape, 1972, pp.70–71
17. Gerald Kaufman, *How to be a Minister*, Sidgwick & Jackson, 1980, p.71
18. William Safire, *Before the Fall: An Inside View of the Pre-Watergate White House*, Belmont Tower, 1975, p.249
19. Charles Peters, *How Washington Really Works*, Addison-Wesley, 1980, p.38
20. William Safire, *ibid*, pp.249–250
21. *Ibid*, pp.259–260
22. 'How Mrs T Changed Britain', *Sydney Morning Herald*, 24 November 1990

23. James Callaghan, *Time and Chance*, Collins, 1987, p.497
24. John Kenneth Galbraith, *A Life in Our Times*, Corgi, 1983, p.425
25. 'Department Commemorates 200th Anniversary', *Update from State* (Washington DC), September 1989, p.1
26. 'Lee Merely Eases His Grip on Singapore', *Australian*, 28 November 1990
27. Richard B. Bilder, 'The Role of States and Cities in Foreign Relations', *American Journal of International Law*, Vol. 83, 1989, p.822
28. Daniel N. Nelson 'Not All Quiet on the Eastern Front', *Bulletin of Atomic Scientists*, November 1990, p.36
29. John Langmore, 'The International Perspective', *Canberra Bulletin of Public Administration*, October 1990, p.37
30. 'Global Effort to Curb Drug-Cash Laundering', *Australian Financial Review*, 23 May 1990
31. 'How Not to Fight the Drug War', *World Development Forum* 15, December 1989

5

THE UNITED NATIONS

*What enhanced role is a global
political authority likely to have?*

THERE IS NO SINGLE REPLACEMENT for the nation-state. Centralisation of power was itself a Second Wave characteristic. Instead, we are heading into an era of power being divided up among different organisations.

The earth's twenty-first century will have the following layers of government. First, national governments. They will still exist, but will not necessarily be very significant. Second, a global political authority. This will seek to find transnational solutions to transnational problems. Third, transnational corporations. They will have even more power. Fourth, local government. This will have more delegated power. There will be more self-reliant local communities and more involvement of non-governmental organisations in decision-making.

This chapter deals with the main current form of 'global political authority': the United Nations (UN).

The UN itself is hindered by the fragmentation of power. Citizens expect too much of the UN — and governments are reluctant to give it the power it needs to meet the aspirations of the citizens. Indeed, most (if not all) national governments would prefer not to have to work through the UN at all. But — as this chapter will show — governments have been forced by events to cooperate through some form of international organisation, initially the League of Nations and now the UN. But the UN is far from being a world government. Indeed, for the foreseeable future there can be no central world government because some of the world's main economic actors — transnational corporations — cannot be brought under UN control.

THE FIRST GLOBAL EXPERIMENT:
THE LEAGUE OF NATIONS

The League of Nations was the great experiment of the period between the two world wars. The League was an entirely new organisation. There had been some previous attempts at getting cooperation via international conferences, but none had been as institutionalised.

The League's Covenant was much shorter — 26 articles — than the UN Charter — 111. Its authors realised that they were launching an untried experiment and so they wanted to avoid hindering its future development by too precise and detailed a set of provisions. They were content to give it the bare outlines of the constitution it needed for a start on its career.

Major changes in international relations generally follow on from major wars. After the defeat of Napoleon, the victors had met in Vienna in 1815 to create a new international order to learn from their recent wartime experiences. Never again, they reasoned, should any one nation (most recently, France) be allowed to dominate Europe. The post-1815 European order — effectively the 'world order', since they controlled much of the globe — consisted of European nations which, via a balance of power, would maintain European peace since no nation would want to fight against the rest. A sophisticated game of nations was thereby developed in which nations had to balance each other.

The rise of a united Germany spelt the end of that system. It was too large and too ambitious to fit easily into the European balance of power system. Land warfare before the 1920s consisted of large conventional armies and these had to be drawn from large civilian populations. France's population, 1815 to 1914, remained constant at about twenty-five million; Prussia's had been fourteen million in 1815, but Germany's was forty million in 1914.

Who was to blame for World War I? There are a variety of explanations. They range, at one end, from the role of key individuals, such as Gavrilo Princip, an Austrian Serb, who assassinated the Austrian Archduke Franz Ferdinand and his wife on 28 June 1914 while they were visiting the Bosnian capital of Sarajevo.

At the other end of the scale, there were the questions of whether the entire international system of a balance of power was at fault or whether the system was satisfactory but some nations had not played the game by the rules. The European victors argued that the system was satisfactory but it had run into trouble through some political miscalculations. According to this approach, then, Austria did not play the game properly because it overreacted to the assassination, Russia mobilised for war too quickly, the UK was encircling Germany via alliances, France was too ready to take risks, and Germany was too ambitious for overseas empires and was too eager to gain control in the Balkans.

Germany, in particular, was blamed for the war. After unification forty years earlier, it was set on a path of challenging the UK as the world's superpower and it organised itself for a showdown. The 1919 Versailles Peace Treaty, in Article 231, blamed Germany for the war.

The American president, Woodrow Wilson, and some Europeans did not share that interpretation. They blamed the entire system which had fostered an intricate system of alliances and large standing armies and navies on constant readiness. They argued that the 1815 Vienna system required consensus and was not designed to cope with major changes (such as the unification of Germany and Italy and the continued decay of the Ottoman Empire).

The victorious leaders at Vienna in 1815 and at Versailles in 1919 had a common problem: how to create a system whereby one nation could not dominate Europe? If, then, the old balance of power system was discredited, what should now replace it? Since many of the victors still did not accept that the old system itself was to blame, it is not surprising that the new system — the League of Nations — was not a revolutionary organisation. It accepted that international relations were still dominated by nations and so the new system had to find a satisfactory way to enable the nations to carry out their business. The League did not replace the old system of nations cooperating with each other; it merely supplemented that system. Despite this modest role, it was still seen as the major international experiment in the 1920s and 1930s.

The League consisted of an assembly, a council and a secretariat. All member-nations (around forty) were represented in the assembly, where they had one vote each. It was the main debating body. The council, by contrast, was smaller so as to act more quickly to deal with international crises. It consisted of four permanent members (the UK, France, Italy and Japan) and six nations elected each year.

The League was hindered from the outset. First, the League's membership remained incomplete. Not only did the United States, whose own President Woodrow Wilson had been so keen an advocate of the organisation, fail to become a member, but vast regions of the world, under colonial rule, lacked the opportunity for direct representation.

Second, in spite of theoretical provision for collective security, the League had no real power; even the application of sanctions achieved little or nothing — some maintaining they were actually counter-productive.

Third, the League secretariat lacked an independent voice with which to articulate the aspirations of the membership and commitment to the Covenant at moments when these appeared in conflict with the national interests of powerful individual States.

Fourth, the two superpowers of that era, the UK and France, did not accord it a high priority in dealing with international crises. Official opinion towards the League was generally neutral or hostile — never one of complete enthusiasm.

It was not so much that the principles of the League were rejected. Few people hated it. Most people desired peace. But governments seemed to think that all they needed to do was to give a general and somewhat tepid approval to its work.

The League's career, however, was not a complete disaster. For the first few years its work grew and there was a sense of progress being made. It enjoyed extensive public support. For the period 1925 to 1931, it consolidated its gains.

The downturn began in 1931. In September, Japan invaded Manchuria and the League, via its two main superpowers, did little. The 1932 World Disarmament Conference failed. There was an international economic depression. Hitler came to power in Germany in 1933 and pulled Germany out of the League. Italy invaded Ethiopia in 1935 and for the only time the League tried economic sanctions, which failed. The system of collective security, which had replaced the discredited balance of power system, was now itself discredited. But its career — and even more its failure — haunted the Allied leaders in World War II. They were determined to avoid World War III.

THE SECOND GLOBAL EXPERIMENT:
THE UNITED NATIONS

Foremost in the minds of the UN's founders was the experience of the League, with its successes and failures. The overriding concern of the founding members of the UN was for the organisation 'to maintain international peace and security'.

As one principal organ alongside the General Assembly, the Security Council was structured in such a way that the five great powers of the time, the United States, the Soviet Union, the United Kingdom, France and China, were to be permanent members with shared responsibility for maintaining international peace and security. To back words with the potential for action, the Security Council enjoyed the authority to use force to ensure compliance with its decisions. A military staff committee, whose members were drawn from nationals of the Security Council's permanent members, was to be established to advise and assist the Security Council on all questions relating to its military requirements. Unlike the General Assembly, the Security Council was considered to be in continuous session.

Responsibility in the new organisation had to be commensurate with power. The Security Council could only function through the cooperation of the Big Five. But before the Charter was signed, there was dissension between the Big Five. The US, Soviet Union and perhaps the UK deserved that status. France forced itself into the magic circle. China was the American candidate; Stalin tried to oppose it for that reason; Churchill regarded it as too weak and too close to revolution to justify that status.

The Security Council, consisting of the Big Five (though mainland China was excluded between the 1949 Revolution and 1971) was always vulnerable to disruption. Its influence required the World War II alliance to continue. The alliance ended when the war did. The Security Council was weakened from the outset. In other words, the

Security Council has not operated in international crises as forcefully as the creators of the UN hoped and UN peacekeeping operations have been ad hoc arrangements.

Another change occurred with the UN membership. The original membership consisted of fifty-one nations, drawn almost entirely from Western and Eastern Europe, North and South America, Australia and New Zealand. With the exception of China and a few others, they were nations which to some degree shared the heritage of classical antiquity, Christianity as it had evolved over the centuries, and European political philosophy. They represented only a part — albeit an influential part — of the world's population.

There are, in mid-1992, 178 member-nations, comprising for most practical purposes all nations of the world except Switzerland. It was a member of the League, but feared that its obligations under the Charter, in particular those arising from Security Council decisions, could compromise its strict neutrality policy. In practice, Switzerland is permanently represented at the UN by an observer and is a member-nation of almost all the main components of the UN system. New nations upon achieving independence almost automatically seek admission. It has become practically unthinkable for any nation to withdraw. Indonesia, which left the UN in the 1960s over decisions relating to Malaysia, subsequently returned.

All these changes mean that, in a sense, there have been several 'United Nations' in only forty-seven years. In the beginning, Western nations dominated the UN. But they misused their opportunity by treating the UN as a way of furthering their propaganda purposes. This meant that the UN was neglected in terms of its potential as a facilitator of international cooperation. Additionally, it set a bad example for the newer nations to follow. Writing twenty-four years ago, a former UN official Conor Cruise O'Brien explained the special role that the US then had at the UN in this way:

In the Assembly, any delegate soon learns that the most important thing to know in relation to any proposition is how the United States stands on it. Where the United States has been flatly opposed, the proposition has had no chance of being carried. Where the United States has been indifferent — a rare event — the proposition, even if carried, has had no practical significance.

There has been all the difference in the world between an Assembly resolution actively supported by the United States, and a resolution passed by a similar numerical majority but with the United States abstaining, or even casting a merely tactical vote in favour. In the former case, the resolution has constituted a 'moral warrant' for a policy which the most powerful country in the world either intends to execute or finds it otherwise useful to have proclaimed; resolutions not actively supported by the United States have remained unheeded 'recommendations', like the long series of Assembly resolutions on apartheid.[1]

That era of Western dominance of the General Assembly is now over. The Third World now has the voting strength. But the ability to muster votes is not necessarily an indication of influence in international relations. After all, General Assembly resolutions are not binding on any nation (even those which voted for them).

Political power is now much more dispersed. Only forty-seven years ago, it was easier to decide which were the 'powerful' nations (although the UK and France were slow to accept their slippage down the international league table). The US and the Soviet Union, possessing between them ninety-five per cent of the world's nuclear weapons, could easily destroy the world. However, President Reagan was troubled not only by the Soviet Union, but also by a country the size of Iowa, with a population of less than three million: Nicaragua. The

Soviet Union had difficulty with an even smaller group of guerillas in Afghanistan.

THE ROLES OF THE UNITED NATIONS

All the UN's activities may be distilled into three basic roles: first, to bring nations together; second, to keep nations apart; and third, to move nations forward.

1. *To bring nations together*

In doing this, the UN is doing what the authors of the UN Charter basically had in mind: fostering international, economic, political and social cooperation. Such is the extent of the UN's work in this role, that if the UN did not exist it would need to be created. This is the daily grind of helping nations to find common solutions to common problems.

The world is a small place and nations keep bumping into one another. Consequently, there has to be one central clearing house for diplomacy, especially the expression of governmental opinion (General Assembly), and making international arrangements for such activities as postage, health, food, radio wavelengths, telecommunications, merchant shipping, civil aviation, combating narcotic drugs, protecting human rights and monitoring weather patterns.

2. *To keep nations apart*

This is much more controversial. The UN is occasionally obliged to keep nations — or peoples within a nation — from fighting one another. UN peacekeeping operations are not explicitly provided for in the UN Charter. Each one is usually surrounded by bitterness. Each one is usually an example of the nation concerned having made a mess of a crisis (the UK winding up its empire in Palestine and Cyprus, for example) and wanting to pass the disaster onto someone else. The buck stops with the UN. Each one is said to be the UN's last peacekeeping operation — until the next crisis comes along.

3. *To move nations forward*

The UN provides a global strategic vision. It was born out of a sense of hope in a period of despair and tragedy. The UN Charter's roots go back to 14 August 1941 and a meeting between Prime Minister Winston Churchill and President Franklin Roosevelt. The UK was still virtually alone, defending the free Western world: Britain's 'finest hour'. Germany had invaded the USSR two months earlier and was making good progress against it. The US was still out of the conflict.

The 'Atlantic Charter', as this agreement was called, was a statement of eight principles designed to impress enemy opinion with the justice of the Western cause. The war was not just *against* Germany, but was also *for* creating a better world.

This vision was incorporated into the UN Charter: the UN was created 'to save succeeding generations from the scourge of war', and to work for the outlawing of force 'save in the common interest', the promotion of equal economic and political rights and the rule of law — all of which implied the existence of a sense of international community.

Like all human institutions, the UN has fallen far short of what was hoped for it. But it is difficult to find an alternative to persevering with the UN. If the UN did not exist, it would be necessary to invent it. We cannot turn the clocks back to an earlier era when nations had few contacts with each other. The UN did not create global interdependence: global interdependence has created the need for the UN.

The UN, then, looks forward to a new political era. The protection of the Mediterranean's marine environment is an example of this. Little ET flying in from outer space via Hollywood would see the Mediterranean as one vast inland lake for which there should be one governing authority to protect its environment. However, around the Mediterranean are groups of people which in some cases have fought one another for hundreds of years. For little 'ET' to fly between Cairo and Jerusalem is a journey of an hour; for an Arab or an Israeli it is a journey of 3 000 years.

However, in recent years it has become obvious that traditional disputes and animosities are being overshadowed by a common threat: the destruction of the Mediterranean. The UN Environment Program for the Mediterranean is attempting to bring together these Mediterranean nations to focus their attention not on their past but on the current common threat. They are making progress in cleaning up the Mediterranean.

THE ORGANS OF THE UNITED NATIONS

The Charter established six principal organs of the United Nations: the General Assembly, the Security Council, the Economic and Social Council, the Trusteeship Council, the International Court of Justice and the Secretariat.

1. *The General Assembly*

The General Assembly is the main deliberative organ. It is composed of representatives of all member-nations, each of which has one vote. Decisions on important questions, such as recommendations on peace and security, admission of new members and budgetary matters, require a two-thirds majority. Decisions on other questions are reached by a simple majority. Under the Charter, the functions and powers of the General Assembly include the following:

* to consider and make recommendations on the principles of cooperation in the maintenance of international peace and security, including the principles governing disarmament and

the regulation of armaments;

* to discuss any question relating to international peace and security and, except where a dispute or situation is currently being discussed by the Security Council, to make recommendations on it;

* to discuss and, with the same exception, to make recommendations on any question within the scope of the Charter or affecting the powers and functions of any organ of the UN;

* to initiate studies and make recommendations to promote international political cooperation, the development of international law and its codification, the realisation of human rights and fundamental freedoms for all, and international collaboration in economic, social, cultural, educational and health fields;

* to make recommendations for the peaceful settlement of any situation, regardless of origin, which might impair friendly relations among nations; to receive and consider reports from the Security Council and other organs of the UN;

* to consider and approve the budget of the UN and to apportion the contributions among members; to elect the non-permanent members of the Security Council, the members of the Economic and Social Council and those members of the Trusteeship Council that are elected;

* to elect jointly with the Security Council the judges of the International Court of Justice;

* to appoint the Secretary-General on the recommendation of the Security Council.

The General Assembly's regular session begins each year on the third Tuesday in September and continues usually until mid December. In addition to its regular sessions, the Assembly may meet in special sessions. At the beginning of each regular session, the Assembly holds a general debate, in which member-nations express their views on a wide range of matters of international concern.

The decisions of the Assembly have no binding legal force for governments. But they carry the weight of world opinion on major international issues, as well as the moral authority of the world community. The work of the UN year-round derives largely from the decisions of the General Assembly — that is, the will of the majority of the members as expressed in resolutions adopted by the Assembly. That work is carried out in the following ways:

* by committees and other bodies established by the Assembly to study and report on specific issues, such as disarmament, outer space, peace-keeping, decolonisation, human rights and apartheid;
* in international conferences called for by the Assembly;
* by the Secretariat of the UN — the Secretary-General and his staff of international civil servants.

2. *The Security Council*

The Security Council has primary responsibility, under the Charter, for the maintenance of international peace and security. The Council has fifteen members: five permanent members — China, France, Russia (which has replaced the Soviet Union), the United Kingdom and the United States — and ten elected by the General Assembly for two-year terms.

Each member of the Security Council has one vote. Decisions on procedural matters are made by an affirmative vote of at least nine of the fifteen members. Decisions on substantive matters require nine votes, including the concurring votes of all five permanent members. This is the rule of 'great power unanimity', often referred to as the veto power. All five permanent members have exercised the veto right at one time or another. If a permanent member does not support a decision but does not wish to block it through a veto, it may abstain.

Under the Charter, all UN members agree to accept and carry out the decisions of the Security Council. While other organs of the UN make recommendations to governments, the Security Council alone has the power to take decisions which member-states are obligated under the Charter to carry out. Under the Charter, the functions and powers of the Security Council are:

* to maintain international peace and security in accordance with the principles and purposes of the United Nations;
* to investigate any dispute or situation which might lead to international friction;
* to recommend methods of adjusting such disputes or the terms of settlement;
* to formulate plans for the establishment of a system to regulate armaments;
* to determine the existence of a threat to the peace or act of aggression and to recommend what action should be taken;
* to call on members to apply economic sanctions and other measures not involving the use of force in order to prevent or stop aggression;
* to take military action against an aggressor;
* to recommend the admission of new members and the terms on which nations may become parties to the Statute of the International Court of Justice;
* to exercise the Trusteeship functions of the UN in 'strategic areas';
* to recommend to the General Assembly the appointment of the Secretary-General and, together with the Assembly, to elect the judges of the International Court.

The Security Council is organised so as to be able to function continuously, and a representative of each of its members must be present at all times at United Nations headquarters.

When a complaint concerning a threat to peace is brought before it, the Council's first action is usually to recommend that the parties try to reach agreement by peaceful means. In some cases, the Security Council itself undertakes investigation and mediation. It may appoint special representatives or request the Secretary-General to do so or to use his good offices. In some cases, it may set forth principles for a peaceful settlement.

When a dispute leads to fighting, the Security Council's first concern is to bring this to an end as soon as possible. On many occasions since the UN was founded, the Security Council has issued ceasefire directives which have been instrumental in preventing wider hostilities in many parts of the world. It also sends UN peacekeeping forces to help reduce tensions in troubled areas, keep opposing forces apart and create conditions of calm in which peaceful settlements may be sought. The Security Council may decide on enforcement measures, economic sanctions (such as trade embargoes) or collective military action.

3. *The Economic and Social Council (ECOSOC)*

ECOSOC was established by the Charter as the principal organ to coordinate — but not to control — the UN's economic and social work and the specialised agencies and institutions known as the 'United Nations family'. The Council has fifty-four members which serve for three years, eighteen being elected each year for a three-year term to replace eighteen members whose three-year term has expired. Voting in the Economic and Social Council is by simple majority; each member has one vote. The functions and powers of the Economic and Social Council are:

* to serve as the central forum for the discussion of international economic and social issues of a global nature and the formulation of policy recommendations on those issues addressed to member-nations and to the UN system as a whole;
* to initiate studies, reports and recommendations on international economic, social, cultural, educational, health and related matters;
* to promote respect for, and observance of, human rights and fundamental freedoms for all;
* to call international conferences and prepare draft conventions for submission to the General Assembly on matters within its competence;
* to negotiate agreements with the specialised agencies, defining their relationship with the UN;
* to coordinate the activities of the specialised agencies by means of consultations with and recommendations to them and by means of recommendations to the General Assembly and the members of the UN;
* to consult with non-governmental organisations (NGOs) concerned with matters with which the Council deals.

The subsidiary machinery of the ECOSOC includes the following:

* six functional commissions: the Statistical Commission, the Population Commission, the Commission for Social Development, the Commission on Human Rights, the Commission on the Status of Women, and the Commission on Narcotic Drugs;
* five regional commissions: the Economic Commission for Africa (headquarters in Addis Ababa), the Economic and Social Commission for Asia and the Pacific (Bangkok), the Economic Commission for Europe (Geneva), the Economic Commission for Latin America (Santiago) and the Economic Commission for Western Asia (Baghdad);

* six standing committees: the Committee for Program and Coordination and the committees on Natural Resources, Transnational Corporations, Human Settlements, Non-Governmental Organisations and Negotiations with Intergovernmental Agencies;
* a number of standing expert bodies on such subjects as crime prevention and control, development planning, tax treaties between developed and developing countries, and transport of dangerous goods.

ECOSOC may consult with non-governmental organisations (NGOs) which are concerned with matters within the Council's competence. ECOSOC recognises that NGOs should have the opportunity to express their views and that they often possess special experience or technical knowledge of value to ECOSOC in its work. NGOs which have been given consultative status may send observers to public meetings of ECOSOC and its subsidiary bodies and may submit written statements relevant to its work.

4. *The Trusteeship Council*

In setting up an international trusteeship system, the Charter established the Trusteeship Council as one of the main organs of the UN and assigned to it the task of supervising the administration of trust territories (colonies confiscated from Germany and Japan) placed under the trusteeship system. Major goals of the system are to promote the advancement of the inhabitants of trust territories and their progressive development towards self-government or independence.

The aims of the trusteeship system have been fulfilled to such an extent that only one of the original *eleven* Trusteeships remains — the Trust Territory of the Pacific Islands (administered by the United States). The others, mostly in Africa and the Pacific, have attained independence, either as separate nations or by joining neighbouring independent nations.

5. *The International Court of Justice*

The International Court of Justice is the principal judicial organ of the UN. Its statute is an integral part of the UN Charter.

The Court is open to the parties to its statute, which automatically includes all members of the UN. A nation which is not a member of the UN may become a party to the statute on conditions determined in each case by the General Assembly upon the recommendation of the Security Council.

All nations which are parties to the Statute of the Court can be parties to cases before it. Other nations can refer cases to it under conditions laid down by the Security Council. In addition, the Security Council may recommend that a legal dispute be referred to the Court.

Both the General Assembly and the Security Council can ask the Court for an advisory opinion on any legal question; other organs of the UN and the specialised agencies, when authorised by the General Assembly, can ask for advisory opinions on legal questions within the scope of their activities.

The jurisdiction of the Court covers all questions which nations refer to it, and all matters provided for in the UN Charter or in treaties in force. Nations may bind themselves in advance to accept the jurisdiction of the Court in special cases, either by signing a treaty which provides for reference to the Court or by making a special declaration to that effect. Such declarations accepting compulsory jurisdiction may exclude certain classes of cases.

The Court, in deciding disputes submitted to it, applies the following principles:

* international treaties establishing rules recognised by the contesting nations;
* international custom as evidence of a general practice accepted as law;
* the general principles of law recognised by nations;
* judicial decisions and the teachings of the most highly qualified publicists of the various nations, as a subsidiary means for determining the rules of law.

The Court consists of fifteen judges elected by the General Assembly and the Security Council, voting independently. They are chosen on the basis of their qualifications, not on the basis of nationality, and care is taken to ensure that the principal legal systems of the world are represented in the Court. No two judges can be nationals of the same nation. The judges serve for a term of nine years and may be re-elected. They cannot engage in any other occupation during their term of office.

6. *The Secretariat*
The Secretariat services the other organs of the UN and administers the programs and policies laid down by them. At its head is the Secretary-General, who is appointed by the General Assembly on the recommendation of the Security Council.

The first Secretary-General was Trygve Lie, of Norway, who served until 1953. Dag Hammarskjold, of Sweden, served from 1953 until his death in a plane crash in Africa in 1961. U Thant, of Burma, served as Secretary-General until 1971. He was succeeded by Kurt Waldheim, of Austria, who served from 1972 to 1981. The next Secretary-General was Javier Perez de Cuellar, of Peru, who served for ten years until 1 January 1992. The current UN Secretary-General is Boutros Boutros Ghali of Egypt.

As one of many functions, the Secretary-General may bring to the attention of the Security Council any matter which, in his or her opinion, threatens international peace and security, and may use his or her good offices to help in resolving international disputes.

The Secretariat, an international staff of more than 16 000 people from over 170 countries, carries out the day-to-day work of the UN both at headquarters in New York and in offices and centres around the world. As international civil servants, they work for the organisation as a whole; each takes an oath not to seek or receive instructions for any government or outside authority. Under Article 100 of the Charter, each member-nation undertakes to respect the exclusively international character of the responsibilities of the Secretary-General and the staff and not to seek to influence them in the discharge of their duties.

The work of the Secretariat is as varied as the list of problems dealt with by the UN. It includes the following:

* administering peace-keeping operations;
* organising international conferences on problems of world-wide concern;
* surveying world economic and social trends and problems;
* preparing studies on such subjects as human rights, disarmament and development;
* interpreting speeches, translating documents and servicing the world's communications media with information about the UN.

7. Specialised agencies

The Security Council and General Assembly receive the most publicity. Most people when they think of the UN, think of its attractive building in New York. But over eighty per cent of the UN's total finances are devoted to projects other than the Security Council and General Assembly. In terms of direct impact on the ordinary person on a daily basis, the UN works in a way unknown by the League of Nations.

There are fifteen specialised agencies. The oldest, the International Telecommunications Union (ITU), originated in 1865 and so pre-dates the UN by eighty years. The youngest, the International Fund for Agricultural Development (IFAD) came into operation in 1976. Most of them were conceived, if not born, in the later years of World War II. Accordingly, they vary in their constitutions and membership and in their relationship with ECOSOC. Each of course has its special interest, expertise and field of activity. Each sets its own agenda.

But there are several features common to all specialised agencies. These common features are:

* they are autonomous and are financed by their member-nations chiefly on a basis similar to their contributions to the UN;
* they have all-member conferences, usually meeting annually, but some twice a year or every two or more years and they each have a headquarters and secretariat, usually in a capital city;
* they report regularly to ECOSOC to minimise overlap and duplication of effort;
* they supply technical assistance by means of reports on research, statistical and other information, and assist members individually with planning, expert advisers and on-the-spot supervision;
* they conduct regional and global research projects, which are often funded by special voluntary contributions pledged by member-nations;
* either singly or in team with other agencies, they may carry out projects approved by and part-financed by the UN Development Program (UNDP) or the World Bank (International Bank

for Reconstruction and Development — IBRD). They also cooperate in schemes with the UN Environment Program (UNEP).

The agencies may be grouped according to their activities:

(a) *There are those concerned with the basic needs of food, health, work and education.* They are the Food and Agriculture Organisation (FAO), the World Health Organisation (WHO), the International Labour Organisation (ILO), the UN Educational Scientific and Cultural Organisation (UNESCO), and the International Fund for Agricultural Development (IFAD).

FAO covers food and other resource crops, animal husbandry, forestry and fisheries and works in research and training in all forms of land use including water, fertilisers and pesticides. IFAD was set up to provide extra money for the expansion of food production. WHO, whose objective is the 'attainment by all peoples of the highest possible level of health' not only fights disease, but seeks to have set up everywhere at least a basic health service and a safe water supply. The ILO, by an International Labour Code of more than a hundred conventions, has set standards for labour conditions in all types of industry.

(b) *There are the financial institutions.* These are the International Monetary Fund (IMF), the International Bank for Reconstruction and Development or World Bank (IBRD) with its affiliates, the International Development Association (IDA) and the International Finance Corporation (IFC).

The IMF holds credit in gold and in the currencies of its members to use to assist them in times of financial crisis. Its 'special drawing rights' (SDRs) are a further means of extending international credit. The IBRD, with funds subscribed by nations, private corporations and individual holders of its bonds, lends money for both national and international development projects at about current rates of interest. The IDA was set up to provide soft loans at nominal rates and repayment usually over twenty-five years especially to poor nations. The IFC assists investment in private companies working for world development.

(c) There are institutions concerned with travel, transport and communications. These are the International Civil Aviation Organisation (ICAO), the Universal Postal Union (UPU), the International Telecommunications Union (ITU), the World Meteorological Organisation (WMO) and the Intergovernmental Maritime Consultative Organisation (IMCO).

They are all highly technical, but together they serve to standardise conditions and to regulate and expedite with safety the movement of people and goods throughout the world by land, sea and air and to promote the exchange of information. In a world covered by a complex network of roads and railways, air and shipping lines, weather stations and communication systems of post, telegraph, telephone, radio and television, their value is shown to us all daily.

(d) There are the agencies to increase trade and industry. These are the General Agreement on Trade and Tariffs (GATT) and the World Intellectual Property Organisation (WIPO). GATT's member-nations meet to reduce tariffs and other discriminating barriers so as to expand world trade. WIPO concerns itself with copyright and patent rights. UN Industrial Development Organisation (UNIDO) has coordinated the industrial expansion of industry in developing nations by the dissemination of information, research and technical assistance in training and planning new lines of production.

THE LIMITATIONS OF THE UNITED NATIONS

In arguing that the UN is a necessary creation, it has to be admitted that it has some significant limitations. These are largely based on its political work.

1. *The UN is not a world government.*

The UN the general public expected never existed. Public perception of the UN is that of some supra-national global governing authority which can instruct national governments to change their policies.

The frustration that some people feel at the UN's lack of perceived action is due to their misconception of the UN's role and powers. The UN has little scope to interfere in the domestic affairs of nations (unless those affairs are a threat to international peace and security). In a macabre way, starvation in Ethiopia is the price those people pay for the privilege of being controlled by a national government rather than some form of world government.

2. *The Security Council's 'Big Five' have at times not acted responsibly.*

Even accepting that the UN is not a world government, the UN Charter was not designed to be impracticable. The Security Council's Big Five (US, USSR, UK, France and China) were the main Allied nations. If their wartime unity had been maintained, then they could have made more of a success of the UN.

The Security Council veto is the main example of this. One disadvantage of the veto system is that it has created two classes of nations: those with and those without the veto. Coincidentally, the five nations with the veto are also the five main nuclear powers (with about ninety-nine per cent of the world's nuclear weapons). The veto can block Security Council action on a threat to international peace and security — the nations most likely to be involved in such a threat being, ironically, the Big Five.

On the other hand, the veto was part of the price to be paid to get the US and USSR into the UN. The veto power reassured Americans that the new UN would not act as an anti-US body, while reassuring the USSR (which was in the minority in the 1940s) that the UN could not act against it and its immediate allies.

The Big Five play a double game. On the one hand, they do not give the UN the full support they should while, on the other, they prevent other nations from playing a more responsible role in it. For example, it is difficult to see why France and the UK should both remain as permanent members, when their power is declining and when Germany and Japan are on the rise. But neither would ever accept the suggestion that their privileged positions should be taken by Germany and Japan.

3. *The UN operates a minute budget.*

The UN's budget in New York is US$5.5 billion, compared to US$7 billion for New York City Council, or US$25 billion for the European Community. The peacekeeping operations are also cheap: the US contribution to the 1989 Namibian operation was US$175 million — approximately four per cent of the annual operating budget for the US 82nd Airborne Division (on the ground, not in action) and one-third of the purchase price of one highly controversial B-2 Stealth bomber. UNESCO's budget is less than that of the Australian Broadcasting Corporation's.

Additionally, the UN system has comparatively few staff. To respond to the entire spectrum of international cooperation for five billion people, the staff of all the UN system's organs and agencies amounts to little more than 50 000. That is only one UN staffer for every 100 000 human beings alive in the world — less than the civil service for Victoria's four million citizens or one-third the staff of British Railways.

Even its legendary use of paper is not so large as is claimed. The UN system uses 2 170 tons of paper per year — less than the *New York Times* uses for one Sunday edition.

4. *Only two parts of the UN system can actually make decisions binding upon governments.*

These are the Security Council and the International Court of Justice. All other bodies adopt resolutions which (apart from domestic organisational decisions) are not binding. The Security Council is occasionally prevented by the veto power of the permanent members from adopting a resolution.

Even where a resolution is adopted, the nations being instructed to carry out a course of action sometimes ignore the instruction and get away with doing so. The International Court of Justice is hampered because many nations refuse to take their international disputes to it. They sometimes refuse to appear before it in a dispute. There is no 'world police force' to enforce the ICJ's decisions.

5. *The UN is far more able to create visions and standards — rather than implement them.*

The UN has, for example, made far more progress in the international protection of human rights than could ever have been envisaged in 1945. The UN has created the following:

* the 1948 Universal Declaration of Human Rights;
* the 1966 International Covenant of Civil and Political Rights, and the 1966 International Covenant of Economic, Social and Cultural Rights (which together form the International Bill of Human Rights);

* the 1948 Convention on the Prevention and Punishment of the Crime of Genocide;
* the 1952 Convention on the Political Rights of Women;
* the 1965 International Convention on the Elimination of All Forms of Racial Discrimination;
* the 1989 Convention on the Rights of the Child.

But all these treaties have one basic flaw — there are no sanctions when these rules are violated. Rules for their implementation are either lacking, or weak and ineffective. In the coming decades, one of the most important tasks will be to establish legal machinery to enforce the norms.

An important step in the right direction would be the creation of the office of a high commissioner for human rights who would be able to keep an eye on human rights situations causing special concern and to render assistance to nations at their request. Proposals to this effect have been submitted to the UN General Assembly in the past, but unfortunately most member-nations still have strong reservations about UN involvement in their affairs.

6. *The UN system itself suffers from a fragmentation of power.*
The specialised agencies have their own governing boards consisting of representatives of member-nations. They are not controlled centrally by the General Assembly, ECOSOC or the Secretary General. Each sets its own agenda and each is accountable to the member-nations on its governing board.

This format was designed in 1945 for a world in which problems were comfortably divided into specialised compartments. It is now clear that global problems require a different approach. The Secretary-General is only first among equals of the heads of the UN's specialised agencies and programs. He does not have the authority either to coordinate their work or to demand the vigorous intellectual analysis of problems that should animate the activities of the UN system.

To manage problems such as global warming, refugees, over-population, environmental damage and the eradication of hunger and disease requires both the bringing together of divergent interests and the generation of ideas large and practical enough to work. Such ideas, if they are to be effective, must also be presented powerfully and persuasively to the public. But, for the moment anyway, the UN lacks a centralised sense of direction.

To conclude, it is important not to overestimate the UN's power. It is not a world government. Indeed, to talk of a world 'government' is itself a Second Wave form of thinking.

THE ACHIEVEMENTS OF THE UNITED NATIONS

A way of assessing the UN is by comparing it with its predecessor, the League of Nations. The League expired in a world war at the age of twenty, and the UN is still going strong with no world war in sight. The League had an extremely limited membership, not including the United States or in its later days either the Soviet Union or Germany. The UN contains virtually every nation, including the greatest powers, all of which have stayed in and have no intention of leaving.

I believe there have been four major achievements of the United Nations: its intervention to solve disputes by the use of peace-keeping forces; its ability to make a virtue of its apparent weakness; its humanitarian work; and its ability to reshape the global agenda by focussing attention on a crisis.

1. *The UN's successful intervention to resolve disputes by the use of peacekeeping forces.*

The UN has been adept at fielding ad hoc peacekeeping forces. As one formal avenue has been blocked, so alternative avenues have been devised. Each peacekeeping operation is said to be the last — until the next crisis comes along.

A well-known successful UN operation took place in the Congo. The Republic of the Congo (now the Republic of Zaire), a former Belgian colony, became independent on 30 June 1960. In the days that followed, disorder broke out and Belgium sent its troops back to the Congo, stating that the aim was to protect and evacuate Europeans. On 12 July 1960, the Congo asked for UN military assistance to protect it against external aggression. The Security Council called upon Belgium to withdraw its troops from the Congo and authorised the Secretary-General to provide the Congolese government with such military assistance as might be necessary until the national security forces were able to meet their tasks fully.

In less than forty-eight hours, contingents of the UN Force, provided by a number of nations, began to arrive in the Congo. At the same time, UN civilian experts were rushed to the Congo to help ensure the continued operation of essential public services.

Over the next four years, the task of the UN was to help the Congolese government restore and maintain the political independence of the Congo; to help it maintain law and order throughout the nation; and to put into effect a wide and long-term program of training and technical assistance.

To meet the vast task before it, the UN had to assemble an exceptionally large team. At its peak strength, the UN Force totalled more than 20 000 personnel.

By August 1961, the main problem was the attempted secession, led and financed by foreign elements, of the province of Katanga. In 1961 and 1962, the secessionist forces under the command of foreign mercenaries clashed with the UN Force. Secretary-General Dag Hammarskjold lost his life on 17 September 1961 in the crash of his plane on the way to Ndola, where talks were to be held for the cessation of hostilities. In February 1963, after Katanga had been reintegrated into the national territory of the Congo, a phasing out of the Force was begun. The Force was completely withdrawn by 30 June 1964.

2. *The UN has been adept at making a virtue out of apparent weakness.*

The UN plays a vital role as a scapegoat. Its political organs can be used by a government to show that it is doing 'something' when it also wants to avoid a head-on collision or when it lacks the power to interfere in a crisis. Conor Cruise O'Brien provides examples of this:

The Soviet Union has also now experienced, over the Middle East, just as the United States did over Hungary, the value of the United Nations in a situation where a policy of prudent but inglorious inaction has to be reconciled with an earlier posture of ostensible militancy.

In the Middle Eastern crisis of 1967, the Soviet Union made a double use of the United Nations stage. First it used the Security Council to demonstrate its real resolve not to let the crisis escalate into a military confrontation of the great powers. This it did by calling, in concert with the United States, for a ceasefire. Next it used the United Nations to 'take the harm' — as we say in Ireland — out of its failure to support the Arab cause. This it did by having the General Assembly convened for a propaganda orgy, strongly reminiscent of the 'Hungarian' denunciation rituals of 1956, but with different objects of verbal immolation.

Nor should it be assumed that the Soviet government was notably chagrined by the defeat of its resolution. A defeat which could be plausibly and even accurately blamed on United States opposition may well have been almost as acceptable as an actual victory. In any case it was the convening of the Assembly, combined with the tabling of the resolution and the speeches in its favour, that served the real Soviet purpose, which was to compensate for its failure to come to the aid of the Arab countries in the war, by dramatic demonstration in their favour after the war was over. And since popular opinion in Arab countries is widely believed to be not always quite clear about the existence of a distinction between rhetoric and reality, the compensation may well have been judged to be remarkably effective in proportion to its price — bearing in mind the relative costs of military action and military speeches.[2]

Although the Security Council has not functioned in such a way as to enable the UN Charter to operate as it should, the Security Council — and General Assembly — both have a vital role in global diplomacy. They are essential for governments to assess how other governments are thinking on particular issues. Moreover, much valuable work is done in private by the discreet meetings of diplomats.

The General Assembly sessions also provide a reason — if not a cover — for heads of government to meet one another without the formality of specific summit conferences.

3. *The UN has achieved much in its humanitarian work.*
Canada's former Ambassador to the UN has set out this success:

I've often thought to myself, as surely you have, that UNICEF [The UN Childrens' Fund] almost single-handedly legitimises the nature and character of the United Nations. Just reflect on it for a moment. Four hundred thousand youngsters under the age of five saved every year by UNICEF. Saved from death every year by UNICEF.

When I stood in a refugee camp five or six weeks ago in the Sudan, right on the border with Ethiopia, to which 80 000 Tigreans had made a migration desperately seeking survival. . . when I stood in that camp and chatted with the doctors from Medecins sans Frontieres, and asked them how it was possible to keep children alive in circumstances of such eviscerating desolation, they said to me that 'part of the reason is that we have these little packets of oral rehydration therapy to distribute — 15 000 of them a day and in that way, Mr Lewis, we keep hundreds of children alive'.

Now it is important for the world to be reminded over and over again, with unselfconscious vigour, that you'd never have that outcome without the United Nations. That's the kind of thing which the world body achieves.[3]

A second example is the program to eradicate smallpox. In 1979, the World Health Organisation (WHO) declared that for the first time in history, a disease — smallpox — had been eradicated from the globe. Smallpox hospitals are no longer needed and its vaccination everywhere has stopped. The annual savings are at least US$1 000 million — more than three times the cost of the entire program.

This 'sunken iceberg' of the UN is certainly one reason why the UN will not suffer the same fate as the League of Nations. The League focussed almost exclusively on immediate political issues. The UN has a permanently expanding agenda. It is gradually spreading a mantle of care around the globe.

4. *The UN has the ability to reshape the global agenda by focussing political attention on emerging crises.*
One such is the destruction of the environment. The first UN Conference on the Human Environment was held in Stockholm in June

1972, following a 1968 decision of the General Assembly that action at the national, regional and international levels was needed to limit the impairment of the human environment. The conference adopted the Declaration on the Human Environment, which proclaims the right of human beings to a quality environment and their responsibility to protect and improve the environment for future generations.

It also adopted an Action Plan, containing over 100 recommendations for measures to be taken by governments and international organisations to protect life, control contamination from human-made pollutants and improve cities and other human settlements.

Late in 1972, on the basis of the conference's recommendations, the General Assembly created the United Nations Environment Programme (UNEP) to monitor changes in the environment and to encourage and coordinate sound environmental practices. The first UN agency to be based in a developing country, UNEP has its headquarters in Nairobi.

UNEP's programs include 'Earthwatch', an international surveillance network with three main components:

* a Global Environmental Monitoring System, which monitors selected environmental parameters to provide governments with the information necessary to understand, anticipate and combat adverse environmental changes;
* INFOTERRA, a computerised referral service to 20 000 sources in 100 countries for environmental information and expertise;
* the International Register of Potentially Toxic Chemicals, which works through a network of national correspondents to provide scientific and regulatory information on chemicals that may be dangerous to health and the environment.

Other major programs of UNEP include implementation, in the

Sudano-Sahelian region of Africa, of the plan of action to combat the spread of deserts adopted by the 1977 United Nations Conference on Desertification. The plan comprises integrated national and international programs of land reclamation and management.

UNEP's efforts against marine pollution, begun with a pilot program in the Mediterranean, now also include anti-marine pollution programs for the Kuwait region, the Red Sea and the Gulf of Aden, the wider Carribean, East, West and Central Africa, the east Asian seas and the south-east and south-west Pacific.

In the area of environmental law, UNEP's efforts have included the development of guidelines or principles regarding the harmonious utilisation by nations of shared natural resources, offshore mining and drilling, and an international convention on the ozone layer. Other important activities include the preparation of regional conventions for the protection of the marine environment and related technical protocols.

The June 1992 UN Conference in Environment and Development will also lead to other major changes in international cooperation.

THE INEVITABILITY OF THE UNITED NATIONS

The UN's creation and expansion have been inevitable. The value of particular decisions and programs will always be open for debate. But the UN, as a fixed fact of international life, is here to stay. Governments, though they do not necessarily enjoy sharing their power, now accept the UN. The world we live in makes reliance on the UN inevitable.

The world is infinitely more closely knit than the one before World War II. Virtually everyone in some way is dependent on someone else, and so there are unprecedented problems in creating mechanisms to cope with global interdependence among nations which still pretend they alone are guardians of their individual national destinies.

Churchill clearly saw the UN's significance for all governments and citizens:

It may be through the United Nations alone that the path to safety and salvation can be found. To sustain and aid the United Nations is the duty of all. To reinforce it and bring it into vital and practical relation with actual world politics by sincere agreements and understanding between the Great Powers, between the leading races, should be the first aim of all who wish to spare their children torments and disasters compared to which those we have suffered will be but a pale preliminary.[5]

The importance of the UN is underlined by the USSR's changing attitude over the years. The USSR was sceptical from the outset about the UN — after all, the last major decision of its predecessor was to expel the USSR for invading Finland! The USSR boycotted much of the UN's economic and social work, refused to pay for most of the peacekeeping operations, obliged UN secretaries-general to appoint its own selected citizens to the UN Secretariat (rather than permitting them a choice of Soviet applicants) and it invaded independent nations, such as Afghanistan in 1979.

The change in Soviet attitude began in 1985 when Mr Gorbachev became the Soviet leader. He was anxious to pull the USSR out of its losing war in Afghanistan — and asked the UN to create a mediated settlement. The USSR paid all its back debts to the UN. It applied to join such UN specialised agencies as the World Bank, International Monetary Fund, and Food and Agricultural Organisation. Mr Gorbachev recognised that the USSR could not stand aloof from international cooperation. *Perestroika* — restructuring — could only work if the USSR traded more with the rest of the world and imported foreign technology.

Russia and the rest of the Commonwealth of Independent States are continuing this policy. In the sort of world we are living in, there is a certain inevitability to such a policy towards the UN.

I have attempted to show in this chapter that the UN is not as powerful as its critics fear or as its supporters would like. It is not a world government. But it does play a useful role in fostering international cooperation.

Endnotes:

1. Conor Cruise O'Brien, *The United Nations: Sacred Drama*, Hutchinson, 1968, pp.23–24
2. *Ibid*, pp.72–73
3. Stephen Lewis, *Address to the National Convention of UNA–USA*, 29 April 1985 (available from UNA–USA, New York)
4. Winston S. Churchill, *If I Lived My Life Again*, Allen, 1974, p.240

6

TRANSNATIONAL CORPORATIONS

What stake does their growing wealth and power give them?

WHAT TRULY COUNTS CANNOT BE COUNTED. Fellowship with God and others, family life, the arts, a peaceful environment, good health and a long life are all examples of factors that are important in life — and yet are not easily reducible to economic terms.

But money makes the world go around. We live in an era where we know the price of something but not its value. The 1980s slogan of 'greed is good' is no longer so fashionable — but the idea is still with us.

A major reason for the popularity in the former USSR of *perestroika* was the desire for economic reform which (it was hoped) would lead to Western goods and services being available. No-one, on either side of the former Iron Curtain, would admit to being greedy — but many would like 'just a little more money'.

Another perspective on money is that more lives are destroyed each day through economic injustice and deprivation than are destroyed by weapons. Forty thousand children die each day, for example, through a lack of basic necessities which we take for granted: clean water, food and sanitation. For these children and their parents, then, World War III is a daily occurrence. Linked to these casualties are children who are part of the 'living dead': they evade death, but suffer permanent brain damage because of infant malnutrition.

The issues of economic overdevelopment and underdevelopment go beyond this book's scope. But a key factor for both those issues and this book is the rise of transnational corporations.

THE GLOBAL FACTORY

The transnational corporations are now major players in world economic affairs and their evolution is taking the world from a collection of separate national economies to a single global economy.

Richard Barnet puts it this way:

Increasingly, global resource systems are being managed by multinational corporations. The mining, melting, refining and mixing of animal, vegetable, mineral and human resources into products for sale is an integrated operation on a planetary scale. Viewed from space, the global factory suggests a human organism. The brain is housed in steel and glass slabs located in or near a few crowded cities: New York, London, Frankfurt, Zurich and Tokyo. The blood is capital and it is pumped through the system by global banks assisted by a few governments.

The financial centres — New York, London, Frankfurt and Tokyo — and their fictional extensions in such tax havens as Panama and the Bahamas function as the heart. The hands are steadily moving to the outer rim of civilisation. More and more goods are now made in the poor countries of the southern periphery under direction from the headquarters in the north, and most are destined to be consumed in the industrialised countries.[1]

The transnational corporation is the first institution in human history dedicated to centralised planning on a world scale. Its primary purpose is to organise economic activity around the world in such a way as to maximise global profit. The corporation is an organic structure in which each part is expected to serve the whole. It measures its successes and its failures not by the balance sheet of an individual subsidiary, or the suitability of particular products, or its social impact in a particular nation, but by the growth in global profits and global market shares.

Transnational corporations present a serious challenge to prevailing ideas about the world being constructed out of a collection of building blocks called nation-states. An even more recent challenge is that Japanese-based corporations are heading the list of the world's largest corporations:

Rank	Market Value $US billion	Net Profit $US billion
1 Nippon T/graph and T/phone (Japan)	118.8	1.78
2 IBM (US)	68.9	5.263
3 Industrial Bank of Japan (Japan)	67.6	0.554
4 Royal Dutch/Shell Group (Neth/UK)	67.1	6.545
5 General Electric (US)	62.5	3.946
6 Exxon (US)	60.0	2.987
7 Sumitomo Bank (Japan)	55.8	1.218
8 Fuji Bank (Japan)	53.2	1.209
9 Toyota (Japan)	50.4	2.2710
10 Mitsui Taiyo Kobe Bank (Japan)	49.8	0.47 [2]

Transnational corporations used to be called 'multinational corporations'. A multinational corporation operated in many nations, behaved as an individual firm in each nation, and was only tenuously coordinated at a global level. It was valid to treat the corporation as an extension of the local large corporation, with the added feature of remitting profits overseas rather than locally.

But over the last twenty years these corporations have embarked upon a new corporate strategy which justifies the new term 'transnational corporations': they have started to transcend national boundaries. This corporate strategy is to locate each level of production to take advantage of local conditions. The firm is passing out of the period when it operated as a set of independent but related individuals and is now integrating operations on a global scale. Decisions about what to do are being concentrated in the home country. The execution of those decisions is being located wherever they are best carried out.

International trade is, of course, not new. It has a long history from the Phoenicians' investments in the tin mines of Cornwall in England. For many decades before World War I, international economic ties were critical to the economies that today are thought of as 'developed'. Migration was high; capital was flowing across international boundaries at impressive rates; and there were considerable movements of goods among these nations.

From World War I to World War II, the technology of international transportation and communication steadily advanced. But while world production went up something like forty per cent in the interwar period, world trade increased by only half the production rate. International investment also was restricted; after a period of growth in the 1920s, the flow of investment was curbed and reversed in the 1930s. The level of post-World War II international trade is, then, unprecedented.

The British merchant companies and the Dutch VOC (United East India Companies), all established in the seventeenth century, are examples of earlier forms of transnational corporations. They did not establish production units overseas. Their main activities were the trade in gold, silver, spices and commodities like coffee, tea and sugar. Production was in the hands of the native princes who performed the traditional mode of production.

By contrast, modern corporations continuously update their modes of production and expand their production on an ever-widening international scale. In other words, the early corporations were not involved in the actual process of production, whereas the modern corporations are the real agents of modern forms of production.

Current transnational corporations can be divided into four broad categories:

1. *There are the resource-based companies, whose main mission is to produce raw materials.*
These often have roots in the colonial era, but most of them have been reorganised, as host countries have striven for control of their natural resources.

2. *There are public utility companies (including defence).*
They differ from other economic sectors in that they are either natural monopolies (it makes no sense to have two identical telephone systems or power systems serving the same community) or they serve a monopsonistic — single buyer — market, such as the national airline of the host nation.

3. *There are manufacturing and banking companies.*
They have been the largest growth sector of transnational business

since the 1950s. Host nations have been instrumental in attracting these corporations. Foreign investment incentive programs have been the common practice to lure inbound investments. Intricate schemes of tax privilege, protection against import competition, relaxation of foreign exchange restrictions and governmental loan guarantees are part of such arrangements. Governments have seen such corporations as providing employment opportunities and bringing in new technology.

4. *There are service industries.*
A corporation in this category differs from counterparts in other sectors in that the main factor is technological and managerial know-how rather than investment capital.

Many international hotel companies, for example, own none, or very few hotels in their global chain. The buildings and grounds are mostly owned by a variety of local nationals or other financial interests, all quite distinct from the company which runs the hotels. These separately-owned properties are bound into a transnational system producing quality hotel service by a set of long-term contracts which not only transfer the management of the hotels to the company, but also provide for profit-sharing to assure a strong incentive for efficiency.

American tourists staying at a Hilton hotel, for instance, will feel reassured that even if they are in another nation, they will receive the usual Hilton treatment.

THE GLOBAL ECONOMY
There is only one economy — the global one. Governments like to pretend that there are still 'national economies'. But they are mistaken.

For example, even though Australia and the UK are oil producers, their oil prices are set by foreign governments and events in the Middle East.

The growth of world trade is now running each year at a faster rate than the annual growth in mining and manufacturing. The average citizen is unaware of the extent to which he or she relies on imports and exports — of raw materials, goods and finance. Money makes the world go around.

Jean-Jacques Servan-Schreiber provides this example of the way the international trade in raw materials and manufactured goods works:

Take, for example, a typical day in the life of an American businessman. He wakes up, showers and heads for his breakfast in the kitchen. This breakfast may be accompanied by toast made on an imported asbestos grill. Will he have his breakfast before or after shaving? No doubt about it, he'll shave before a mirror made of silver or aluminum — both of which have been imported. He'll be using an electric razor with imported lithium batteries, equipped with an imported copper wire; or with an electric razor whose blades are made of an alloy of tungsten and vanadium steel — both imported. He may even want to dry his hair with a dryer made of imported steel.

While eating, he may listen to the news over a transistor radio that has silicon circuits and batteries made of lithium (both imported). Now he goes out — dressed in imported wool or cotton, after turning off the heating unit, in which the imported copper piping brings steam to (imported) nickel or chromium radiators.

It's raining. Water is spouting from the (imported) zinc rain-pipe. Should he take the car? It's hard to start — something wrong with the battery, which is made of a combination of lithium, manganese and lead (all imported), surrounded by (imported) antimony plates.

Finally, he's in the office elevator which has been fireproofed with imported antimony. It takes him to the sixth floor where his office is located. The telephone (with a receiver that employs thin strips of imported aluminium and imported copper wiring) starts ringing. It's a cloudy day and he needs light, so he switches on a bulb that has an imported tungsten filament — or neon lights having long bulbs with filaments made of magnesium tungstenate, zinc mercurate — all imported.[3]

In a similar way, developing countries are important markets for US exports and investments. They purchased more than US$95 billion worth — about forty per cent — of total merchandise exports in 1988. They are also an important market for US agricultural goods. Of the US$37 billion of agricultural products exported in 1988, more than US$19 billion worth — about five per cent — went to developing countries.

Another example of this transnational activity comes from the world of finance:

Three central developments in the 1980s have driven the globalisation of financial markets. First, deregulation ended many controls around the world on foreign investments in financial services and on international capital flows. Second, advanced technology enabled financial institutions to use computers to create new products unimagined only a few years ago and to apply sophisticated communications technology to link markets and offer financial products globally, often on a twenty-four hour basis.

Finally, volatility of prices, exchange rates and interest rates led to a demand for innovative ways to hedge against or take advantage of new risks.[4]

For business purposes, the boundaries that separate one nation from another are no more real than the equator. They are merely convenient demarcations of ethnic, linguistic and cultural entities. They do not define business requirements or consumer trends. The world outside the corporation's home nation is no longer viewed as a range of disconnected customers and prospects for its products, but as an extension of a single market.

Armand Hammer (who died in 1990) was one of the first Americans to understand this. He was the first American businessperson (aged twenty-four) to strike a deal with Lenin following the 1917 Russian Revolution. On returning to the US after his first visit to the USSR (which was not at that time recognised by his government), he was interviewed by journalists:

I said to the reporters: 'When I conferred with officials of the Soviet government, I told them that I was a capitalist, that I was out to make money, but entertained no idea of grabbing their land or their empire. They said, in effect, 'We understand you didn't come here for love. As long as you do not mix in our politics, we will give you our help.' And that is the basis on which I conducted negotiations.

It is curious for me to read these words today and see that I have been explaining myself, in exactly the same terms, in answer to the same kinds of questions for over sixty years. Western reporters are always asking me how I describe myself in Russia and I always reply that I tell the Russians that I am a capitalist, that I believe our system is better than theirs and that I want us to coexist peacefully in order that history may decide which of our systems is better. If my words haven't changed much over sixty years, neither have the reporters.[5]

Ironically, dictatorships are not necessarily repugnant to corporations. They are often more stable than democracies. Their plans for their people are stern, bold and backed by a powerful police force; if trouble threatens, they can always shoot someone. A dictatorship is centrally directed, with the reins gathered in a single fist. It is also much easier for a corporation to understand than a democracy: once you understand the character of the leader, you have figured out the government.

Transnational corporations have had little trouble making deals with foreign governments. Sometimes consumers themselves can be the losers. In April 1990 the then largest deal ever between a US corporation and the USSR resulted in Pepsico Inc signing an agreement to barter vodka for Pepsi-Cola. The USSR had little foreign 'hard currency' (like US dollars, UK pounds or German marks). Consequently to meet Soviet consumer demands, Moscow agreed that Pepsico Inc could sell Pepsi-Cola in the USSR; with the roubles (which are worthless outside the USSR) Pepsico Inc bought vodka in the USSR, shipped it to the US, where it was sold in US dollars.

Pepsi-Cola has been sold in the USSR since 1974, but trade increased considerably under Mr Gorbachev:

Pepsico was the first large US company to enter the Soviet market, led by its former chairman, Mr Donald Kendall. Mr Kendall, a former co-chairman and now a director of the US-USSR Trade and Economic Council, has actively encouraged other Western businesses to invest in the Soviet Union. He once told an interviewer: 'If we can get the Soviet people to enjoy good consumer goods, they'll never be able to do without them again.'

Pepsico, which is based in Purchase, New York, had sales in 1989 of more than $15 billion, making it one of the largest consumer product companies in the world. Its well-known brand names include the Kentucky Fried Chicken and Pizza Hut restaurants and Doritos tortilla chips.

Mr John Swanhaus, president of Pepsico's Wines and Spirits subsidiary, said: 'This deal is going to make the Soviet Union a very big business for us.'[6]

Indeed, US soft-drink trail-blazing in the USSR was first identified a decade ago — at the onset of a new 'Cold War' when US corporations were most concerned with seeing the Soviets as customers rather than as enemies.[7] Ronald Reagan has come and gone — but the Russians are still buying US soft drinks.

Owing to the inefficiency of communism, Soviet production always lagged behind consumer demand. After the Japanese, the Soviets had the world's biggest bank deposits — they had little on which to spend their pay. But corporations are now solving that problem: the largest McDonald's and Pizza Hut outlets in the world are in Moscow. This means more roubles for the corporations, more purchases of Russian vodka and more sales of vodka in the US.

H.C. ('Nugget') Coombs (Australian economist, banker and public official) tells in his memoirs an interesting story about the Governor of the Bank of England, Montagu Norman's dealings with the USSR:

It was Norman, too, who established the tradition that central banks act as agents for one another, without charge, and maintain communication by confidential letters and visits. There is a story that not long after the 1917 Bolshevik revolution the new government caused havoc in the London gold market by selling large quantities of gold, causing a dramatic fall in prices. Norman got in touch with the State Bank of the USSR, drew their attention to the losses they had incurred by their lack of expertise and offered to act for them confidentially and without charge. The offer was accepted and a working relationship established which both protected London gold traders and gave the Soviet Union a significantly better return.

I cannot vouch for the truth of the story, but in my time the Bank of England was better informed about the Soviet economy than any other official agency of which I was aware.[8]

Money, then, recognises no national frontier or political ideology. It can bring together even the bitterest of enemies.

In 1981, for example, it was reported that each year in carefully concealed movements, thousands of carats of rough diamonds from Soviet mines in Siberia were transferred to vaults owned by a South African-run enterprise based in London. In exchange, the Soviets were paid millions of dollars by the South Africans. As the major competitors on the Western market for such important commodities as gold, coal, asbestos, iron, manganese and platinum, Pretoria and Moscow shared a common interest in seeking a high or at least a stable price for these products. Despite their ideological distaste for each other — and Moscow's support for economic sanctions against South Africa in international political forums condemning apartheid — friendlier relations prevailed in the discreet world of international business.

It would be going too far to say there was collusion between South Africa and the Soviet Union to fix mineral prices, especially in the case of gold. But their covert contacts undoubtedly provided them both with valuable information and contributed to 'orderly marketing'.[9]

Transnational corporations are economically-orientated rather than politically- or ethnically-orientated. As they continue to expand their activities, they will contribute directly to continuing economic integration and indirectly to a reduced prospect of conflict between nations. They have a strong vested interest in a smoothly functioning international system and a reduction in global instability. To the extent that economic integration continues to make war a less practical instrument of foreign policy, the transnational corporation will help ensure that the prospects will improve for creating a socially and politically unified global community.

Concerns about Transnational Corporations

It would seem, then, that transnational corporations are a force for good: they will bring nations together and reduce the risk of war. But transnational corporations are human institutions and therefore suffer from the fallibility of humankind. As a result, it is also necessary to recognise that they contain flaws.

1. *Transnational corporations represent a vast accumulation of wealth and power beyond the regulatory control of any national government.*
Their wealth is comparable to that of many nations, without adequate control by and responsibility to the people affected. There is no global regulatory authority to control corporations. The UN's work (to be examined below) merely monitors their activities and has been trying to create a code of conduct.

The continuing scandal of the Bank of Credit and Commerce International (BCCI) provides an example of how difficult it is to regulate these corporations. BCCI operated at two levels: it provided ordinary banking services for small customers and 'special services' for rich ones. These 'special services' helped people who were anxious to get their money out of countries that had strict currency controls, corrupt officials seeking to hide their ill-gotten gains and an assortment of arms dealers, drug dealers and even terrorist groups who liked BCCI's policy of not asking awkward questions.

In the US, for example, BCCI used Miami as a staging ground for the largest single drug-running operations yet discovered. It was the October 1988 Florida indictment of the bank and six of its officials for allegedly laundering drug money that helped focus attention on BCCI's activities. A US Senate enquiry into the alleged drug-running activities of General Manuel Noriega revealed the connection between BCCI and Washington's largest bank, First America.

Like a spreading oil slick, the BCCI scandal is expanding and drawing into itself a range of respected figures. President Carter, for example, received a donation for his library and Lord (formerly Sir James) Callaghan received a donation for his favourite charity. Many people receiving attention happened to be in the wrong place at the wrong time; they are not criminals.

BCCI was beyond the control of any one nation. It began in Pakistan (many of its small customers who have lost out are overseas Pakistanis and Indians, 120 000 of them in the UK alone). It was incorporated in Luxembourg (notorious for its inadequate company regulations). It operated in seventy nations.

Its main shareholder is Sheik Zayed of Abu Dhabi, one of the world's richest men, who thought he was buying into a respectable bank; he has lost US$2 billion of his own money and US$7 billion of Abu Dhabi's state funds. Total losses for all of BCCI's customers could come to US$12 billion.

This is the largest banking scandal in history. National governments are trying to sort out BCCI's problems within their boundaries — but there is no global authority to monitor global banking. Although the UN's World Bank lends money — about $20 billion per year — it has nothing to do with controlling world banking as such.

How does such a situation arise in transnational corporations? Part of the answer is that no-one is in control over a long enough period to have the long-term interests of the organisations at heart. General Motors (GM) is a good example of this.

John de Lorean was a gifted executive at GM — one of the world's biggest car manufacturers. American writer J. Patrick Wright recalled de Lorean's work at GM and the changing nature of ownership and control:

The big individual owners of GM, like Sloan or du Pont and others, who owned hundreds of millions of dollars worth of the corporation's stock, had long tenure. Their decisions were biased as much in favour of the long-term growth and health of the company as they were in favour of the short-term profit statement. When they managed the business, sound planning was a fundamental aspect of management because that was the only way the company could grow and prosper. Their tenure gave a continuity to management.

There are no great owner-managers at GM today. 30 000 or 40 000 shares are considered a large position of stock. But that is almost insignificant compared to the 250 million shares that have been issued. Much of the corporate stock, however, is controlled by institutions of one sort or another. These organisations are usually short-term and results-orientated, and they do not take an active hand in management. When they are dissatisfied with the company's performance, they just sell the stock.

The people running GM today tend to be short-term, professional managers. They are in the top spots only a short time, less than ten years. In a sense, they just learn their job about the time they have to leave. So the concern at the top today is for the short-term health of the company. These professional managers want to produce a good record while they are in office. They do not have the perspective and incentive that a long-term owner with a large financial position in the company has because they are in a top spot for only a short while and then gone. They are running the business for themselves.

Several times in the late '60s and early '70s, outside board members asked management why we weren't getting into small cars. Management brushed aside their inquiries and never gave the questions serious consideration in running the company. Sloan or du Pont wouldn't have stood for this.[10]

Another example of a transnational corporation's activity that is difficult to control is 'transfer pricing'. This occurs when corporations buy and sell to and from their own subsidiaries at artificially high or low prices. This practice enables corporations to declare artificially low profits in nations with high tax rates, with high profits showing primarily in offshore tax havens, such as Panama or the Cayman Islands. A high percentage of world trade is composed of intra-firm transactions, and home and host nation governments are seldom able to examine the different sets of books kept by most corporations. The temptation to engage in transfer pricing is strong and the difficulties involved in regulating the practice are many.

This is a simplified illustration of how a UK branch of a US bank could carry out transfer pricing — in banking, it is called 'booking'. Suppose a London branch of a US bank receives a $10 million deposit; management decides to lend the money out. However, for tax reasons, it decides that it would be more advantageous to 'book' the loan with its Bahamas' branch or subsidiary — that is, to make it appear on the bank's accounts that the loan was made by the Bahamas entity rather than by the branch in London.

To make this possible, all that is needed is for the London branch to 'lend' — that is, deposit the $10 million with the Bahamas entity, which in turn makes the loan to the outside borrower. Formally, for accounting and tax purposes, this will appear as a Bahamas transaction: in fact, the real arrangements may have been made by the head office in New York, while the money comes from the London branch.

Of course, the bank has to pay taxes in the UK on the interest earned on the London branch's 'loan' to the Bahamas subsidiary, but inter-bank lending rates are lower than the rates charged to non-bank borrowers, so the bank still comes out ahead on its consolidated earnings.

2. *Transnational corporations' products are sometimes lethal (armaments) and often ill-designed to meet the basic needs of the masses of people because of the decision-making strategy methods of such companies.*

An example of such a product is the Corvair car. John de Lorean has recalled the ill-fated product, launched in 1959 (over the objections of some GM staff who had raised questions about the Corvair's safety):

The results were disastrous. I don't think any one car before or since produced as gruesome a record on the highway as the Corvair. It was designed and promoted to appeal to the spirit and flair of young people. It was sold in part as a sports car. Young Corvair owners, therefore, were trying to bend their cars around curves at high speeds and were killing themselves in alarming numbers.

It was only a couple of years or so before GM's legal depart-ment was inundated with lawsuits over the car. And the fatal swath that this car cut through the automobile industry touched the lives of many General Motors executives, employees and dealers in an ironic and tragic twist of fate.

The son of Cal Werner, general manager of the [GM] Cadillac Division, was killed in a Corvair. Werner was absolutely con-vinced that the design defect in the car was responsible. He said so many times. The son of Cy Osborn, an executive vice-president in the 1960s, was critically injured in a Corvair and suffered irreparable brain damage. Bunkie Knudsen's [head of GM] niece was brutally injured in a Corvair. And the son of an Indianapolis [GM] Chevrolet dealer also was killed in the car. Ernie Kovacs, my favourite comedian, was killed in a Corvair.[11]

Ralph Nader, who has become the world's leading consumer advocate, made his reputation with a study of the Corvair, entitled *Unsafe at Any Speed*. But GM's initial response to the discovery that Ralph Nader was examining the question of automobile safety was to hire detectives to trail the reformer in the hope of discovering some bit of scandal that might be used to dissuade him from either further investigation or disclosure. GM did not devote the same attention — at least initially — to Nader's claims.

Ironically, Nader later successfully sued GM for its spying on him and the damages he received — plus the fame — helped expand the non-governmental organisation (NGO) he had founded to investigate products. As de Lorean commented:

> There wasn't a man in top GM management who had anything to do with the Corvair who would purposely build a car that he knew would hurt or kill people. But, as part of a management team pushing for increased sales and profits, each gave his individual approval in a group to decisions which produced the car in the face of the serious doubts that were raised about its safety, and then later sought to squelch information which might prove the car's deficiencies.[12]

The Corvair saga is a case study of how moral people make immoral decisions. It often happens when you have a form of decision-making where no-one is finally responsible. Transnationals have a propensity to be like this.

3. *Transnational corporations' research and development funds are not always related to the basic needs of the people.*

The potentials of scientific knowledge and technology are thus deflected from serving the people towards the interests of easy profit for a few. Rich people make better customers than poor ones. Consequently, medical research, for example, revolves around the consequences of over-indulgence of rich people (heart attacks, strokes and alcohol-damaged livers and kidneys) rather than helping to fight the diseases in poor nations.

AIDS, for instance, was not a problem while it was in tropical poorer countries — it only became a major tragedy when it hit San Francisco.

4. *Transnational corporations have a preference for capital-intensive technology which aggravates the unemployment problem.*

In other words, corporations employ machinery rather than human beings. This helps explain a paradox. In spite of the sizeable investments that have been made, in spite of jobs created by transnational corporations in poorer nations, the number of absolute poor is increasing. The industrialisation of the poorer world is not ending poverty.

UN figures place direct employment by transnational corporations at a minimum of some sixty-five million people in the world's market economies. Approximately forty-three million jobs are at home and twenty-two million abroad, of which roughly seven million are in developing countries. These conservative estimates do not include all banking, financial and service activities (which might add at least another three million employees worldwide). Nor do they take into account indirect positive employment effects created by the corporation's demand for local products, transport, market facilities and other services (about seven million additional jobs depend on this in the developing countries alone).

But an International Labour Organisation survey[13] has found that corporations' employment is stagnating, if not shrinking, in some places. One reason is that in the wake of the recession during the 1980s, a good proportion of foreign direct investment in the US and Western Europe took the form of acquisitions of existing firms. Although such investments may have increased the share of transnational corporations in total employment, they are unlikely to have led to the creation of further jobs — especially since many recent mergers have been accompanied by major efforts to cut costs and streamline production, inevitably lowering the number of employees.

At the same time, foreign direct investment in developing countries has diminished. Only those developing countries that have a relatively skilled labour force or are well situated geographically may have some hope of export-orientated foreign investment to boost employment. Western-based corporations may subcontract more work to firms in the developing world.

Yet even under the most optimistic scenario, jobs generated by transnational corporations will constitute a small percentage of total employment. At present, the world's economically active population is growing at a rate of more than two per cent a year. If full employment is to be approached, forty-seven million new jobs throughout the world are needed annually over the next four decades.

5. *Transnational corporations can exercise undue influence upon national governments and can interfere with the freedom of people to choose their own form of government.*

The standard example is the campaign in the early 1970s against Chile's socialist politician Salvador Allende. Chile was one of Latin America's few traditional democracies. But International Telephone and Telegraph Company (ITT) perceived Allende as a threat. Allende was not going to nationalise ITT's company in Chile, Chiltelco, but it would be forced to give up a certain percentage of its stocks to the Chilean government and a certain percentage, therefore, of its profits. (The same applied to Anaconda Copper which had taken out of Chile US$500 million in profits between 1960 and 1970, without putting much back in.) ITT and other corporations funded Allende's opponents in the 1970 election. But Allende still won.

US journalist Seymour Hersh said that President Nixon was furious:

> There is compelling evidence that Nixon's tough stance against Allende in 1970 was principally shaped by his concern for the future of the American corporations whose assets, he believed, would be seized by an Allende government. His intelligence agencies, while quick to condemn the spread of Marxism in Latin America, reported that Allende posed no threat to national security.
>
> Three days after the popular election, the CIA told the White House in a formal Intelligence Memorandum that, as summarised by the Senate Intelligence Committee, the United States 'had no vital interests within Chile, the world military balance of power would not be significantly altered by an Allende regime and an Allende victory in Chile would not pose any likely threat to the peace of the region'. Nixon's anger at failing his corporate benefactors — Jay Parkinson [Anaconda], Harold Geneen [ITT] and Donald Kendall [Pepsico] — was passed directly on to Kissinger.[14]

Kissinger, according to Seymour Hersh, then set about creating a program of destabilising the Chilean economy, assisting right-wing groups and, in effect, disrupting Chile's tradition of democracy. Three years later, the military rebelled against Allende who was killed in the action, and a brutal dictatorship was installed. Chile's parliamentary system was wrecked — but the US corporations were saved.

6. *Transnational corporations' vast wealth gives them power to influence the mass media, to control the spread of information, to create myths and to obscure the truth, and to remould the culture and its values in the interests of industry and business.*

The power of the mass media is well illustrated by what happened in Eastern Europe. The Russian army could keep the American forces out of Eastern Europe — but it could not keep out the American mass media. Television, radio, and movies are a new force in global politics. Until the recent uprising in Europe, the East Europeans were forced to be politically loyal to Moscow. But their hearts belonged to Hollywood.

In the early 1980s, for example, there was a sudden interest among Czechoslovakians in learning German. However, German has been rarely taught since 1945 — a reaction against the World War II German occupation. But by the 1980s it was possible to tune Czechoslovakian television sets to receive West German signals. A knowledge of German was required to follow *Dallas* and *Dynasty* — and so quite suddenly there was a demand for people in Czechoslovakia to teach German.

A new form of colonialism is developing — electronic colonialism. A handful of nations are hosts to the main media outlets. For example, in regard to the news, the five big news agencies — Associated Press, United Press International, Reuters, Agence France Presse and (at one time) Tass — control some eighty per cent of the global market. This means that the developing countries get eighty per cent of the global news market from London, New York, Paris and (at one time) Moscow. The local media report the stories which are seen by the five big news agencies as important. People may not know about their own country, but they do hear a great deal about the US President or the Queen of England.

For example, seventy per cent of students polled in three secondary schools in Kingston, Jamaica, could not name the prime ministers of Barbados, Trinidad or Tobago, but eighty-nine per cent could name the US President. The survey revealed the rapid erosion of Carribbean culture by the predominantly foreign content in the news media. The majority of English-speaking Carribbean's television output — eighty-seven per cent — comes from outside the region.

The Americanisation of culture has several impacts. One is the incentive to learn English (or at least the American version of it). A thirst for *Dallas* and *Dynasty* will do more for English than all the British government's attempts to encourage the foreign study of Shakespeare, Tennyson, Keats and Charles Dickens. Language is also the key to culture and history. In time, people will forget their own culture and history. An Australian example of this is the way in which all Australians can recall the names of some US Red Indians (like Chief Sitting Bull), but few can recall the names of Aboriginal leaders.

But this is not a conspiracy of the US government to take over the world; electronic colonialism is much more complicated than the old-style colonialism. Cable News Network (CNN), the world's largest global television network, is an American media transnational corporation that well indicates the power of such worldwide institutions.

In January 1992, *Time* magazine announced that its 'Man of the Year' was Ted Turner, founder of CNN. It broadcasts one continuous, simultaneous signal. It is the common frame of reference for the world's power elite, who all get the same signal at the same time. President Bush said he preferred CNN to the CIA briefings because CNN operated much faster than the CIA.

CNN has become the fourth most respected brand name in the US, behind Disney parks, Kodak and Mercedes-Benz and ahead of Rolex,

Levis and IBM. CNN can be received by individuals and organisations which have satellite dishes. American viewers have taken to this technology faster than, say, Australians and Britons. But the technology is here to stay. Transnational corporations' products are given worldwide advertising coverage by CNN. Global products such as McDonald's and Coca Cola are examples of this.

The news journalists may strive for independence, but they tend to view the world through American eyes and American priorities determine which events are 'news'. African nations, for example, need a war or a natural disaster before they attract any attention.

7. *Transnational corporations can be irresponsible and wasteful in the use of scarce resources.*

Corporations — particularly those engaged in the natural resources and life sciences industries — are increasingly becoming major forces in the global environment today. They figure prominently in ocean fisheries, groundwater pollution, the greenhouse effect and global food production. They have a major role in the control of how the planet is used.

They determine which natural resources are developed and how fast; which ones are degraded and depleted; how much pollution there will be; and which technologies will be developed. Their research often determines what pollutants will be replaced and when; what natural resources will be 'outdated'; and what new ones will fuel the industrial processes of tomorrow. All this is due, of course, to their sheer size in mining, processing, manufacturing and marketing.

It is always cheaper to invest in safety than to pay the costs of hazards. The exception seems to be in the developing world, where life is cheap. More than 3 400 Indians have died since a cloud of methyl isocynate gas leaked out of a storage tank at the Bhopal facility and wafted over the city of 672 000 in the early hours of 3 December

1984. In the worst industrial accident in history, at least 200 000 more were hurt, with 15 000 to 20 000 suffering lasting injuries to their eyes, bronchial passages and other organs.

US transnational corporation Union Carbide fought to limit its liability in the case, spending more than $30 million on legal talent. Had the case gone to trial, the corporation was prepared to argue that the gas leak was the result of sabotage by a disgruntled employee, not its own negligence, as the Indian government charged. The sole direct payment to the victims of the disaster has come from the Indian government, which paid $666 to the families of those who died and $100 to families seriously affected whose monthly incomes are below $34 — a total of about $10 million.

In the end, Union Carbide (1988 earnings: $720 million on revenues of $8.3 billion) succeeded in keeping the settlement at a manageable level; it had already set aside $200 million and insurance will cover $250 million more. When the Indian government filed its lawsuit in 1986, it demanded $3.3 billion for Bhopal's victims. In 1987, Union Carbide was reportedly offering to pay $600 million, but New Delhi balked, claiming that the figure was too low. With the corporation prepared to drag out the legal proceedings for another decade, the Indian government in February 1989 accepted $470 million in a lump sum settlement.[15]

Bhopal is the ugly side of industrial progress. Transnational corporations bring the material advantages of modern living — but they are equally significant in contributing to pollution. It follows that if a corporation has as its basic job making things that make life better, it should not, in the course of production, make life worse. Corporations are perceived as responsible for whatever they do — for the quality of their products, for the smoke pouring out of their plants, for the wages and promotion of their employees, and for the health of people living near their factories.

Unfortunately, the very character of the transnational corporation is that it is an amoral institution with no soul. As de Lorean recalled:

> Never once while I was in General Motors management did I hear substantial social concern raised about the impact of our business on America, its consumers or the economy. When we should have been planning switches to smaller, more fuel-efficient, lighter cars in the late 1960s in response to a growing demand in the marketplace, GM management refused because 'we make more money on big cars'. It mattered not that customers wanted the smaller cars or that a national balance-of-payments deficit was being built in large part because of the burgeoning sales of foreign cars in the American market.
>
> Refusal to enter the small car market when the profits were better on bigger cars, despite the needs of the public and the national economy, was not an isolated case of corporate insensitivity. It was typical. And what disturbed me is that it was indicative of fundamental problems with the system.
>
> General Motors certainly was no more irresponsible than many American businesses. But the fact that the 'prototype' of the well-run American business engaged in questionable business practices and delivered decisions which I felt were sometimes illegal, immoral or irresponsible is an indictment of the American business system.[16]

It is important to note that these transnational corporations are not the only companies which are endangering the global environment. Small national firms also contribute to pollution. But the fact that transnationals have global links means that their decisions can affect the shape and direction of our world in a way that smaller, more localised corporations cannot.

TACKLING PROBLEMS WITH
TRANSNATIONAL CORPORATIONS

Given the enormous power of transnational corporations, what can be done to bring abuses into the light of day? After all, very little is known about them.

Who is the head of General Motors? Who is the head of Exxon? This is not secret information. But whereas the mass media report endlessly on politicians, they devote far less attention to the inner workings of transnational corporations. This is not necessarily a media conspiracy. The media have simply assumed that viewers and readers have little interest in these matters. It is certainly amazing that transnational corporations have such a big impact on our lives — for good or ill — and yet they receive so little scrutiny.

The corporations themselves are happy with this arrangement. They like the corporate code of silence. The American economist John Kenneth Galbraith has set out three reasons for this code of silence.[17]

First, the internal politics of the corporations have never been a serious interest of the press, nor of the economists. Financial analysts are more concerned with acquisitions, takeovers, investments, product development and profits.

Second, there is the role of money. An employee who carries news of internal strife and dissent to the press or public does so at grave, even total, financial risk to himself or herself. The whistle-blower in the public service in Washington has recourse to civil service rules and the law. The corporate dissident or combatant who goes public gets sacked, with no legal recourse, and he marks himself as someone not to be wanted elsewhere: who can tell what he might do next?

Third, corporation executives who are the victims of corporate rows are given early retirement. Or after watching over, participating in, or mediating those rows, they serve their terms and then retire. In either case, the habit of corporate containment of thought and its expression is by then complete. The capacity for dissenting thought and expression is gone. Corporate discipline has taken over the executive mind.

1. *One individual's struggle with a transnational corporation*

An example of the problems confronting an individual who reveals information about a transnational corporation is revealed in the story of Stanley Adams.[18] In February 1973 Adams, then a senior executive with Basle-based pharmaceutical giant Hoffman-La Roche, told the EEC's competition department that his corporation was part of a price-fixing cartel which broke the EEC's fair-trading rules. The drugs giant was not exactly brought to its knees by the eventual fine — some £180 000. But it was outraged by the breach of commercial secrecy.

As the Commission hunted for evidence, the corporation hunted the informer. Adams, who left Hoffman-La Roche in late 1973 to start his own pig-breeding business in Italy, was eventually identified from documents handed over by the Commission and traced back to him. The EEC was careless in not keeping Mr Adams informed of its investigation or the risks he ran for providing the information to the EEC.

In December 1974, on a visit to Swiss relatives, he was arrested at the border, charged with giving economic information to a foreign power and put into prison. His wife Marilene, who was told only that he could face a twenty-year sentence, hanged herself twelve days after the arrest. The EEC, too, was kept in the dark. But news of Adams' plight eventually came to Brussels through released prisoners. Adams was let out on bail and later fled from Switzerland, where in due course he was sentenced in absentia to a year in prison.

Mr Adams became entangled in a legal and political octopus as his allegations were followed up in the EEC and the European parliament. The Swiss government regarded him as a criminal and transnational corporations (presumably even including competitors to Hoffman-La Roche) refused him a job. He complained to the European Court of Human Rights about the EEC's handling of his information. In November 1985, Judges of the European Court of Justice ordered the EEC to pay compensation, including damages for ten years of personal misery. Ironically, by the time he won this case, Mr Adams had found a new career — lecturing on business ethics.

His autobiography contains insights, such as the following extracts, into the workings of a corporation. First, on salaries:

Roche operated a scheme whereby they paid the agreed monthly rate for the job, but they could vary the number of payments. I started on thirteen payments a year and by the time I left Roche I was getting fifteen payments a year (double salary in June and treble salary in December). The scheme was used to reward people without other colleagues on the same level finding out about it. Everyone knew officially that the salary for this level of management was so much a month, but no-one knew how many monthly payments were being made to anyone else.

The same kind of principle was applied when paying managers abroad, but the main purpose then was to keep wages down in developing countries. Once Roche and I had agreed the level of salary I was to earn as manager in Venezuela, then Roche would decide how much they would actually pay me in Venezuela, and how much extra they would pay into my Swiss bank account in Basle. Then they would notify the Venezuelan accountant only of the amount I was paid in Venezuela, so that in Venezuela that was the amount I declared and paid tax on. The amount in the Swiss account would not normally be declared in Switzerland and would not be caught for tax in

either place. Although there were obvious tax advantages for overseas managers paid in this way, it was not done for that reason.
What Roche wanted to do was prevent the local people who
worked for them in other countries from realising how much
money those on foreign contracts were earning.[19]

Second, the effect of the corporation's policies on the developing
world:

During my business career I had travelled extensively all over the
world and particularly in poor countries. I had seen the effects of
the drug companies' policies. I had seen so much poverty in the
world and seen people unable to buy medicines and vitamins because of the price. I had also seen that within Roche, when news
came of an influenza epidemic in, for instance, India, instead of
putting vitamin C out in greater quantities and reducing the price,
we would control the quantities going out to the market and usually increase the price. I thought that somebody more powerful than
industrial companies should be able to control the situation.[20]

Third, the link between the corporation and Switzerland:

In other words, even when the facts of 'economic life' that Roche
wanted to keep hidden were illegal and broke the provisions of an
international agreement that Switzerland had signed, they were
still protected under Swiss law. What's more, anyone who attacked Roche by revealing those secrets was deemed to be attacking
the interests of the Swiss State. The two were linked together.
What was good for Roche was good for Switzerland, and woe
betide anyone who challenged that link or dared to report them to
an outside body, even if that body was a partner in an international agreement.[21]

Before going to the EEC, Adams — presumably like other conscientious executives with doubts about their companies — could see little scope for complaining about these activities:

> There was nobody I could report Roche to who could take action. Switzerland does have competition laws, but they would scarcely take any notice of a single individual complaining against one of their biggest companies. And Roche was a great patron, a great benefactor of the arts and music, a great donator to good causes. The city of Basle in particular had good reason to be grateful to Roche. Roche imported orchestras to play to the citizens of Basle. (Roche employees were admitted free.) Roche loaned or donated paintings and works of art to Basle Art Gallery. Roche employed thousands of people living in Basle. Basle was definitely not the place to be critical of Roche, as I discovered later to my cost.
>
> I could, I suppose, as a former British citizen, have reported them to the British, but the government would only be able to take action over any dealings Roche had with British firms and that was only a small part of the whole.[22]

Switzerland, which is not part of the EEC, wanted its companies to trade more easily in the EEC area. In December 1972, Switzerland and the EEC concluded an agreement giving greater access to Swiss companies in the EEC — but it also meant that any Swiss corporation trading in the EEC area would be bound by the EEC's rules of competition.

A few weeks later, Adams wrote privately to the EEC reporting on Hoffman-La Roche's trading activities. He broke the code of corporate silence — and spent a decade paying for it.

2. The United Nations' dealings with transnational corporations

National governments have been slow to respond to the problems created by transnational corporations. Initially they tended to see only the benefits brought by the corporations; they thought the problems created by corporations (such as pollution) could be handled by existing legislation. Techniques such as transfer pricing were beyond their understanding. Graduates in economics employed in the national civil services were equally unprepared; economics textbooks and courses also paid little attention to this revolution.

Since national governments were slow to catch on to this revolution, it is not surprising that the UN — made up of nations — was equally slow. It has only been since 1972 that problems relating to the activities of transnational corporations and their effects on development have been under consideration by the UN.

The starting point was the representative of President Allende's government in Chile who charged the International Telephone and Telegraph Company (ITT) with massive interference in the domestic political processes of his nation. This event marks the beginning of the UN's work to develop rules on the conduct of corporations.

The issue of interference in host-nation politics was not, however, the sole or even the primary cause of UN activity in this field. Corruption was eye-catching, but there were also the concerns of US labour unions with the export of jobs and the growing apprehension of Western European trade unions about relations with inaccessible home-country management, particularly in cases of projected plant closure.

In 1972, the Economic and Social Council (ECOSOC) requested the UN Secretary-General to appoint a 'group of eminent persons. . . to study the role of multinational corporations and their impact on the process of development, especially that of the developing countries, and also their implications for international relations, to formulate conclusions which may possibly be used by governments in making their sovereign decisions regarding national policy in this respect and to submit recommendations for appropriate international action'.

The group reported in April 1974. Its main concern was to strengthen the hands of host nations dealing with transnational corporations and it made a number of recommendations. In particular, it recommended the establishment of a commission on transnational corporations which would, among other things, prepare a code of conduct for governments and transnational corporations to be considered and adopted by ECOSOC. It also recommended the establishment of an information and research centre. Both the commission and the information and research centre were established later in the year.

This concern about the activities of transnational corporations arose from the growing desire of developing countries for fuller control over their political, economic and social development and from their awareness of the possibility of a conflict between their interests and those of the foreign corporations operating in their nations. Trade unions in the developed world were also worried about job losses to developing nations.

The forty-eight member Commission on Transnational Corporations was established in 1974 as an intergovernmental subsidiary body of ECOSOC. Election of member-nations to the commission is based on geographical distribution: twelve members are from Africa, eleven from Asia, ten from Latin America, ten from the developed countries of Western Europe, North America and Oceania, and five from Eastern Europe. Members serve a three-year term and are eligible for re-election. The main home nations of corporations (for example, the US, the UK, Germany and Japan) have always been members of the commission.

The commission's main functions are to discuss and keep under review all issues related to corporations, to draft the UN Code of Conduct on Transnational Corporations and to advise ECOSOC in all matters relating to corporations. In addition, it determines the priorities and the program of work of the Centre on Transnational Corporations. Sixteen expert advisers are elected by the commission to assist it in its deliberations. The advisers are drawn from trade unions, business, public interest groups and universities. They act in a private capacity.

The centre has thirty-five professionals and uses a number of consultants for various specialised activities. Its total annual budget is approximately US$5 million. The centre's technical cooperation program is funded through a voluntary trust fund and by the United Nations Development Program. Since 1976, the following governments have contributed various amounts totalling US$7 million to the trust fund: China, Denmark, Finland, Germany, Greece, Italy, Republic of Korea, Nepal, Netherlands, Norway, Sweden, Switzerland, UK, Zaire and Zambia. The centre is not exactly overwhelmed by government donations — the richest nations which could give money are also the ones that host corporations and derive some income from them.

With an annual budget of US$5 million, the centre has minute resources. By comparison in 1985, the total value of foreign direct investment was some US$650 billion, accounted for by approximately 20 000 transnational corporations with more than 100 000 affiliates worldwide. The centre has four tasks:

* It provides governments with comprehensive information pertaining to transnational corporations, various data on companies, information on contractual arrangements, investments and employment. It collects information on specific

    industrial sectors, contracts, agreements and rules and regulations from different nations.

* It has been engaged in research regarding the social, political, economic and legal aspects of transnational corporations. Very little is known about some aspects of corporations. Even the task of quantifying their size and their importance is difficult. The data on international trade does not differentiate between international trade among individual companies and trade among affiliates of the same corporation in different nations.
* It provides assistance to governments by holding seminars, workshops and other training programs.
* It replies to requests from governments for advisory services on drafting legislation, formulating regulations, and negotiations.

These are all worthy activities — but very small in the face of the problems created by corporations.

The centre is working on the Code of Conduct. First suggested in 1974, the Code is to provide a voluntary set of standards of behaviour of transnational corporations as well as general rules regarding their treatment by the nations in which they operate. Even by UN standards, this is a long-running saga. About eighty per cent of the document was completed by 1990. The demand for such a code is increasing. With *perestroika* in Eastern Europe, the former communist world is joining the developed world in hosting transnational corporations. However, as a former US presidential adviser has explained, the delay has come from the US:

> Unfortunately, the US has been anything but a strong supporter over the last years. In 1987, President Reagan's Assistant Secretary of State for International Organisation, Alan Keyes, said that negotiations on the Code were 'bogged down'. And last November

[1989], the Bush administration testified that it saw little hope for an early agreement on the Code. Fortunately, however, increasing congressional and nongovernmental organisation [NGO] interest, developments in the EEC and a strong commitment to passage of the Code by members of the Commission on Transnational Corporations (including support from the Group of 77 [the Third World]) have given new hope for a successful adoption of the Code.

After reaching agreement on the great majority of its provisions, the Code negotiations have indeed been deadlocked on one or two issues concerning the standard of compensation for expropriation and the formulation of an 'international law' standard. It is mostly agreed, however, that these are antiquated arguments that have lost much of their meaning in today's investment climate. A committee of international experts has proposed solutions to these outstanding issues; what is needed now is the political will to complete the work.

The Code is becoming more and more relevant to Americans at home as the US becomes a major host country for foreign investment. The Code not only serves to protect US corporations against discriminatory practices throughout the world, but is also a vital instrument for the US in its role as a recipient of non-US goods and services. Additionally, it will help to secure a predictable climate for Americans seeking to invest abroad.[23]

Even when the Code is eventually completed, it will still be only a voluntary code. The UN has no power to force corporations to change their activities. The UN is not a world government.

If such a world government existed, then it could, for example, introduce rules about environmental protection, wages, safety standards, transnational investment and banking, and taxation. It could also create a transnational corporation control agency funded by taxes based on the savings that the corporations make by being able to escape or minimise national tax obligations. (Properly taxing the corporations would also help other smaller companies compete more fairly with them.) It could also require the corporations to contribute to funds for social development in the developing countries in which they operate. But since there is no world government, none of these policies can be introduced.

THE FUTURE SHAPE OF
TRANSNATIONAL CORPORATIONS

The only constant in life is change. Corporations are as susceptible to change as any other institution. Having gone from 'multinational' corporations to 'transnational' corporations, we may now be heading towards 'supranational' corporations: not only might the corporations of the future move *across* national barriers; they might move *beyond* them.

This evolution has come partly from the emergence of industrial complementation agreements among nations. Such agreements may involve either the manufacturing of several related products in different nations, or the manufacturing of components which are eventually assembled into a final product.

The first type, manufacturing related products, may be illustrated by four nations interested in developing a petrochemical industry. One nation might supply petrol from indigenous reserves, one might do the refining, one might have a lubricants enterprise, and the fourth might have a plastics industry or some other petrochemical enterprise. These products would then move freely among this group of nations, enlarging the market for all and justifying investments which otherwise could not be considered.

An example of the second variety, manufacturing of components, is the agreement worked out by International Business Machines (IBM) with Argentina, Brazil, Chile and Uruguay in the computer industry.

Components are manufactured in Brazil and assembled in Argentina, a Chilean firm is licensed to produce punch cards and the entire operation is headquartered in Uruguay. In exchange for these arrangements, the four nations now constitute a duty-free zone for all IBM computers, components and punch cards.

Newsweek magazine (1 May 1989) has reported on the growth of a global car partnership:

> The world auto industry is fast becoming one great partnership. Consider this: Mazda designed and built Ford's sporty new Probe. The classic Japanese Toyota Corolla now rolls out of an American plant half owned by General Motors. The preppy 'American' Pontiac LeMans was engineered by Opel (GM's West German subsidiary) and is built by Daewoo in South Korea. The Corvette, often described as the epitome of the American-made sports car, comes with a high-performance transmission built by ZF, a West German company.
>
> Chrysler vice-chairman Gerald Greenwald says, 'No car company will be successful in the 90s that doesn't learn to develop strategic international alliances.'

SIGNS OF FRAGMENTATION IN TRANSNATIONAL CORPORATIONS

Centralisation is a Second Wave characteristic and fragmentation is the Third Wave one. We need also to look for signs of fragmentation, for they will co-exist alongside the move towards supranational corporations. What are these signs?

1. *A failure by transnationals to understand local cultures, customs and languages.*

Dr Rose Hayden, President of the US National Council on Foreign Language and International Studies in 1986, quoted some anecdotes showing how some US corporations have made costly blunders out of ignorance:

> The Chevrolet 'Nova' did not sell in Latin America. When spoken, *Nova* means 'it doesn't go' in Spanish. 'Body by Fisher' was translated in Flemish as 'Corpse by Fisher'. Schweppes Tonic Water was advertised in Italy as 'bathroom water' and 'Come Alive with Pepsi' nearly appeared in China as 'Pepsi Brings Your Ancestors Back from the Grave'.[24]

2.   *A failure by transnationals to be sufficiently diverse.*
John de Lorean eventually resigned from General Motors because he found the corporation too rigid, too stifling and too top-heavy:

> General Motors' strength comes from its diversity within the confines of one industry. This offers many different approaches to the demands of one marketplace for wheeled, motorised vehicles. That diversity is severely diminished today. As GM centralised, management moved to combine, consolidate and intertwine the operating arms of the corporation. The Detroit Diesel and Allison Divisions were combined; parts operations were likewise blended; and the manufacturing-assembly capability of the car divisions was all but taken away and given to an entirely new entity, GM Assembly Division.
>
>   Each of the car divisions was given the design and manufacturing responsibility for parts of all GM's cars. The rationale was that these moves made good financial sense. I suspect, however, and no-one told me this, that these moves were made primarily to thwart or complicate federal government antitrust action. A closely knit and intricately interwoven General Motors would be much

more difficult to break up than a distinctly diverse operation.

These moves destroyed the heart of General Motors' decentralised operations. So the answer to curing the company's ills today includes a rapid move back to the point where the divisions are easily distinguishable entities, responsible, to a large degree, for the success and/or failure of their own operations. Such a move would include giving the divisions back much of their assembly responsibility and cutting back the program of standardisation to the point where it makes economic sense.[25]

Ironically, General Motors used to be the world's biggest car manufacturer. That position is now held by Toyota.

3. *A trend towards self-employment*

One innovation to watch for is the intrapreneurial system, by which some existing employees would become part-time jobbing outworkers, providing labour on contract, possibly on a cooperative basis. With the emergence of the intrapreneurial system, whole chunks of business can be contracted out, or hived off and sold to their current employees on a management buyout basis. More people will want to involve themselves in their work by owning it — either self-employed or in a cooperative, rather than being a tiny fish in an impersonal ocean.

A related development is the increase in 'independent operators' whom British social commentator Francis Kinsman describes in this way:

It may be difficult to employ a gardener, but the same man is happy and fulfilled to be a jobbing gardening consultant with his own business, driving round in a van to work for ten people half a day a week each. Parallel to this is a subtle shifting in the manifestation of employee loyalty. People have a sense of loyalty not only to their company but also to their family, their neighbourhood and their own professional skill. They are more independent now, they have a whole range of imperatives and they feel individualistic.

Through education and the impact of mass media, particularly television, people are looking for opportunities to make choices and to grow. The majority feel that they can find this in small organisational groups much better than in large ones, and therefore the diversified, decentralised workplace looks more attractive, even sometimes to the ultimate of combining it with the home.[26]

4. A trend towards products tailored to individual taste
The age of mass production is ending and there are likely to be short runs of products tailor-made to individual tastes. This is good news for the UK, writes Francis Kinsman:

The British contribution to this change of direction — which is of world significance and not just confined to these islands — will be an important one, since we still understand the nature of craftsmanship and have a proven record of creativeness and discovery. A Japanese MITI report showed recently that of significant discoveries in recent years Japan itself lay bottom of the list with something like six per cent. Germany had fourteen per cent, the US twenty-two per cent and the UK an incredible fifty-five per cent.

In modern technological terms the trend shows through in our world dominance in software — and this is a crucial factor for our potential growth in the next century. In spite of all the problems that now beset us, the future therefore looks as if it will suit us very well if only we can reach it intact.[27]

Such craftsmanship must surely go some way to undermining straightjacketed transnationals.

5. *A trend towards employee stock-ownership plans (ESOPs).*[28]

Ten million US workers, about one-quarter of all corporate employees, are enrolled in an ESOP, up from three million only a decade ago. More than 9 800 American companies offer such programs, including 1 500 in which employees own the majority of the stock. By giving workers a stake in the company's success, the programs boost morale and productivity.

This system works best in small companies, where workers feel they have more of a role in determining 'their' company's productivity and profits. Transnationals, on the other hand, might find that their size and remoteness make stock-ownership less effective because of the workers feeling a sense of powerlessness. If they implement stock ownership, would they sour relations with employees? If they don't, might employees go elsewhere?

Decentralisation, creativity and self-reliance are all characteristics of the new era. Transnational corporations — or supranational corporations — will need to absorb these factors in order to survive.

Endnotes:

1. Richard Barnet, 'Multinationals and Third World Development', *Development Education Forum*, Lutheran World Federation, October 1980, p.20
2. 'Top Aussie is 149th', *West Australian*, 21 July 1990
3. Jean-Jacques Servan-Schreiber, *The World Challenge*, Collins, 1981, pp.116–117
4. Joan E. Spero, 'Guiding Global Finance', *Economic Impact*, No. 1, 1989, p.55
5. Armand Hammer, *Witness to History*, Simon and Schuster, 1987, pp.158–159
6. 'Pepsico Goes Down Well in a US-Soviet Barter Deal', *Australian Financial Review*, 10 April 1990
7. Charles Levinson, *Vodka-Cola*, Gordon & Cremonesi, 1981
8. H.C. Coombs, *Trial Balance*, Macmillan, 1981, p.142
9. 'How Moscow and Pretoria Carve Up the Mineral Market', *Guardian Weekly*, 23 August 1981
10. J. Patrick Wright, *On a Clear Day You Can See General Motors: John de Lorean's Look Inside the Automobile Giant*, Avon, 1979, p.259
11. *Ibid*, p.66
12. *Ibid*, pp.67–68
13. International Labour Organisation, *Transnational Corporations in World Development: Fourth Survey*, UN Centre on Transnational Corporations, 1988
14. Seymour Hersh, *The Price of Power — Henry Kissinger in the Nixon White House*, Faber, 1983, p.269
15. 'Is it "Just" or "Peanuts"?', *Time*, 27 February 1989, p.27
16. J. Patrick Wright, *ibid*, p.63
17. John Kenneth Galbraith, 'Lee Iacocca and the Code of Corporate Silence', *Australian Financial Review*, 18 April 1986
18. 'Painful Path to Justice', *Guardian Weekly*, 17 November 1985
19. Stanley Adams, *Roche versus Adams*, Jonathan Cape, 1984, pp.8–9
20. *Ibid*, pp.17–18
21. *Ibid*, p.107
22. *Ibid*, p.19
23. Esther Peterson, 'New Support for Code on Transnationals', *The Interdependent*, Spring 1990, p.3
24. Quoted in *World Development Forum*, 15 June 1986, p.2
25. J. Patrick Wright, *ibid*, pp.276–277
26. Francis Kinsman, *The New Agenda: Business in Society*, Spencer Stuart

Management Consultants, 1983, pp.74–75
27. *Ibid*, p.75
28. 'They Own the Place: Employee Stock Plans are Hot in the US and Start to Catch on Worldwide', *Time*, 13 February 1989, pp.44–45

7

NON-GOVERNMENT ORGANISATIONS

What power do the people have?

IT HAS BEEN SAID THAT THERE ARE three groups of people: those who make things happen; those who watch things happen; those — the largest group — who don't know what happens.

In the old world order, the first group of people were largely in government positions. This was the 'deferential society', in which people deferred to their leaders (however defined) to make decisions. The leaders were perceived as having more wisdom, secret information and more experience than their followers. In the new world order, the first group are increasingly *outside* the government: it is people power. They are sceptical that the political leaders always do know best. They are no longer, in Western democracies, likely to be just election fodder, voting for the same parties without question at each election.

This helps explain the stagnation in Western political systems in the old world order identified in chapter 4. The political party system, first devised in the eighteenth century, cannot cope with electoral behaviour of the late twentieth century.

Australian political scientist Ian Marsh has described two features of the new world order.[1] He stated that 'left' and 'right' are no longer valid in describing political outlook based on occupation and income. He noted that Don Anderson, a sociologist at the Australian National University, had shown the extent to which new influences (such as tertiary training) shape the political allegiance of professionals, leading to support of political causes at odds with their apparent material interests. His study covered 2 000 Australian lawyers, engineers, doctors and teachers and monitored their political allegiance and voting behaviour from the mid-60s to 1984. He showed how older patterns of political loyalty and alignment became blurred. On a range of issues, he saw occupation and income as no longer reliable predictors of attitude.

Consequently, political parties have difficulty in devising campaigns that appeal to their traditional supporters. Instead, some of the traditional supporters have drifted off to support minority political parties, independents or single issue parties, or have just dropped out of the political party game entirely.

So along with the decay of the main political parties has been the growth of non-governmental organisations, such as the environmental movement. In Australia, for example, the Liberal and Labor parties probably have no more than 100 000 members each. The environment movement through its various affiliated organisations is estimated to enlist over 300 000 people. People are voting with their feet. They are leaving political parties and joining people power movements.

RECENT EXAMPLES OF PEOPLE POWER
People power has been evolving over the decades — if not centuries. But the last few years have seen it get onto the front pages of

newspapers. The following three examples are significant examples of this.

1. *People power reaction to NATO's limited nuclear war strategy*
In December 1979, the North Atlantic Treaty Organisation (NATO) decided to deploy new missiles which changed nuclear strategy: instead of relying upon deterrence, the new nuclear weapons were designed to fight a 'limited' nuclear war. The peace movement in Western nations had been dormant for years, but this policy change helped revive it.

Various movies such as *The Day After* and *Threads* were made which helped shock people into action. The peace movement contributed to the political pressure on presidents Reagan and Gorbachev to begin reducing the US and Soviet stocks of nuclear weapons.

2. *People power and the 1986 Philippines election*
In January 1986 President Marcos, bowing to US pressure, held a presidential election. The main alternative candidate was Mrs Corazon Aquino. I was in Manila at that time and met her on the night of her final election rally. The prevailing view in the Australian media was that the election was a foregone conclusion because President Marcos controlled most of the media, his staff controlled the election process, and they would count the ballots.

Thankfully, Mrs Aquino's supporters did not read Australian newspapers and so did not know they were attempting the impossible. President Marcos' corruption was too blatant. Even his own cronies failed to support him when challenged by the people power in the streets and the military sided with Mrs Aquino. He fled Manila and died in exile. Although Mrs Aquino's term as president failed the hopes of many of her supporters, her method of coming to power remains a vivid example of people power.

3. *People power and the Eastern European revolution of 1989*

The technology that worried the old communist tyrants was not only the new US nuclear missiles, but also the photocopying machine, telephone and computer.

The importance of this new technology was apparent back in early 1986 when I set out the challenge it presented to the communist rulers: it enabled people to access information from data bases, it encouraged the questioning of official statements and statistics, it enabled people to communicate without using official printers, and it provided the means of such communication around the globe.[2]

The new technology was of great assistance to movements like Solidarity in Poland and the independent peace movements throughout Eastern Europe. They have played an important role in restoring the self-confidence of societies damaged by decades of repression and thereby have helped to prepare the ground for the revolutions of 1989.

These are among the more notable illustrations of people power during the past decade or so. But they represent only the tip of the iceberg. They may have suddenly burst into the mass media, but they have been evolving over a very long time.

THE RISE OF PEOPLE POWER

It is impossible to identify the beginning of people power. 'People power' means people working for their own betterment (or for the betterment of others) outside the work of government. People have been doing this in various ways throughout history.

Psalm 105, verses 12 and 13 talks of the time when the Jews 'were but few in number' and they 'wandered from nation to nation, from one kingdom to another'. Moses led them out of Egypt and towards the Promised Land. By today's standards, Moses was leading a national liberation movement. Such movements are out to seize governmental power in a particular country. Moses, then, was a forerunner in a tradition that includes George Washington, Ho Chi Minh, Nelson Mandela and Yasser Arafat.

1. *People power and the church*

Churches provide a good example of both an old form of people power — and an old form of government! The Christian Church began as a minute sect on the fringe of the Roman Empire. Almost 1 700 years ago it became the official religion of the empire and developed close links with the rulers — people power had become government power.

The Catholic Church retains a unique legal status: possessing a small geographic territory in Rome (called the State of the Vatican City), the Holy See is accorded a legal status similar to that of nations. The Vatican operates a full-fledged diplomatic apparatus and has diplomatic representatives accredited in many capital cities. It was the world's first 'transnational corporation' — it now has over 500 million members scattered around the world. Just to complicate matters still further, it also manifests some people power qualities since some of its members are, for example, critical of governments — in Latin America, for example — and have identified more with the poor and weak than with the rich and powerful.

Some other churches are 'established'. The Anglican Church in England is one example of this. It is governed by secular laws, and senior appointments (such as that of the Archbishop of Canterbury) are made by the Queen on the advice of the prime minister. The Russian Orthodox Church, before the 1917 Russian Revolution, was the established church in Russia. The constitutions of the US and Australia, by contrast, rule out any 'established church' and guarantee religious equality for all religions.

Most churches, however, are examples to a greater or lesser extent of people power. The Anglican Church is particularly diverse in this respect. It may be established in England, but it is definitely not established in lands where Christianity is under threat, as in some parts of northern and central Africa and western Asia.

2. *People power organisations in nineteenth century Europe*

No-one said specifically that they wished to design on a particular date a people power organisation. But history is full of examples of such organisations being formed.

One example is the UK's Anti-Slavery Society which has been campaigning for over 150 years to stop slavery in the British Empire, to stop Britons from conducting the slave trade and, more recently, to stop slavery and the slave trade in other nations. Another example is the triumph in 1845 of the UK's Anti Corn Law League which shattered the pattern of politics for a generation. A further example is the 1860 campaign by Swiss businessman Henri Dunant to establish the International Committee of the Red Cross to care for the victims of war. The creators of all three organisations would be amazed if they could see what flowed from their humble origins.

THE IMPORTANCE OF NON-GOVERNMENTAL ORGANISATIONS (NGOs)

The customary term today for people power is the less colourful non-governmental organisation (NGO). At the local or national level, an NGO is an organised group of people which is not part of the machinery of state — that is, not the cabinet, the civil service, the armed service or statutory authorities (like the Australian or British Broadcasting Corporations). At the international level, NGOs may 'observe' United Nations meetings, but cannot vote at them (a right reserved only for member nations).

The relationship between a government and NGOs in its territory is not necessarily antagonistic. Indeed, NGOs can be of help to governments, as the British political scientist Richard Rose pointed out:

> A government seeks four things from pressure groups. Information is the simplest of its needs. By virtue of their contacts with members, pressure groups accumulate much information about society that does not otherwise come to the attention of Whitehall. This is as true of organisations lobbying on behalf of such groups as unwed mothers or narcotics addicts as it is for spokesmen for major unions or trade associations. When a department is reviewing a policy, it will want to collect information from as many different interested parties as possible. The solicitation of information leads to the solicitation of advice. Government departments want to know what pressure groups think ought to be done and how they would react to various policies being canvassed within the department.
>
> Once a decision is taken, a department expects pressure groups likely to benefit from the measure (and those that wish to retain its long-term goodwill) to support the official proposal.
>
> Once a policy is made formally binding, the government looks to pressure groups to co-operate in administering the law. In important fields of economic affairs, such as policies to hold down prices or wage increases, cooperation is a prerequisite for success.
>
> In extreme instances, a government may look to an interested group to carry out policies on its behalf. For example, the Marriage Guidance Council receives an annual government grant to carry out work in a field which the government considers in the national interest, but not suited to civil service procedures.[3]

Indeed, in the long sweep of history, NGOs have helped change the very nature of societies.

British political scientist Graham Wootton reviewed the work of British NGOs between 1720 and 1970 and concluded:

What does all this sound and fury signify over the years? At one level it means what it plainly says — the strivings of men and women, through government, to gain advantage and to right wrongs.

The deeper meaning, however, is that what they undertook and in part achieved contributed importantly to the modernisation of British polity. In seeking their own objectives, they eased the transition from (in shorthand) oligarchy to democracy. That was certainly not accomplished without violence, but it was relatively peaceful for a period of rapid economic development which we now recognise as a potentially dangerous phase for any nation, the strains and stress, tensions and conflicts, discontinuities and incompatibilities tending towards extremist 'solutions' to current suffering and only-too-probably injustice.[4]

Similarly, particular issues have benefited from the involvement of NGOs, such as the campaign against slavery. This is indicated in the following excerpt from an anti-slavery report to the UN in 1965:

While governments alone can legislate, administer and influence economic conditions, NGOs may to a limited extent influence public opinion and so government policy. This they have always done, in the case of slavery, by obtaining information and, if the government concerned is unwilling to act on it, by resorting to publicity inducing that government to do so.

A second and equally important function of the NGO in fighting slavery is to provide continuity. This is well illustrated in history. Between 1839 and 1890, over 300 international conventions against slavery were signed. The Brussels Act of 1890, however, was the first to be effective. This effectiveness was due to the insistence of a non-governmental organisation that machinery be set up to implement that Act. The machinery was the Slavery Bureau, operating from Brussels, with an office at Zanzibar. The greatest progress yet made in eliminating slavery was achieved by the Slavery Bureau, whose work was brought to an end in 1914.

After the First World War, it was only the insistence of non-governmental organisations that secured the adoption of the 1926 Convention on Slavery. Six more years of constant pressure by these NGOs were required to achieve the appointment of the Standing Advisory Committee of Experts on Slavery to implement the 1926 Convention, which in 1933 resumed the work abandoned by the Slavery Bureau, whose work was brought to an end in 1914. The Second World War caused a repetition of these events. Thereafter nine years of work by NGOs secured the adoption of the 1956 Supplementary Convention.

Official bodies, whether governmental or international, tend not to survive international catastrophes. Voluntary bodies, however small, tend to do so and serve a useful purpose.[5]

The 1991 Annual Report of the now renamed Anti-Slavery International shows that the campaign goes on: Bangladesh, slaves in Karachi Central Prison, debt bondage in the Philippines, migrant domestic workers in the UK and elsewhere, Portuguese child labour, and forced prostitution in Turkey, Thailand and India. These are just some examples of the society's work.

Slavery and slave trade have not disappeared from the world (even though some governments would prefer it to disappear from NGO agendas). While the problem still exists, there is an important role for the NGO.

NGOs AND THE UN

1 200 NGOs attended the 1945 San Francisco conference which finalised the UN Charter. Although the original proposals drawn up by the 'Big Four' made no mention of NGOs, they were successful in applying pressure, mainly via the United States delegation, so that NGOs were granted an official status. The result was the following, Article 71 of the Charter:

> The Economic and Social Council may make suitable arrangements for consultation with non-governmental organisations which are concerned with matters within its competence. Such arrangements may be made with international organisations and, where appropriate, with national organisations after consultation with the Member of the United Nations concerned.

The NGOs wanted to widen the UN's responsibilities as much as possible beyond security questions. They strove for the inclusion of some provision for dealing with questions related to educational and cultural cooperation and human rights.

The Economic and Social Council (ECOSOC), in implementing Article 71, has drawn up and regularly reviews a list of NGOs which have been granted 'consultative status'. The work is done through the Committee on NGOs, which has to apply several criteria before accepting any NGO on the list: the activities of the NGO should fall within ECOSOC's competence; and it should have an established head-quarters, an administration, authorised representatives and a policy-making body.

Hundreds of NGOs now have consultative status. They use this status to attend UN meetings — there are 4 000 'meeting days' in Geneva each year alone!

UN officials like this relationship as an additional way of communicating directly with the world's citizens. The General Assembly at its first session encouraged this contact in one specific way. The Office of Public Information (OPI) within the Secretariat was asked to disseminate information about the UN through the NGOs. The OPI has established its own list of organisations with which it has contact in New York. Weekly briefings are given by top personnel, periodic conferences are held and documents on UN activities are supplied. Different UN organs and programs now are developing their own constituencies by using the OPI. Some go direct to the NGOs and the public, as with the monthly newspaper *Development Forum* or the journals, *United Nations Chronicle, Objective Justice* (concentrating on action against apartheid) and *Disarmament*.

One way of enhancing international cooperation is to convene a UN conference on a particular topic. It has now become standard practice, when specialised conferences are called, to set up a small unit to act as a secretariat for the conference, and it is authorised to make contact with NGOs. They are thus involved in the earliest stages of the preparations and provide an input before some governments have even begun to formulate policy.

The intergovernmental preparatory committees for global conferences also work closely with NGOs. When the conferences actually take place, the diplomats become dominant and often allow little formal NGO participation. But the agenda for the conferences and the basic documentation have been prepared long before the delegates arrive and the NGOs have helped to set the frame of reference within which the debates take place. Since 1972, all the major global intergovernmental conferences have had 'unofficial' conferences take place alongside them, involving thousands of participants from hundreds of NGOs from all over the world.

Many of the NGOs which take part in the UN's work are INGOs —

international NGOs. US sociologist Elise Boulding has described them in this way:

> They are globe-spanning associations of private citizens pursuing transnational concerns covering the whole range of human interests — scientific, economic, cultural, religious, political, recreational, artistic. In 1909 there were 176 such organisations. Today there are 18 000. Linking households, communities and nation states in their transnational networks, they are the most concrete embodiment of the global civic culture. Certainly they vary greatly in character. Many have highly specific, even technical interests; others are exclusive to particular kinds of groups, such as political exiles, and may be adversarial in nature; still others are simply humorous, such as the International Stop Intercontinental Drift Society. In general, however, INGOs represent shared concerns for human well-being that cross national boundaries.[6]

Many working people are individual members of INGOs, by virtue of being members of local branches of NGOs. NGO activities are not just the highly publicised events (such as rallies) or other tasks done in a person's spare time (such as writing letters to prisoners of conscience in an Amnesty International group). Professional, scientific and scholarly associations (for example, medical practitioners, geneticists, historians, anthropologists, journalists, doctors) constitute transnational linkages. Through their common interests and concerns about professional standards and values, many of these groups are led to active efforts directed at influencing people and governments in other countries. The abuse of psychiatry to silence dissidents in the Soviet Union, for example, was a major issue at the 1977 World Psychiatric Association Convention.

The international media play an especially important role in providing information and shaping attitudes toward world events. The legal profession's international associations are of special importance for the development of world law and common definitions of human rights.

THE ROLES OF THE NGOS

The international campaign to save the environment did not arise from governments; it came from concerned individuals and non-governmental organisations. The human rights field is guided by NGOs like Amnesty International and the International Commission of Jurists. Concern over the current state of the arms race arose from the peace movement.

But these NGOs are significant not just in changing the nature of public debate, but also in all other areas of life. People with disabilities, for example, are no longer willing to be subject to the medical model of treatment in which decisions over their health are made by medical specialists; they wish to control more of their own affairs. The provision of childcare and services for the elderly as well as emergency relief are all handled far more efficiently by the non-governmental sector than by government departments.

It is difficult to generalise about the roles of NGOs: they are so varied. This chapter will identify five of these roles: investigating likely problems, generating ideas, lobbying governments, providing services, and creating a new global civic culture.

1. *NGOs investigate likely problem areas.*

NGOs are part of the early warning system for societies. As the previous examples of the environment, human rights and nuclear weapons have all indicated, NGOs are often sensitive to emerging problems. In chapter 6, Ralph Nader's campaign to alert people to the risk of driving the GM Corvair is one example.

Another example comes from Jacques-Yves Cousteau, one of the leaders of French environmental NGOs, who has called for greater scrutiny of technocrats (the experts who guide our lives). He writes:

The problem today is to know if science is going to be able to develop a way of getting energy from nuclear reactors without making bombs and waste, to use nuclear science for the benefit of people without the danger of nuclear waste, without the danger of bombs.

The problem is to get rid of the arrogance of technocrats. We want to know the truth when an accident occurs. And we want to fight. We want the right of all people to decide what risks they will or will not take, to protect the quality of life for future generations.[7]

Cousteau has provided this example of the thinking of technocrats in the French nuclear industry:

There is, in France, a new nuclear plant being built in Nogent, fifty-five or sixty miles from Paris on the Seine River. News of this, after Chernobyl, was very disquieting for the population of Paris because an accident in Nogent would be a complete disaster for all of Paris.

My friends from the French television channel Antenne 2 interviewed the director of the plant in a segment to be shown at the end of a documentary on Chernobyl. They asked the Nogent plant director what the plan was in case of an accident. He said, 'Oh, here an accident is not possible, of course.' The interviewer responded, 'But if it were, Paris would be impossible to evacuate.' The director said, 'Oh yes I know. We can't evacuate Paris.' 'Then what will you do?' He scratched his head and said, 'Well, we will give advice to the public.' 'What kind of advice?' 'Well, for example, to close their windows.'[8]

Thanks to environmental NGOs, people are now more sceptical of such bland reassuring statements from technocrats.

NGOs are, then, the nerve-endings of humanity. They are closer to the people than distant governments and civil services; they *are* the people.

2. *NGOs generate ideas.*

We should not underestimate the power of ideas. Less than two decades ago, pollution of the environment received little attention in the mass media. When it did, it was usually in the limited context of dirty rivers and non-returnable bottles.

Problems in the environment are now recognised as among the gravest in human history. People are now being encouraged to look beyond the problems of dirty rivers and non-returnable bottles and, instead, to question their very lifestyles and cultures. That is remark-able. Indeed, it often seems that progress is being made so quickly — especially in the context of social awareness — that we fail to note fully what is happening.

The instruments of social change have rarely been persons who have achieved a lot, but rather persons who came up with powerful ideas which have made their impact on the things people do and on the lifestyles they lead. The balance of ideas and practice makes an explosive combination. Two examples will illustrate this point.

The first example is E.F. Schumacher, a British economist who coined the term 'small is beautiful'. He was often called a crank by his detractors. He used to reply: 'A crank is a piece of simple technology that creates revolutions.'

His criticism of the environmentally destructive form of conven-tional economics led to a growth in alternative economic strategies. His criticism of the Western world's failure to distinguish between the 'good life' and gluttony has encouraged people to create lives which are outwardly simple and inwardly rich.

The second example is Amnesty International, which is based on a very simple idea: people should not be punished if they hold political opinions different from those of their governments. Former British politician Peter Archer tells how this Nobel Peace Prize-winning, multimillion dollar NGO began in a simple way:

> Early in 1961, Peter Benneson, a London barrister, was glancing through a newspaper in the course of a train journey, when his eye fell on an account of some students in Portugal, imprisoned because they had taken part in a peaceful demonstration which had not commended itself to the government. There must have been others who read the story and whose blood boiled. But Benneson determined to channel the energy generated by boiling blood.
>
> To a few friends he suggested that something might be done to focus public attention on the problem. For if governments were to be dissuaded from such conduct, the only weapon to hand was the effect of public indignation. They decided to launch a campaign. The first *Background Notes* (cyclostyled for the use of supporters) announced that 'Appeal for Amnesty 1961' had been launched by a group of lawyers, writers and publishers in London.[9]

3. *NGOs lobby governments.*

Their purpose in doing this is to change policies. They do not face the constraints of governmental responsibility, such as the need not to offend allies. Most governments are concerned with keeping their bilateral relations on a friendly basis. Even where relations are quite close, or perhaps because they are close, governments hesitate to criticise one another.

Governments do make diplomatic interventions in issues relating to human rights (and should be doing much more in this respect), but they act on human rights questions infrequently and with exaggerated caution.

NGOs have the advantage that they act without a political bias. They can submit information to international organisations without its becoming identified as a political gesture of hostility. NGO information may therefore be more easily taken up by governments since it is seen as impartial.

NGOs, through their lobbying, try to create the political will necessary to change policy. A good definition of 'political will' is: 'Enough citizens saying to the politicians, *You will!*' When the followers lead, the leaders will follow.

4. *Some NGOs provide services.*

NGOs are used at times to accomplish tasks which governments cannot or prefer not to undertake themselves. Lifeline telephone counselling and Red Cross blood donations are two examples. Churches are the oldest continuous form of social welfare provider; they go back over a thousand years.

It has been, by contrast, only in the last century or so that governments have become involved in the provision of such services as education; for most of history in nations with a Christian tradition, churches provided all levels of educational facilities.

5. *NGOs are creating a new global civic culture.*

NGOs are helping people to free themselves from the prison of national sovereignty. US political scientist Louis Kriesberg described the new networking this way:

> When the fourteenth World Ploughing Contest was held in
> Christchurch, New Zealand, contestants from every part of the
> globe arrived to take part. An equally diverse group assembled in

Munich for the International Dairy Congress and the British Paper and Board Makers' International Association of Paper Historians convened in the university town of Oxford. Doctors of many nationalities will gather in cities on every continent to discuss recent advances and obstacles in specialised fields of medical research.

NGOs may help ease world tensions. Perhaps they are even an index of the extent to which a world society already exists. They foster the development of international perspectives by reinforcing interests that cross-cut national boundaries. Their activities ameliorate the material and social conditions — the hunger, disease and overcrowding — that underlie certain international conflicts.

Formulas for settling international dissension may be developed in them and then incorporated into international law. They may even develop structural arrangements for handling conflicts among their own members that can later be used by governmental organisations such as the UN and its affiliates.[10]

In the old world order, there was only one label which had any real meaning: nationality. In the new world order, there is still the label of nationality, but there are also other labels by virtue of a person's transnational linkages in the emerging global civic culture — religious, professional, academic and recreational.

THE REASONS FOR THE STARTLING GROWTH OF NGOs

The startling growth in NGOs may be explained in six ways:

1. *The improvements in communications technology are creating a new international spirit of oneness.*
This new awareness is reflected in links both between humans, and

between humans and the natural environment. Traditional divisions between nations and peoples (whether as a result of religion, geographical boundaries or ideologies) no longer seem so significant. On the contrary, they are held partly responsible for most of today's problems, such as the arms race.

NGOs are concerned more about what common features unite peoples (such as life and a healthy environment), rather than the old divisions. After all, humans do have much more in common than that which divides them. Thanks to modern communications, we are now able to recognise this fact of life.

However, despite the increasing mobility of populations and the modern communications technology, most people function almost exclusively in a limited segment of the world, as limited socially as it is geographically. Local problems are for them of far greater magnitude and urgency than the global problems of earth. NGOs — much more than any national government — are able to show the linkages between local problems and global problems.

2. *International crises are changing.*
Even as recently as the early 1980s, such crises were often of the Cold War type (for example, over Afghanistan). But there is now a new global agenda of political action, in which the main crises have been outside the mainstream of old Cold War disputes — the pollution of the environment, depletion of the earth's non-renewable resources, inflation, unemployment, starvation and housing — problems that NGOs are well-placed to address.

Cold War considerations, of course, contributed to the crises — especially because of the wasteful expenditure by the world on weapons. The ending of the Cold War means that the world can now concentrate on the problems it should have been addressing before it got sidetracked by the Cold War. The solution of common problems requires long-term and international cooperation — and this, in turn, requires a new approach to international peace and security.

3. *Governments are shrinking in importance.*
As I pointed out earlier, national governments are being submerged by new power groupings.

A basic principle of governance is that every function in the public domain should be performed at the level closest to the people at which it can be performed most effectively. Unfortunately, the nation-state has become too big for small things and too small for big things. The small things are local economic and social development; the big things are matters of global coordination and regulation such as environmental protection.

4. *NGOs are part of the new global self-help movement.*
People want to do things for themselves — and not be instructed by governments or bureaucrats. Once people begin to receive some independence in some areas of their lives, they build on this for other parts, a point made below by American social commentator Bruce Stokes:

> Chilean sociologist Ignatio Balbontin's studies of employees in worker-managed factories indicate that they are more active in politics and community life than employees in traditionally-organised businesses. Similarly, the women in the mothers' clubs of Indonesia and South Korea have not been content to narrowly focus their energies on family planning. They realise that the welfare of their villages rests on the resolution of a whole range of economic and environmental issues and their efforts to solve these problems include exerting political pressure on their governments.
>
> The various community self-help movements in Western Europe and the United States have led to experiments with

neighbourhood government as a way for people to exercise greater control over social services. Italy now has neighbourhood governments in more than 130 cities, more than a dozen American cities have neighbourhood councils or advisory commissions, and New York City alone has more than 10 000 block clubs that have some say over life in their communities.[11]

5. *There is a growing awareness that involvement in NGOs is mentally healthy.*

A key to good health is to have a second employment — an interesting and worthwhile job for which no payment is received. NGOs are part of this voluntary work revolution.

In the UK, for example, it has been calculated that three million people put in eighteen million hours per week of unpaid work. With the continuing recession in Australia (and the UK) a new trend has emerged, as journalist Anabel Dean pointed out in a Sydney newspaper article:

> Voluntary work will always be a worthy occupation, often carrying with it the image of a good Samaritan pushing a wheelchair, shopping for necessities or offering solace to the deprived, the disabled and the elderly.
>
> But the popular view ignores the personal value of voluntary work, not least of which is employment.
>
> And in these tough economic times, those who are awake to the hidden opportunities are making the most of them. Volunteer agencies have seen a massive increase in applications for voluntary work, and many of these people later obtain permanent positions in their fields of interest.
>
> The most recent survey found that more than half of young volunteers, many of whom had been long-term unemployed, were

in paid work after four months of volunteering.

Traditionally, it has been the employed who gave up their spare time to help others while helping themselves in a 'spiritual' or social sense.

One of the chief advantages of voluntary work is the experience it may give. It may assist in forging new contacts and, perhaps equally important, keep spirits high during the demoralising process of finding a new job.[12]

6. People are sceptical of traditional methods of settling international crises.

There is some evidence that people are tired of their governments responding to the crises, rather than looking ahead at what problems are looming on the horizon and acting positively. People are tired of their governments following unimaginative and conservative policies. Governments seem too concerned to follow what has worked in the past, rather than to develop policies for the future.

This is a by-product of entrusting too much power to the public service (which is more influential in policy-making and execution than parliament). There is a tendency to deal with the short term, while ignoring the long term — thereby overlooking the fact that many of today's problems were yesterday's long-term problems (which were ignored so that the short-term problems could be resolved). The result is often that the short-term problems were not resolved and we still have the long-term ones. Governments have us on a permanent treadmill.

NGOs provide hope and vision. They provide an alternative to the narrow nationalism of governments. Their members cross national boundaries. National governments speak for nations — NGOs speak for the earth.

Endnotes:

1. Ian Marsh, 'Issue Movements, Australian Writers and the Decline of Two Party Politics', *Canberra Bulletin of Public Administration*, August 1989, p.101
2. Keith Suter, *Reshaping the Global Agenda: The United Nations at 40*, United Nations Association of Australia, 1986, pp.96–99
3. Richard Rose, *Politics in England Today*, Faber, 1974, p.262
4. Graham Wootton, *Pressure Groups in Britain 1720–1970*, Allen Lane, 1975, p.99
5. Anti Slavery Society, *Reply to UN Questionnaire*, March 1965, p.2
6. Elise Boulding, 'Building a Global Civic Culture', *Development* (Rome), 1990: 2, p.39
7. Jacques-Yves Cousteau, *Attacking Power with Wisdom: The Need for Long-Term Thinking*, Nuclear Age Peace Foundation, 1990, p.7
8. *Ibid*, p.8
9. Peter Archer, 'Amnesty International: The Maturity of a Crusade', *Contemporary Review*, June 1972, p.281
10. Louis Kriesberg, 'Non-Governmental Organizations', in *Peace and the War Industry*, Kenneth Boulding (ed.), Transaction, 1970, p.44
11. Bruce Stokes, *Helping Ourselves: Local Solutions to Global Problems*, Norton, 1981, p.141
12. Anabel Dean, 'The Rush to Volunteer', *Sydney Morning Herald*, 22 March 1991

PART C:

The new global warfare

8

SECOND WAVE WARFARE

Is warfare as we know it on the way out?

A NEW ERA OF WARFARE IS EMERGING. The First Wave of warfare consisted of guerilla operations. Conflicts were fought by bands of individuals raiding one another's territory, stealing property and persons. These marauders did not fight in uniforms and were not necessarily organised along strict military lines.

The Second Wave's transformation in warfare occurred with the rise of the nation-state. A strong centralised government could accumulate more resources and personnel, and thus had the ability to organise warfare in a more sophisticated way. Mercenary forces gave way to nationally-recruited forces: defence forces were the world's first nationalised industry. Scientists were mobilised to provide new equipment. Large troop formations required colourful uniforms so as to set one side apart from another, requiring developments in the textile industry. This form of warfare over the centuries has become so common that it is now called 'conventional warfare'. The Second Wave culminated in World Wars I and II. 1945 represents the peak of that Wave: it was the end of the world's largest conventional war and saw the use of atomic weapons.

The Second Wave is now coming to a close. Nuclear warfare is too destructive to fight and conventional wars are too expensive to fight.

As in the Third Wave of technology and government, so the Third Wave of warfare is forcing us to think afresh about old ideas. 'If you want peace, prepare for war' is an example of the old thinking. We are beginning to realise that if you prepare for war, then you will get war. Instead of thinking that nuclear weapons preserve the peace, we must recognise that peace deters the use of nuclear weapons. The only defence in the nuclear era is peace.

The Third Wave of warfare has seen the return of guerilla warfare. It has also seen a new emphasis on trade and conflict resolution. As with Third Wave changes in technology and government which we have already explored, so the Third Wave's new warfare state will be very different from the previous two Waves.

First Wave Warfare

Humans were slow to invent warfare. American peace researcher William Eckhardt wrote:

> For several million years, when humans made their living by gathering and scavenging, there was presumably no warfare at all, since there were no tools, let alone weapons, until about two million years ago when men began to hunt. Humans biologically similar to ourselves emerged at least 40 000 years ago and left a large number of cave paintings, some of which depicted hunting,

but none of which depicted war. Bands of gathering-hunters, numbering about twenty-five to fifty people each, could hardly have made much of a war. There would not have been enough people to fight about.

Then, 10 000 years ago, we settled down to farming and herding in villages, we developed a vested interest in our land and cattle, and something like a war became possible. This agricultural revolution eventually resulted in food surpluses, making civilisation (living in cities, learning to write, etc.) possible, starting about 5 000 years ago. Then war really began to come into its own, and it has been growing with civilisation ever since then to this day.[1]

Warfare began, then, as guerilla warfare. The term 'guerilla' is from the Spanish and means 'small war'. It was carried out in the early nineteenth century when the UK encouraged the Spanish and Portuguese to rebel against Napoleon's forces. By that time, conventional warfare was the normal way of fighting and so it was necessary to create a new name for this rediscovered form of warfare.

The earliest weapons were all easily carried by individuals: the bow, the sling, the dagger or short sword, and the mace. They were made for mobility; they enabled their users to move and strike quickly. Uniforms were not important; combatants knew who were their colleagues.

Guerilla raids were enhanced by horses: an attacking force became even more mobile and could operate over larger distances. Genghis Khan mastered this form of warfare. He began in Mongolia and then rampaged through northern China. By the year 1199, he dominated an area from the Pacific Ocean to the Ural Mountains. His main obstacle into Europe were other horsemen: the Tartars.

In Europe, the First Wave government gradually evolved into feudalism, with people owing their political loyalty to their local barons. Warfare helped shape that evolution, especially the invention of the stirrup. As Australian General Sir John Hackett pointed out:

> Feudalism, of course, rode into Europe on the stirrup. I wonder how many people here realise that the stirrup is the most important military instrument that has ever been invented, more important than the internal combustion engine and gunpowder, and nuclear power. Why? Because the stirrup enabled the horse to be used as a weapons platform for the first time.
>
> If, without a stirrup, you try to use a heavy weapon from the back of a horse, you'll fall off. With stirrups, you can use a horse as a weapons platform. And feudalism rode into Europe on the stirrup and helped to set up that weapon system which controlled the development of civilisation for a thousand years. The feudal system is a system, a weapon system, based on the armoured mounted man-at-arms and his defended base, the castle. If you really want to romanticise it, you can call it the 'knight and castle system'.
>
> It would have been impossible without the stirrup; and with the stirrup the feudal man-at-arms was enabled to offer his services to somebody in return for what he wanted more than anything, which was a bit of land to cultivate. Military service, in return for land tenancy, was the basis of the feudal system, in which almost all of our legal system was developed.
>
> Most of our constitutional history emerged under it and a very great deal of our poetry. And talking of poetry, let me remind you that war, men fighting other men, has been more written up in verse than any other topic in the history of man's civilisation, including the love of men for women. War has occupied more lines of verse than anything else that's been written up in poetry. It has adopted a very important place in our way of life and we cannot pretend otherwise.[2]

The Rise of Second Wave Warfare

The Second Wave of warfare is characterised by larger fighting formations, more destructive weapons, greater military expenditure, and far more organisation and bureaucracy.

1. *The Second Wave before World War I*

As in the First Wave, so the Second Wave of warfare helped shape technology and government. Professor Paul Seaver of Stanford University has explained it in this way:

> It may be said that the modern state came into being in order to support its army. The revolution in military technology that took place between 1450 and 1700 necessitated a vast increase in the powers of the centralised states — Spain lost out in the competition in part because it was unable to rationalise and centralise state power — and this increase and centralisation of power was, necessarily, at the expense of local autonomy and liberty.
>
> Hence the great power in late seventeenth century Europe after the collapse of Spain was not England, which retained its medieval parliament and a peacetime standing army of 5 000, but rather France, the first absolutist state, with a peacetime army of 300 000. The new mass armies brought a forced modernisation of the state, which had to create the machinery for enforcing the power of taxation over the wide population base required to support the army. Absolutism, then, was the logic of the military revolution.[3]

Armies of that size required a distinct organisation. Rome, which had pioneered conventional warfare in a much smaller way 1 500 years previously, was looked to as a model of organising fighting formations. Uniforms, ranks and professionalism all became far more important and soldiers were now accommodated in their separate barracks, rather than being billeted in civilian homes.

Napoleon mobilised the entire nation for war. He led 600 000 troops into Russia in 1812. Through the nineteenth century, techniques improved. The American Civil War was the first war in which railways were used to move large bodies of troops. It was the first war which used preserved rations, so that you had meat in tins instead of 'on the hoof'. It was the first war in which the electric telegraph was used extensively and it was the first war in which the lethality of small arms fire from single-shot weapons was fully demonstrated.

2. *The Second Wave in World War I*
Both railways and science were of particular importance in this war. Railway timetables may even have helped cause the war of 1914. At a certain stage when the armies began to move, they were all tied to fixed railway timetables. When the German military leader was asked to change his plans and instead of invading France to invade Russia, he replied it was quite impossible: it would take at least six months to make the change and draw up different timetables!

Science was mobilised in the interests of warfare. As early as 1914, scientists were determining military strategy rather than serving it. The machine gun, for example, made it difficult for mass attacks across open country to take place. On the other hand, it made defensive tactics more secure. Scientists were then mobilised to provide better offensive means: tanks and aircraft.

3. *The Second Wave in World War II*
World War II was a mechanised war. In 1941, the UK had 100 000 vehicles in the Middle East alone. During the D Day period in June 1944, there was one vehicle to every five men.

All fighting formations have 'teeth' (who do the fighting) and a 'tail' (who supply the needs of the teeth, such as cooks, builders, plumbers, doctors and engineers). In the Middle East during World War II, for example, the UK had 100 000 men doing the actual fighting and 650 000 people providing the support services. A division (of 28000 people) required over 6 000 tonnes of supplies per day.

World War II was also notable for the high level of civilian deaths. Conventional warfare had grown out of the specific creation of a professional fighting force who wore uniforms and lived separately from the civilian population. They were given a special status in society precisely because they had been set apart for possibly laying down their lives in order to protect civilians.

As recently as World War I, comparatively few civilians had been killed — they were living beyond the range of the weapons. But World War II covered a geographically far greater area and the weapons were more destructive. Out of the estimated 38 351 000 people who were killed, about 15 000 000 were military. This meant that three civilians were killed for every two military. The home front had become the front line.

WHY SECOND WAVE WARFARE HAS DECLINED

The decline of the Second Wave of warfare has been characterised by the ineffectiveness of war as an instrument of national policy. The main reasons for this are the limitations of nuclear weapons and the high cost of conventional weapons, hurried along by a number of recent events.

☐ **The first reason for the decline in Second Wave warfare is the limitations of nuclear warfare.**

Nuclear weapons have transformed warfare. A recurring theme in military biographies before 1945 is the complaint that the military leaders concerned did not have enough firepower or troops or ships or aircraft.

Leaders with access to nuclear weapons could not make that complaint. The total firepower of World War I, thanks to modern technology, could be placed in a nuclear warhead small enough to fit under a person's bed. Nelson at Trafalgar in 1805 or Wellington at Waterloo in 1815 could have destroyed the enemy with one nuclear missile — thereby removing the need for Nelson's fleet or Wellington's army.

In the early 1980s, the US and USSR had stockpiled the equivalent of 546 kilograms of dynamite for every human being — more weight in destructive power than there was food for every person on earth. The US and USSR continued accumulating more nuclear weapons throughout the eighties — even though they had more nuclear firepower than there were people in the world to kill. This was called 'overkill' — a surplus of weapons over targets.

The US and USSR had between them ninety-five per cent of the world's supply of nuclear weapons. The UK and France each had only two per cent. This seems a small amount of firepower, but that two per cent would have been enough to destroy the USSR (or US for that matter).

The sheer destructiveness of nuclear weapons made them useless. British historian Peter Calvocoressi has said:

Nuclear weapons are an astounding invention. By producing them, man has invented weapons of war which are useless for war. Since 1945 we have been hag-ridden by these weapons because of their awful destructiveness, and we must not forget or ever try to minimise their terrible power; but no less remarkable is their uselessness. This combination of power and purposelessness is, to say the least, disconcerting.[4]

One problem, then, with nuclear weapons is that they are too destructive. For the first time in human history, a government cannot defend its own people from an incoming attack. Technology does not exist to shoot down every incoming missile — not even Patriot missiles can guarantee that. Only a handful need get through to destroy a nation.

Major General Jack Kidd (formerly of the US Air Force) has tried to alert his fellow citizens to the dangers of nuclear destruction:

It helps to understand the destructive power of the current stockpile when we translate it to over 6 700 times the firepower
released by all Allied bombers in the six years of World War II.
Another useful mental image is a train 4 000 miles long loaded
with conventional bombs, as the equivalent of the world stockpile
of nuclear weapons. You've seen the photos of Berlin at the end of
the war, with eighty per cent of its buildings gutted with conventional bombs. It just hasn't sunk in yet — the destructive power of
nuclear weapons.

A single weapon on Washington or New York would produce
the worst calamity brought on by human beings. Destruction
could be 500 times that in Hiroshima. In the case of Washington,
chaos would result from the loss of the national political and
military chain of command. In the case of New York, economic
disaster could result from just the loss of records in our financial
capital, not to mention the millions of people killed or maimed.
Just imagine the court cases involved in stockholder ownership of
business across America.[5]

This problem required a new strategy: nuclear deterrence. Nuclear weapons were built in the expectation that they would never be used. If a nuclear weapon had to be used, then it had failed. But such a system required a total success rate — a nuclear deterrence system which was successful for only 99.999 per cent of the time would have been a failure.

This overlooked the 'human element' in decision-making: the errors, omissions and downright stupidity of humans. Three incidents, one from World War II and the other two from the Cold War period, illustrate this point.

Japan entered World War II by attacking Pearl Harbour on 7 December 1941. The Japanese at the same time began an invasion of the north coast of Malaya. Admiral Sir Tom Phillips sailed from Singapore with the *Prince of Wales* and *Repulse* to intercept the attack. He was convinced that he could achieve this with surprise and fighter cover. But he was told that the aircraft could not be made available — and so he had to rely on surprise. He lost the element of surprise because of water buffaloes many kilometres away.

James Leasor explains what happened:

Some water buffaloes strayed into a minefield near Kuantan, on the Malayan east coast, and set off the charges. Indian troops opened fire, thinking a Japanese landing was in progress, and informed headquarters at Singapore that they were being invaded. Singapore radioed Phillips to change course; as he did so, he was spotted by a Japanese submarine. Within the hour, dozens of Japanese planes were swooping down on these two great ships. Ninety minutes later, aerial torpedoes had sunk them both, and the sea was littered with debris and the bodies of the dead. British destroyers and aeroplanes combed the area but, not for the first time, help arrived too late; 673 men lost their lives.

Ironically, the Japanese did not reach Kuantan for another month and, when they came, they travelled overland and did not come by sea.[6]

If such accidents can occur in the pre-nuclear age, then the cost of accidents in the nuclear age would be all the greater. And yet political leaders still believe that, despite their own experiences, nuclear deterrence works. Americans print 'In God We Trust' on their coins — but they really worship nuclear deterrence.

The next two examples of human error are from the Cold War period. Americans conducted simulated USSR attacks on the White House on at least two occasions — and yet the disasters that resulted did not force the leaders to change their reliance on nuclear weapons.

The first of these mock attacks was 5 May 1960. The US was 'attacked' by the USSR and President Eisenhower's National Security Council (NSC) had to be evacuated to High Point, North Carolina. American historian Stephen Ambrose tells the story:

> The meeting was part of a continuing civil-defence exercise, designed to test the ability of the members of the NSC to get to High Point, with no previous knowledge of the date or time, as soon as possible. The exercise did not go well — [CIA Director] Allen Dulles' Cadillac broke down and he almost did not make it; General Twining, chairman of the [Joint Chiefs of Staff], did not make it at all; [Defence] Secretary Gates had to be driven to the airport by his wife in her nightgown, had no pass when he arrived at the entrance and almost did not persuade the guards to let him through.[7]

Later, another Administration and another exercise. Zbigniew Brzezinski was President Carter's Assistant for National Security Affairs. He recalls in his journal how, on the evening of 28 January 1977, after he had explained the evacuation procedure to the president, Carter wanted to test the helicopter system immediately. Brzezinski, armed with a stopwatch, called in the person responsible for the evacuation. Brzezinski records:

The poor fellow's eyes. . . practically popped; he looked so surprised. He said, 'Right now?' and I said, 'Yes, right now.' He reached for the phone and could hardly speak coherently when he demanded that the helicopter immediately come for a drill. I took one of the secretaries. . . along to simulate Mrs Carter, and we proceeded to the south lawn to wait for the helicopter to arrive.

It took roughly two and a half times as long to arrive as it was supposed to. We then flew to a special site from where another evacuation procedure would be followed. To make a long story short, the whole thing took roughly twice as long as it should have. Moreover, on our return we found that the drill somehow did not take into account the protective service and we were almost shot down.[8]

Towards the end of the Eisenhower Administration, a secret bunker was carved into a Virginia mountainside: Mount Weather. It contains an underground city: offices, computer system, a pond holding drinking water, a television and radio station from which the president would address the nation after the catastrophe, a hospital, a cafeteria and bedrooms. Would it ever have worked?

Assuming the helicopter system worked, it would take twenty minutes to get there — but a Soviet nuclear submarine off the coast could have destroyed both it (and the White House) while the helicopter was still in the air between both sites. *Time* magazine asked whether it had all been worthwhile:

Mount Weather's greatest vulnerability may lie not with nuclear weapons but with human nature. The government officials designated to be evacuated in case of an emergency are not permitted to take their families with them, and many former officials say they would find it unimaginable to abandon husbands, wives or children. The issue has dogged the doomsday planners from the beginning. 'I never took it very seriously,' says Alexis Johnson, who was Deputy Under Secretary of State during the 1962 Cuban missile crisis. 'It was an unrealistic thing, it seemed to me, that we'd all pick up at the ringing of a bell and run for the hills, leaving our families behind.'

That raises another troubling question about Mount Weather's mission. Over the past thirty-three years, tens of millions of dollars have been spent on maintaining and upgrading the complex to protect several hundred designated officials in the event of nuclear attack. During the same period, the US government has dramatically reduced its emphasis on war preparedness for ordinary citizens and currently spends less than fifty cents a head each year on civil defence. In a 1989 brochure titled *Are You Prepared?*, FEMA offered the suggestion that citizens could use 'furniture, books and other items commonly found around the house' to build makeshift fallout shelters. But who would be left to be governed after the fires had died down and the chosen few emerged from the mountain?[9]

People have become hostages to computers. The nuclear system is increasingly a computerised one. But computer systems can fail because of incorrect or incomplete system specifications, hardware failure, hardware design errors, software design errors and poor maintenance. The 1986 Challenger and Chernobyl disasters are reminders of the fallibility of humans and machines.

To believe the nuclear arms race could have continued without a major disaster required an optimism unjustified by history. To put it another way — humans are just beginners. As social scientist Marianne Frankenhaeussur said: 'The history of humankind tells us that human species spent three million years in the forest, 3 000 years on the fields, 300 years in the factories, and now — barely — thirty years at the computer terminal.'[10]

Finally, what *is* being deterred by nuclear deterrence? One nation's nuclear security constitutes another nation's feelings of insecurity. This insecurity becomes fear, which then leads to its acquiring more nuclear weapons. These, in turn, erode the first nation's sense of security and so a fresh round of the arms race begins. Nuclear deterrence is not a deterrent to war, but to peace itself. Until all people of the world feel secure in their everyday lives, there will be security for none.

❑ **The second reason for the decline in Second Wave warfare is the limitations of conventional warfare.**

On 28 May 1987, nineteen-year-old Mathias Rust, a novice pilot of West Germany, flew single-handedly a Cessna 172 across 800 kilometres of heavily guarded Soviet territory and landed in Red Square, literally outside the windows of the Soviet government.

This one incident reveals much that is wrong with the reliance on nuclear and conventional weapons. A US$70 000 aircraft did what the defence forces of both sides had been spending billions of dollars trying to achieve. The B2 bomber which is supposed to evade radar detection, the most expensive aircraft ever built, will cost at least US$815 million for each aircraft.

A number of points need to be made about the limitations of conventional warfare:

1. *Warfare, particularly conventional warfare,*
   is becoming too expensive.

In 1961, President Eisenhower put a new phrase into the political language: the military-industrial complex. Stephen Ambrose, his biographer, has explained that this was not a sudden interest. Eisenhower had spent most of his life in the army. He was worried that the US after 1945 had become accustomed to maintaining too high a level of defence expenditure. Ambrose writes, 'On every possible occasion, Eisenhower told the press, the politicians and the public that the only way to reduce the budget, stop inflation and cut taxes was through disarmament. So long as the arms race went on, the US would be putting $40 billion or so, nearly sixty per cent of the total budget [into the military].'[11] The military-industrial complex means that defence policy is distorted by the financial benefits that beneficiaries receive from defending a nation.

The direct costs are enormous. A modern fighter aircraft, for example, is one thousand times more expensive than a World War II Spitfire. The B1 bomber project cancelled by President Carter would have been cheaper if it had been made out of solid gold — it would not have flown, of course, but it would have been cheaper. If the American motor car had increased in price in the same ratio as current aircraft have evolved from the 1940s, it would cost US$300 000. Governments can only afford to have a few items of equipment. This means that victory has to come quickly (as in the Falklands, 1982, the Middle East, 1967 and 1973, and the Gulf War, 1991) or else both sides will be confronted with a stalemate.

The total annual cost of the arms race is around US$1 000 billion. If this sum were converted into a stack of silver dollars, it would go to the moon, back to earth, go a second time to the moon, with enough left to encircle the earth.

The nature of warfare has therefore changed. Originally, conventional warfare entailed humans killing one another. Somewhere around the time of World War I, the nature of warfare changed from humans killing humans to machines killing machines. Given the cost of machines to kill other machines, it is, therefore, necessary to win a conventional war within six weeks. If a war is not won in that time, then there can be no easy victory for either side. The Iran/Iraq conflict (1979–89) is a good example of how neither side could muster enough force to destroy the other.

2. *Modern conventional weapons are too sophisticated for battlefield conditions and too vulnerable to destruction.*

The late Norman Cousins wrote about the Bradley M-2 Infantry Fighting Vehicle, a battlefield taxi he called 'the mobile crematorium'. The Bradley (costing US$2 million each) would, in theory, enable high-speed movements by the infantry on the battlefield. The Bradley (named ironically after Eishenhower's World War II colleague General Omar Bradley) is a dud. Norman Cousins wrote of it:

> Though designed as a troop-carrying vehicle, the Bradley, it turned out, had room for three crewmen and only six soldiers — a mere half a squad. If one is to believe the manufacturers, these six soldiers were safe and secure because they were protected by five-and-one-half inches of rock-hard aluminium armour. But under the right conditions — namely, a square hit by a mortar shell, a land mine, or even the right kind of grenade — this aluminium armour might ignite and burn fiercely, incinerating the occupants. The thicker such armour, the more intense and devastating the conflagration it would fuel.
>
> If the vehicle's commander tried to stave off attack by firing his guided missiles, he had a problem. The carrier must lurch to a dead stop if the missile were to be fired accurately. During that time the Bradley is a sitting duck — especially for the $150, shoulder-fired rockets now in existence in other countries.[12]

The Bradley is destined to go the way of the M-16 rifle. This was the standard rifle used by US troops in Vietnam. But it kept jamming, it could not cope with Vietnam's humidity and it was too difficult to aim.

Even the Vietcong, usually short of weapons, had no interest in it. When the Vietcong won a firefight, they would pick the dead clean of everything useful — boots, canteens, knives, grenades, rations and so on. Even relatively outmoded rifles of World War II vintage were eagerly snatched up. Yet the Vietcong disdained the M-16s, leaving them behind on the ground.

3. *Second Wave military expenditure is an inflationary form of government spending.*

A worker making cars or a waitress in a restaurant is providing an item or service to consume. These people are paid wages, which they use to buy the goods or services that other workers are producing. But defence goods or services are not 'consumed' in the normal sense. At the end of the financial year, the defence industry has contributed nothing to the nation's wealth.

Additionally, defence establishments compete with civilian activities in purchasing raw materials, resources and services. The world's largest single consumer of petrol, for example, is the US Air Force.

All civilian corporations are obliged to run at a profit and all government businesses are expected at least to break even. Military contractors, by contrast, are able to operate with scant regard for how much a project exceeds the originally quoted price. Military contractors operate on a cost-plus-profit basis. They have little or no incentive to improve efficiency or cut waste; they get guaranteed profits no matter what the costs incurred. Their profits are frequently calculated as a percentage of their costs and so the higher the cost, the greater the profits.

Defence contracts are often given out under less competitive conditions than those found in almost any other sector of the economy. Fewer firms compete for the highly sophisticated new weapons systems, so the competitive structure needed to hold down costs is missing. Therefore, having a large cost overrun on this contract does not mean the same corporation will not get the next one. This cosy arrangement is augmented by senior officers, upon retirement, joining the directors of defence contractors, and so helping to keep the business all in the family.

In the US, and to a lesser extent in many other countries, defence expenditure goes to favoured areas. Selection of location for new installations or new contracts shows an amazing correspondence with legislative membership on key committees. Once the installation or contract commences, it creates jobs in the locality and becomes a matter of some interest to local chambers of commerce, as well as politicians. Every such installation is viewed by its supporters as a vital link in the national defence, no matter how obsolete or expensive it may have become.

The close relationship between the military and industrial contractors means that the military are relaxed in scrutinising the bills of the contractors. Norman Cousins has provided the following information on inappropriate bills submitted by defence contractors and exposed by a congressional investigation:

* Boeing charged the US taxpayers $11 750 for its sponsorship of the World Paper Airplane Championship.
* Boeing passed along charges totalling $2 485 for golf tees, cart rentals and liquor at executive meetings in Carlsbad, California, in April 1979 and Tucson, Arizona, in November 1979.
* General Dynamics passed along to the government its costs in attempting to sell its weapons to foreign countries.

* Rockwell charged the government for its executive dining room and cafeteria operations in the amount of $1 040 588.
* The Fort Worth division of General Dynamics sent in a bill for $10 713 to cover the losses of the company barber shop.
* Sperry tried to charge the government $160 480 for expenses incurred in connection with the sale of the company's commercial products in Europe.[13]

4. *Beyond a certain point, Second Wave military strength can become a national weakness.*

This may be seen in two ways:

(a) The US and USSR damaged their economies because of running the arms race. The US during the time of the Reagan Administration's arms buildup (the largest peacetime military expansion in US history) transformed itself from the world's largest creditor nation to the world's largest debtor.

No nation has ever managed to be a great power and a great debtor at the same time; debt destroyed Spain in the sixteenth century and it destroyed the UK in the twentieth century. The US's economic role is now being overshadowed by Japan. For the first time this century, the younger US generation is now worse off than its parents. The US has ceased to be a land of rising expectations.

The USSR was even more damaged by the arms race. It had a smaller gross national product and yet was spending a larger proportion of it on the arms race than was the US. Mr Gorbachev came to power realising that the USSR had to pull out of the arms race. The difference between him and the US was that he admitted his nation could not continue running the arms race; the US has yet to make that admission.

(b) The military can become a lethal political parasite. A former President of Costa Rica (the only nation in the world without a defence force) has said:

A country with an army only becomes its own jail keeper; sometimes because the military forces take political power for their own benefit and at other times because they maintain their power by demanding more and more money each year from the national budget using the excuse of 'national security'. What is clear is that every time there is an army in a nation, the people end up working hard to benefit the military. Today it is even more urgent than ever for people to understand that the military is a lethal parasite.[14]

5. *Second Wave warfare is not effective against the Third Wave of warfare: guerilla warfare.*

Between one and two million people were killed in the Vietnam conflict. The conflict cost the US about US$3 billion. It used thirteen million tonnes of high explosives (more than six times the weight of bombs dropped by the US in World War II). But the US still lost. The USSR made a similar error in Afghanistan.

A well-motivated guerilla force, enjoying the support of the local populace and knowing the local terrain, will almost always defeat an invading force, despite the latter's technology. Indeed, an addiction to technology is a distinct disadvantage in guerilla warfare. The key to guerilla warfare is winning the hearts and minds of the local populace.

An addiction to weapon technology creates a barrier between troops and the local populace. For example, there is a temptation to use fire power to quell guerillas, but in the process ordinary civilians get injured. The civilians are likely to be sympathetic to the force which creates the least problems for them. Since guerillas often have to be careful about how they use their ammunition and explosives, they tend to get local sympathy by default. You do not win hearts and minds by putting them in coffins — something the US never recognised in Vietnam or the USSR in Afghanistan.

It would be pleasant to predict an end to nuclear and conventional warfare. But international politics are not that rational. For example, there is now little to justify the UK's independent nuclear force — except a nostalgia for the past, when the UK really was a world power. But that nostalgia still triumphs over reason: Mrs Thatcher said the UK must have Trident nuclear weapons to bring about the USSR's collapse and Mr Major is now saying that the UK should have the Trident because the USSR *has* collapsed. The UK is paying a high cost for its nostalgia.

RECENT EVENTS PRECIPITATING A DECLINE IN SECOND WAVE WARFARE

Three main events have contributed to the decline in Second Wave warfare — the ending of the Cold War; the fact that Russia has come in from the cold and the inadequate response of the one remaining superpower; and the 1991 Gulf conflict.

1. *The end of the Cold War*

It is an irony of history that a great power cannot diagnose its own decline. One has only to look at the British Empire to see the speed of its own unanticipated decline. A century ago, while it was building statues and monuments celebrating its rise to great power status, its lead was already being eroded by Germany (freshly united and the main power in Europe) and the US (well on the way to recovery from the Civil War). Now the US and the Soviet Union have been bankrupting themselves with their military manoeuvres while other nations, notably Japan, have been able to leap ahead with much less of a military expenditure burden.

The Cold War was the central defining event of the period from 1945 to 1990. Many national and international events were viewed through the prism of the Cold War. The US lawyer Michael Reisman has pointed this out:

The geo-strategic confrontation of the Cold War was sustained by two mutually incompatible ideologies or 'contending systems of world public order', deriving, curiously, from the same cultural and historical sources. Each viewed the other in Manichean terms and disseminated or inculcated its message intensively in its own sphere. One was intent on 'containing', if not 'rolling back' its adversary; the other, bent on 'burying' its adversary. At the height of the Cold War, there were two worlds on the planet between which trade and other human contact were drastically reduced. In many ways, there were two systems of international law and two systems of world public order. The Cold War had virtually become part of the natural environment. Few thought it would ever end.

Within each of the adversaries, the anxiety generated by the anticipated conflict reached into and influenced many sectors of life. Both superpowers took on, in varying degree, garrison-state features. In the West, the effects were felt in ordinary democratic processes, in civil and human rights, in school curriculums, in literature and art, in environmental protection, in individual health, in the skewing of economies for defence, in the allocation of public funds for weapons development and the maintenance of a large standing military — indeed, in every sector of life. In the East, the ideology was totalitarian; millions of people were subjected to high degrees of control and deprived of accurate information about what was occurring elsewhere. A larger and larger proportion of the national wealth was diverted to military and security matters.[15]

There are various theories about when the Cold War began. Many of them focus on the details of World War II, US/Soviet tensions and the immediate aftermath of that war. I prefer to see the Cold War as simply a variation on the old theme of new great powers becoming accustomed to each other and their new roles on the world stage. Thus capitalism and communism are incidentals.

There have been cold wars in the past and there may yet be cold wars in the future — although I think that they will lack the intensity of the last one simply because cold wars are the product of the Second Wave nation-state system and, since this is in decline, nation-state rivalries will also become less intense.

In the sixteenth century, the cold war was between Portugal and Spain. In the early seventeenth century, with Portugal and Spain in decline, the new rivals were the Netherlands and France. A century later, the UK rivalled and then defeated France. By the late nineteenth century, Germany challenged the UK's supremacy. Each challenge was often built up on the ruins of the earlier rival.

The beginnings of what we call the Cold War are seen in 1917. In that year, the US assumed at last an important place on the world stage. In that year, too, Russia left the stage to return as the Soviet Union and, like the US, had different ideas (from the Allies) on how the world ought to be run.

But they were both prevented in large measure from following through their ideas at the time. The US was the chief supporter of the League of Nations idea, but for reasons of politics became of its own accord an isolationist nation. The Soviet Union made a separate peace with Germany, thus acquiring the opprobrium of the world and both were isolated from the world by other nations (although Germany had important ties). For a while the Soviet Union was largely unconcerned about this isolation since it had several problems at home to deal with.

The Cold War was, then, essentially about the adjustment that the US and the Soviet Union had to make in becoming superpowers and getting used to each other and their roles in the world. World War II brought the two nations together, but the problems of adjustment were hidden by the larger issue of beating Germany. Both in this period and the post-1945 period, it is possible to see how the two nations were suspicious of each other and very cautious in their international relations. They also tended to see issues in clear-cut terms. There were always hints of 'plots' that could be discerned in the foreign policy of the other bloc. This meant that those attempts which were made in the late 1940s to end the Cold War usually failed.

Cold wars bring together unlikely rivals. The rivals arise simply as a matter of timing and not necessarily due to deep-seated traditional animosities. Cold wars are intense, but brief; subsequent generations make up and even later ones forget there was one. How many Britons, for example, are still angry with France? If there is bad feeling between the British and French, it is far more likely to be over sporting fixtures or inadequate tourist facilities rather than a rehash of eighteenth century cold war rivalries. Ethnic tensions, by contrast, can last centuries — the British/Irish tensions have outlasted all the cold wars mentioned in these paragraphs.

The US and USSR were not obvious enemies. Prior to the Cold War they had never fought each other; they have no common borders (except a close contact in the Bering Strait), no overlapping ethnic minorities anxious to reunite their 'motherland' and no disputes over natural resources. But that is the nature of cold wars: as nations rise, so they are thrown against each other.

In summary, while there could be other cold wars, the diminished importance of the nation-state is likely to limit their significance as we move from a Second Wave to a Third Wave world.

2. *Russia comes in from the cold and the US has no forward-looking policy to handle this.*

In the first half of the twelfth century, an ostrog (block house) was built on the side of a minor river. This minor fortification eventually became the city of Moscow. The Duchy of Muscovy gradually expanded. It became the core of a Slav empire originally drawn from a Nordic tribe called the Rus.

Ivan the Great (who ruled Muscovy from 1462 to 1505) created the first Russian nation-state around the Moscow region. This nation-state was to become a huge empire by absorbing non-Russian nations to its west and the Islamic tribes to its south. By 1725, Russian control had spread through Asia to the Pacific Ocean.

Unlike most empires, the Russian one was territorially contiguous — it was one vast land mass, rather than being separated by oceans (as were the empires of Portugal, Spain, France, the Netherlands and UK). This made it easier for Moscow to claim to be governing one nation rather than an empire.

Control is one thing, progress is another. Moscow leaders were able to govern the land mass, but not reform it. It was traditionally the poorest part of Europe: the communist revolution failed to end the centuries-old pattern of its being the most backward part of Europe. Mr Gorbachev has now joined the ranks of failed reformers. He found — as did all his predecessors, especially Peter the Great (1672–1725) — that it is easier to reform foreign policy than it is to reform economic and social policy.

The 1917 Russian Revolution did not leave the nation with a system for the orderly transfer of power. Elections were meaningless. There was no Western-style democracy. The Communist Party, with its highest level the *nomenklatura*, ran the nation and selected who should head it. Because there was no agreed way of removing leaders via elections, by late 1970 there was a tendency to select old men — if the Party made a mistake, it would not have to live with its error for very long.

Richard Pipes of Harvard University set out in late 1984 the decay that was then apparent to him within the USSR's economy:

The economic crisis is due to inadequate productivity; this, in turn, is caused by two factors: excessive centralisation of economic decision-making in the hands of Party organs, and inadequate incentives offered to workers and farmers, who are essentially paid not in proportion to output but according to the time spent working. Declining rates of economic growth adversely affect the ability of Moscow to engage in its ambitious military and imperial ventures. For more than a decade now, Soviet planners have been forced to transfer resources from the capital investments sector into the military sector, which ensures in the long run further declines in industrial growth.

The country's productive resources are stifled by an economic system that is designed primarily to ensure the security and power of the *nomenklatura*. The government theoretically could, but in reality does not dare to, decrease further the impoverished consumer sector for fear of strikes and riots in industrial centres, preferring instead to risk undermining the country's industrial future. One of the by-products of the economic crisis is declining birth-rates, caused in good part by fantastic abortion rates (estimated at ten per Russian female): for the first time in recorded history, the Russian population, once with the highest reproduction rate in Europe, is not replacing itself, as each year more Russians die than are born.[16]

In March 1985, an embattled Communist Party gambled on a young reformer: Mikhail Gorbachev. He believed the USSR could be reformed while remaining governed by the Communist Party. He tried to ease the level of spying on his citizens and the terror of the KGB — without realising that these were the factors that kept the USSR together. Instead of reforming the USSR, he permitted its fragmentation.

Russia was the only country surrounded by hostile communist nations. It controlled territories whose citizens resented the Russian and communist presence. In 1982 there was a remarkable novel published, in which Donald James set out the fall of the Russian Empire:

> Nobody now doubts that for the Soviet Union and the world, 1980 to 1985 were the fateful years. At the root of its looming problems was the simple fact that the Soviet Union was an empire comprising fifteen totally different nations, one hundred languages, a racial spectrum from Slav to Mongol, a half dozen different residual religions.
>
> At the centre of the empire stood the Russia of the Czars, proud, patriotic, the first among equals. But as the 1980s began, it was not necessary to be a Ukrainian, an Estonian, an Armenian or an Uzbek to be aware the Soviet triumphs were now ringing from a cracked bell.
>
> In so many ways it was the Soviet army in which many of these nationalist stresses were concentrated. Not surprisingly, people in the West reading of the vast defence budgets announced by the Kremlin, thought of the Soviet army as a highly trained and integrated force.
>
> Yet the truth was far from that. The truth was that the army was the point at which all those promises to the Soviet Union's non-Russian peoples ended. Every training camp for conscripts might well have had a sign over the gate reading:
>
> *Local Languages and Cultures Stop Here.*
>
> The truth was that the Soviet army was one vast school for the russification of the Union's one hundred different nationalities.[17]

James predicted that the end of the Russian Empire would come from internal factors. Its Cold War opponent hardly receives any attention; Russia's problems all emerged from within its own borders. The empire struck back. The collapse was so inevitable — and yet so completely unforeseen by Mr Gorbachev.

In late 1990, the USSR was forced to go to international financial institutions (the International Monetary Fund, World Bank and the Organisation for Economic Co-operation and Development) to get financial aid. This was the first time it had done so. It was obliged to open up its economy to outside scrutiny. The result was stunning, as the *Australian Financial Review* pointed out:

Tucked away in the report was the revelation that the once feared red bear was a mouse. Everyone knew the Soviet economy was backward. But with all those people and the ability to stay with the United States in arms development, it was assumed it was big.

According to the special joint IMF-World Bank-OECD report, however, the Soviet economy is only as large as Canada's and not much larger than Australia's.

This would barely gain it membership of the Group of Seven.

The report, commissioned by the G7 industrial nations at the Houston economic summit in July as a guide to Moscow's aid requirements, found that the Soviet Union had a GNP of US$512 billion (A$660 billion) in 1989.

Divided among 288 million people, this amounted to per capita income of US$1 780 — the equivalent of a South American nation like Costa Rica.

Average per capita income in OECD nations is US$17 606. Even in Eastern Europe it is higher than US$2 000.

The findings of the 2 000-page report, released in a 51-page summary in Washington, were based on data provided by Soviet authorities.

The report delivers the most complete statistical picture of the Soviet Union yet available.

It quashes previous US intelligence estimates that had put the Soviet economy at about one-third the size of that of the United States. The report shows the Soviet economy to be less than one-tenth the US's 1989 GNP of US$5.2 trillion.

In comparison, Canada has a GNP of just over US$500 billion and Australia US$360 billion.

If the report is correct, the US annual defence budget of US$300 billion is more than half the size of the whole Soviet economy.[18]

Russia has come in from the cold. Since 1917, it has remained aloof from many international organisations and played a disruptive role in those it did join. It had a Second Wave mentality of trying to go it alone. Now it has accepted the Third Wave philosophy of inter-dependence and so is allowing the absorption of its economy into the global economy.

What has been the US reaction? To lose your best friend is a tragedy — but to lose your best enemy is a disaster. The sudden end of the Cold War revealed the US had limited aims for the Cold War and no policy for peace.

George Washington's advice to his citizens as he left the presidency was that the new US should avoid entanglements in the messy politics and conflicts of the Old World. His successors followed his advice. The US went west. It absorbed the remnants of the Spanish Empire and regarded Latin America as its zone of influence. It was more concerned with trading with the nations in Europe than with fighting them.

In 1917, it was dragged into World War I by Germany's submarine attacks on its shipping. But it was never an Allied nation as such — the US led a separate group of nations fighting Germany. In the negotiations following the war, the US encouraged the Old World victors not to treat Germany too harshly. It also championed a new idea: the League of Nations.

During the 1920s and 1930s, the US again withdrew from the Old World and concentrated on making money. It reduced its military forces to the extent that during the 1930s its army was smaller than that of Greece. In 1941, the US was dragged into World War II by Japan's attack on Pearl Harbour. With the former great powers (the UK, France and Germany) now exhausted, it found itself as the world's top economic and military power. This time, there would be no dramatic demobilisation. The US was on the world stage to stay.

The US had only one policy: to remain the world's main superpower. It became obsessed with military security. George Washington's advice was ignored: a nation of traders became a nation of warriors. The US obsessions became particularly fixated on the USSR: US economic strength was siphoned off into the military-industrial complex. Whatever the question, the answer was a military one.

The peace movement was correct all along. The USSR was not the threat the US argued it was, and the US could not afford such a high rate of military expenditure based on the assumption that the USSR was as evil as the US claimed. If the USSR had been as strong as the US had claimed, then it would have had enough force to put down the internal and satellite rebellions of the late 1980s. The USSR collapsed not because of the US's external pressure, but because of the USSR's internal failure to produce economic growth. The alleged drive for world domination fizzled out. In the 1980s, the USSR lost control over Eastern Europe and in 1990 Russia lost control over the USSR.

The US, ironically, actually helped the Soviet government to control its own citizens. By its threats, the US gave the Soviet government an opportunity to control its citizens in the interests of 'protecting them'. The KGB was necessary (so the government could claim) to prevent CIA espionage and terrorism.

The US failed to understand the USSR's fear of attack. The US has not been invaded for two centuries. Moscow, by contrast, has had both French and German troops on its outskirts in that same period. The USSR lost in World War II fifty times as many soldiers as did the US. The Russians may not have liked communism, but they would die defending their Motherland from the US.

The US, then, handled the Cold War badly. First, it overestimated the USSR's power. Second, its obsession with the USSR (such as President Reagan's 1983 description of it as the 'evil empire') enabled the Soviet government to take even greater control over its citizens.

Third, the US competed with the USSR on the USSR's terms. The USSR's system of centralised economic planning enabled the government (at great cost) to make the weapons sufficient to keep it in the arms race. But centralised planning (as Mr Gorbachev admitted) is not nearly so efficient in creating goods for individual consumers. This was — and remains — the real strength of the Western economic system. But the US did not exploit it fully.

Soviet citizens were obliged to be loyal to Moscow, but their hearts belonged to New York and Hollywood. George Washington would have treated them less as enemies than as potential consumers. The Red Army could keep NATO out of Eastern Europe, but it could not keep out *Dallas*, *Dynasty* and Levi jeans.

The US had no plans for the end of the Cold War. It has been casting around for new enemies (such as Iraq and Libya), but these are no substitute for the perceived Soviet threat. Many of its nuclear weapons are still intact; the US-Soviet disarmament agreements have not scrapped all of the weapons — far from it. But against whom are they now targeted?

Many in the US — and elsewhere — will look back on the Cold War with a sense of nostalgia. Life was so simple then. You either supported the US (First World) or the USSR (Second World), or else you disapproved of both (Third World).

Now everything is so much more complicated. As I pointed out earlier, if the Second World is trying to join the First World, what number should be accorded to the 'Third' World? What does 'neutrality' mean for nations like Sweden, Austria and Switzerland when there is now no 'Second' World to be neutral between? How can we regard nations like Singapore and Taiwan as poor Third World nations when they have higher economic growth and lower unemployment than the UK and Australia?

The end of the Cold War also creates the opportunity for greater moral consistency. During the Cold War, all dictatorships, for example, were viewed through the prism of the Cold War: Washington may not have liked a particular ruler, but at least he was pro-US.

Underhand activities were justified because the USSR itself used such activities and so it was necessary to fight fire with fire. For example, Indonesia invaded the Portuguese colony of East Timor in late 1975; Australia (and the US) ignored — if not supported — the invasion on the grounds that an independent East Timor could have become a pro-Soviet Cuba immediately to Australia's north. Australia's support for Kuwait in 1990/91 was far greater than its support for East Timor.

Now that the USSR has disappeared, each human rights violation will need to be viewed on its terms — and not in terms of that violation being a small pawn in the greater US/USSR chess game. All these issues the US — and the rest of us — need to think through.

If the US overestimated the threat from the USSR in the Cold War, it runs the risk of overestimating what the world will be like without the Cold War and the USSR. A good example of this optimism is the 1989 essay (now revamped for a book) by Francis Fukuyama called 'The End of History'.[19]

Fukuyama, an historian of ideas, claims that the forces of freedom have triumphed over dictatorship, most recently communist dictatorship. This would come as a surprise to the Chinese — over a billion people are still governed by a communist dictatorship. More importantly, this optimism overlooks the fact that the Cold War was about two nations competing with each other — and not two systems of ideas. Ideas don't kill people; people kill people. The planet is not on the verge of some golden era of peace and tranquillity; other problems are already emerging (such as Islamic fundamentalism).

Human nature has not changed simply because the Cold War has ended. Competition and conflict still exist. The challenge is to find ways of converting conflict into something worthwhile, rather than being worried about one ideology defeating another.

Because of the US's superpower status, it is important that they find new approaches to the new situation that has arisen with Russia's coming in from the cold. But the problem is one that we all must address, whether the US does or not.

3. *The 1991 Gulf conflict: war without winners*
The Gulf conflict was the most intensive conflict fought in that part of the world since 1914. It involved, on its first day, the Allies dropping more tonnes of bombs than in any single day of the Vietnam conflict. For the UK, with the deployment of 45 000 personnel, it was the most comprehensive deployment of UK forces outside Europe since 1945. As many people were killed in the Gulf conflict as were killed in the four Arab-Israeli conflicts between 1948 and 1973.

The Gulf conflict was the world's first post-Cold War conflict. The USSR was anxious to improve relations with the US and to receive foreign aid from Western nations, and so it was willing to go along with the US-led coalition at the United Nations.

This consensus has been maintained in the post-conflict era, in which Iraq has been subjected to the most stringent set of intrusions inflicted on any nation since World War II. Although the conflict itself was not a UN operation — the US coordinated the twenty-eight allied nations — the UN has been given the tasks of locating and destroying Iraq's weapons of mass destruction (chemical, biological and nuclear) as well as the facilities which make them. The USSR, which supplied missiles to Iraq, is now giving information on those missiles to the UN inspection team to help it locate all the missiles.

The conflict was unusual in that it was a conventional one. It was the first major conventional conflict since the 1982 Falklands War. The conflict, I predicted in the media at the time, could only run for about six weeks (forty-two days): it lasted forty-three days.

The conflict cost the allied nations US$60 billion — enough to run the UN's central budget for a quarter of a century. Taking the lowest estimate of Iraqi casualties — that of 100 000 people killed — it 'cost' about US$600 000 to kill each Iraqi.

It will take about ten years before Kuwait is free of mines. Iraq ignored international conventions which state that, after a ceasefire, a detailed map of the positions of mines should be made available. Before they left the country, the Iraqis mined Kuwait City, the desert and the sea at random. Then they set fire to the oil wells, the palaces, hotels and official buildings.

Kuwait can be rebuilt. But the unexploded mines — rather than the oil wells and buildings — will have the longest impact. They will affect the nomadic people who seasonally move across Kuwait's borders.

The conflict showed the futility of war as an instrument of national policy. President Hussein failed to maintain his grasp over Kuwait. He looked at how some nations had got away with taking over the territory of other nations (such as Indonesia's invasion of East Timor) and he expected to be equally successful. After all, when he began the conflict against Iran in 1980, he received help from the West and USSR.

The US won the war, but lost the peace. General Schwarzkopf achieved a brilliant success with his 670 000 troops. But President Bush lacked a clear set of peace aims. If President Hussein had been killed, there was no guarantee that his successor would be any more cooperative than President Hussein had been. If Iraq's Kurds had rebelled and obtained independence for their part of Kurdistan, then they would have inspired the Kurds across the border in Turkey — the US's ally — to rebel. Turkey opposed this. If Iraq were broken up, then the resulting power vacuum would have been filled by either Syria or Iran — neither of which is friendly towards the US. Consequently, President Hussein and Iraq were allowed to survive; there is no guarantee that Iraq will be peaceful in the future.

The only people who did well out of the conflict were the arms manufacturers. Ninety-five per cent of the weapons sold to Iraq in the years prior to the conflict came from the US, USSR, UK, France and China. The UN's Big Five are, then, both the world's main law enforcers and main gun-runners.

Beginning in 1983, Iraq used chemical warfare against Iran. Most of the international community ignored what was happening since Iran was even less liked than Iraq. The warheads and delivery systems had to be imported, but nothing was done to stop this trade. In 1987, Iraq began using chemical warfare against its own citizens, the Kurds. This was the largest single use of chemical warfare since World War I. Again the international community was slow to criticise Iraq.

Iraq was also building nuclear weapons at this time. Having got away with building chemical weapons by capitalising on nations' desire for trade over integrity, perhaps Iraq also expected to get away with nuclear weapons. As we now know, President Hussein timed his attack on Kuwait badly. He was premature. A later invasion and a later consequent Allied response would have involved nuclear weapons.

In June 1981, Israeli jets destroyed Iraq's ostensibly civilian reactor near Baghdad. Israel alleged that Iraq was using it to manufacture plutonium. The reactor was built with French help and used uranium from China, Brazil and Niger. Iraq was also in the market for triggering devices for nuclear weapons. These were being purchased in the US.

An Iraqi official was caught at London Airport in March 1990 (five months before the attack on Kuwait) allegedly smuggling such devices from the US to Iraq via the UK. This procurement had been underway for years, but no doubt the intelligence service was still looking for Soviet spies rather than dubious Iraqi traders. This is another example of how the Cold War diverted attention from emerging problems.

International inspection teams are now checking on Iraq's weapons of mass destruction and ensuring their destruction. Ironically, some of the nations which have authorised this destruction would have sold the weapons or their basic components in the first place. In due course, Iraq may well go back to buying weapons from abroad.

Leaving aside the gun-runners (who win in every war), there were no winners in the Gulf conflict. President Hussein was wrong to have invaded, but he remains in power. The US won the war, but lost the peace. The Kurds and other ordinary people in the entire region are still the losers.

The Gulf conflict, therefore, has played a part in undermining the effectiveness of Second Wave warfare in solving world problems.

So if the Second Wave 'solutions' to problems no longer work, what is there to replace them? The next chapter provides some pointers in answer to this question.

Endnotes:

1. William Eckhardt, 'Conditions of Peace Suggested by Some Quantitative Studies of Primitive Warfare', *Peace Research* (Brandon University, Manitoba), August 1989, pp.3–39
2. John Hackett, 'The Profession of Arms', *Journal of the Royal United Services Institute* (Sydney), June 1985, p.28
3. Paul Seaver, 'Armies, Nations and Liberty', *Peace Review* (Palo Alto, CA), Winter 1989, p.8
4. Peter Calvocoressi, 'World Power 1920–1990', *International Affairs* (London), October 1990, p.663
5. Jack Kidd, *The Strategic Co-operation Initiative*, Three Presidents, 1988, p.17
6. James Leasor, *War at the Top*, Michael Joseph, 1959, pp.52–53
7. Stephen E. Ambrose, *Eisenhower: The President*, George Allen & Unwin, 1984, pp.571–572
8. Zbigniew Brzezinski, *Power and Principle*, Weidenfeld & Nicholson, 1983, p.15
9. 'Doomsday Hideaway', *Time*, 9 December 1991
10. Marianne Frankenhaeussur, 'To Err is Human: Nuclear War by Mistake', in *Breakthrough: Emerging New Thinking*, Walker, 1988, p.53
11. Stephen E. Ambrose, *ibid*, p.394
12. Norman Cousins, *The Pathology of Power*, Norton, 1987, pp.130–131
13. *Ibid*, pp.121–122
14. Rodrigo Carazo Odio, 'The Seed of Peace', *Peace Review* (Palo Alto, CA), Winter 1989, p.22
15. W. Michael Reisman, 'International Law After the Cold War', *American Journal of International Law*, October 1990, p.859
16. Richard Pipes, 'Can the Soviet Union Reform?', *Foreign Affairs* (New York), Fall 1984, p.50
17. Donald James, *The Fall of the Russian Empire*, Granada, 1982, pp.26–27
18. 'Super Foe Turns Out to be Mighty Mouse', *Australian Financial Review*, 28 December 1990
19. Francis Fukuyama, *The End of History and the Last Man*, Hamish Hamilton, 1992

9

THIRD WAVE
WARFARE

What shape will new world order conflict take?

CONVENTIONAL WARFARE IS BECOMING a thing of the past. A nuclear war is unwinnable — it will not decide who is right; only who is left. But this does not mean that the world will live completely at peace. I predict a return to guerilla warfare.

THE ERA OF GUERILLA WARFARE
Guerilla warfare is now the most widely used form of warfare. This form of conflict is far from being as destructive as the 1991 Gulf conflict. But it represents a steady erosion of life and property. Guerilla conflicts are widespread, occurring at present all over the world — Northern Ireland, the old Yugoslavia, Georgia, Azerbaijan, Lebanon, Iraq, Somalia, Mozambique, Afghanistan, Burma, Cambodia, Colombia, Bougainville, East Timor, Iran, Japan, Sri Lanka, Kashmir, to name a few.

Guerilla warfare will remain the most common form of warfare in the future for the following six reasons:

1. *Guerilla warfare allows virtually everyone to participate, making it very effective.*
During my research in the Vietnam conflict, when I travelled through rural areas in daylight, I was well aware that some of the people working in the fields were active at night laying mines, building traps and interfering with the telecommunications system. Guerilla warfare removes the distinction between combatant and civilian — a person can be both, depending on the time of day or the action to be performed.

Similarly, guerilla warfare is not limited to adults. Children have taken part in the conflicts in Ethiopia, Lebanon, El Salvador, Nicaragua and Cambodia. Children throwing rocks in Northern Ireland are a public order problem because the police and soldiers obviously do not want to be seen treating them harshly, but their rock and bottle throwing is a health hazard.

2. *Guerilla warfare's exploitation of the vulnerabilities of modern life makes it effective.*
Airports and aircraft are easy targets. With millions of people per day flying, it is perhaps a wonder that there are not more Lockerbie-type disasters. It is not possible to scrutinise all passengers, crew and ground staff plus baggage thoroughly.

The 1988 disaster over Scotland is believed to be due to a bomb placed in a radio, which was itself placed in a case. All these precautions — so elaborate and yet so ordinary — made the bomb undetectable by usual security methods.

3. *Modern technology has benefits for guerillas.*
The Lockerbie disaster, which resulted in the death of 259 passengers and crew and eleven people on the ground — making it the UK's biggest mass murder — was achieved via ten to fourteen ounces of Semtex explosive. Semtex is made in Czechoslovakia and is odourless, tasteless and quite safe to carry around. It is ideal for guerilla warfare. The communist governments sold Semtex as a foreign exchange earner. Ominously, the present government cannot track down where all of it went.

Similarly, the cost of producing conventional weapons has far outpaced the cost of producing simple weapons to destroy them. The Mujaheddin guerillas in Afghanistan, for example, acquired from their supporters in Western nations portable missiles (the 'Stinger') which a single person could fire at Soviet helicopter gunships. The Bougainville Revolutionary Army (BRA), fighting for the independence of its mineral-rich island from Papua New Guinea, is even less sophisticated: it has home-made shotguns, bows and arrows, and abandoned World War II arms — weapons that are effective enough to cause a lot of trouble.

4. *The mass media create a 'multiplier effect' that helps the guerilla cause.*
A bomb explosion, for example, is now heard around the world. An effective way of a dissident group drawing attention to its plight is to kill the citizens of nations which have a disproportionate influence in the mass media, notably the US and the UK (in the English-speaking world) and France. Their media ensure wide coverage of violent events.

The guerillas do not need to cause a large number of casualties to gain publicity. High casualties may even provoke a domestic backlash and so rarely help their aims. Guerilla warfare is economical warfare.

Guerillas want a lot of people watching — not necessarily a lot of people dead.

5. *Guerillas can win by losing yet exhausting the other side.*
If the troops do not become exhausted, their folks at home might be. Some guerilla struggles have gone on for over a decade (Mozambique's has gone on for seventeen years — after an even longer struggle against the Portuguese colonisers). What might start as a limited internal conflict may mutate into a complex struggle fought between competing parties, such as the Lebanese conflict, which began in 1975.

6. *Guerilla warfare's rewarding of the inventive*
encourages guerilla activity.
Among the dangers we have yet to encounter are guerillas poisoning a water supply system, putting chemical weapons through a building's air conditioning system and contaminating a large-scale catering operation.

Additionally, there is the risk of nuclear terrorism. Guerillas could sabotage a nuclear reactor in such a way as to dispense its radioactive material across the local area. More likely, however, guerillas could try to build their own nuclear weapon or steal someone else's.

The two main worries are the former USSR and China. The latter, a minor player in the arms race, is willing to sell nuclear equipment to any nation with the money to pay for it. It is not selling to guerilla groups, but they could obtain the equipment from China's customers.

The long-range (strategic) nuclear weapons of the old USSR are based in four republics: Russia (with about eighty per cent of them), Ukraine, Belorussia and Kazakhstan. But the smaller (tactical) nuclear weapons were deployed in almost all the USSR's republics. Of the USSR's 27 000 nuclear weapons, 15 000 come into this latter category.

They are more portable and harder to detect than the strategic weapons.

A related concern is the way that unemployed Soviet nuclear scientists will take their expertise to whoever will provide them with employment. Russia and the other republics cannot afford to keep running the arms race, but they cannot afford either to pay their scientists to destroy the weapons (which could take two decades to do).

It may be only a matter of time before the mafia get into the nuclear business. Nuclear explosives can be made with less than six kilograms of plutonium, in size about enough to fill a coffee cup. The world's present inventory of plutonium produced in civilian reactors is roughly 700 000 kilograms, greater than the total amount in the world's nuclear arsenals. This plutonium is being produced in thirty-six countries. By the year 2000, there will be more than three million kilograms of plutonium in the world, enough for at least 500 000 nuclear weapons.

The plutonium produced in a reactor must be separated before it can be used in a weapon. While commercial facilities are more complex, a separation plant suitable for military purposes can be built for less than US$50 million in several months' time. Every nation with a commercial nuclear power plant has such resources, since they are small compared with those needed for acquiring the power plant itself. Each year, the reprocessing plant can extract approximately 250 kilograms of plutonium from a single commercial reactor, enough for forty nuclear weapons at the very least.

The most difficult technical barrier for the production of nuclear weapons is access to the required nuclear material. But thirty-six countries with nuclear power plants produce at least enough plutonium for forty nuclear weapons per year from each such plant. Fissionable material suitable for use in weapons is produced as an unwanted by-product at every civilian nuclear power plant in the world. More than 100 000 nuclear weapons could be built from the world's current nuclear wastes.

It can be seen, then, that the possibilities — and consequent rewards — for the inventive guerilla are endless.

In short, warfare will continue in the Third Wave. But it will be different from the Second Wave's warfare. Indeed, even the defence forces may have a different role. If I am correct in the prediction of the Third Wave fragmentation of national power, then defence forces will be used far more to defend governments from their own citizens than from external enemies.

THE ERA OF THE DISINTEGRATION OF NATIONS

One of the characteristics of the Third Wave (as set out in chapter 4) is the fragmentation of power. A national government has to share its power with international organisations, transnational corporations and non-governmental organisations.

Another characteristic is that the nation-state itself is under threat. Most of the guerilla struggles currently underway around the world are going on within nations — not between them — and are based on an attempt to break away from the existing nation.

The most obvious example is currently the old USSR. It spanned eleven time zones, had 130 languages and included over 100 ethnic groups. The USSR has broken up into the republics which constituted the Soviet federation. Now the republics themselves are having their own internal difficulties as groups wish to redraw frontiers. There is also the problem of Russians who have moved into the other republics to administer them — are they now to be expelled?

The old Russian/Soviet empire differed from the European empires in how the masters were viewed by the colonised. For example, the British and Indians, and the French and Algerians have a love-hate relationship based partly on the tradition of Indians wanting to emulate the British (they now play better cricket) and the Algerians emulating the French. The Russians, by contrast, were despised by their colonials for being culturally inferior; they were seen as having nothing worth emulating. The newly-independent people would like the Russians out as quickly as possible.

The purpose of the West's most important military alliance, the North Atlantic Treaty Organisation (NATO), was to keep the USSR out of Western Europe, to keep the US in and to keep Germany down. It was successful for four decades.

But now Europe's map is being redrawn. A strong, united Germany in central Europe disrupted the neat balance of power drawn up in 1815 in Vienna (to cope with post-Napoleonic Europe) and this contributed to World War I. That war's inability to solve 'the German Question' ('What do we do about Germany?') led to World War II. NATO and its East European equivalent (the Warsaw Pact Treaty) maintained post-war stability.

Germany is now the most important member of the European Community. There is no immediate prospect of a revived German militarism. Instead, Germany is likely to use economic power to obtain political influence. The Poles, who have long been between the 'hammer and the anvil' (Germany and Russia), may not be so easily reassured. With no natural barrier (such as a mountain range), Germany flows smoothly into Poland. But for the moment, anyway, Poland has no reason to fear German military power.

Europe's problem, instead, comes from the disappearances of the Warsaw Pact and the perceived Soviet threat. The USSR is no longer around to maintain order in Eastern Europe, where some borders are in doubt, such as those between Hungary and Romania, and Bulgaria and Turkey.

With no Soviet threat to unite Western European nations, there is now a fresh interest in such local nationalism as that of the Basques in Spain and the Bretons in France.

Europe's main conflict is in the former Yugoslavia. This was outside the USSR's direct military control, but it was governed by an authoritarian communist ruler (President Tito), whose successors lacked his flair for playing the provinces off against each other. Yugoslavia was always seen as a fragile nation, but few predicted it would dissolve into a civil war requiring a UN peacekeeping force. Yugoslavia'a fate is a warning that other European nations may yet develop internal conflicts.

Africa's plight is even more desperate. European colonisation paid little attention to tribal boundaries. A patchwork of national lines was superimposed on the traditional frontiers. For example, in traditional Africa, rivers were high streets with families living on either side. But for Europeans, rivers provided neat lines on maps and so families suddenly found themselves divided upon European nationalist lines. Colonial boundaries then became national boundaries following independence after World War II.

The British Empire is also a story of fragmentation. Some of the independent nations have split up. For example, India, the Jewel in the Imperial Crown, was divided up at independence between India and Pakistan; Pakistan later lost East Pakistan which became Bangladesh.

By contrast, no two ex-British colonies have formed a close union after independence, except the East and West Malaysian states. Even the UK itself is under threat, with demands by Scottish Nationalists for independence (Scotland has the world's thirtieth largest economy and in the European Community it would be larger than Greece, Portugal and Ireland). It could survive as an independent nation within the European Community.

Within existing nations there are demands for autonomy — even independence — from such original inhabitants as Australia's Aborigines and New Zealand's Maoris. In the US, about half of the two million native Americans live on reservations. Like Australia's Aborigines, they live in disproportionate poverty (compared with the whites) and are largely reliant on welfare payments.

As in Australia, there was a tradition of removing children from parents and educating them at mission posts or Bureau of Indian Affairs boarding schools to make them into middle-class Americans. That failed (as in Australia) and now their children (as adults) are rediscovering their noble pasts. Hollywood is responding: John Wayne machismo is out and *Dances With Wolves* is in. Environmentalists are acknowledging the skill they had in surviving in the US. (I am amazed at how Australians idolise early European explorers who died through a lack of food — if they were not so arrogant they could have learned from Aborigines, who had lived in the barren outback for 40 000 years; early explorers died in the Aboriginal equivalent of a fast-food restaurant!)

American Indians have picked up white habits: they have formed political organisations to campaign for land rights and have engaged 600 lawyers to do their work.

A similar process is also underway in Canada. In February 1992, a Canadian Royal Commission recommended wider powers (including a right to self-government) for the original Canadians. As the French-speaking residents in Quebec have campaigned for self-government (if not independence), so the nation's 450 000 native Indian and Inuit people (wrongly called 'Eskimo') have also demanded a special recognition. Additionally, thanks to President Gorbachev's *perestroika*, Canada's Inuit have been allowed to contact the Inuit in Siberia.

Minority original populations are forming their own networks across national boundaries. These networks are an example of Third

Wave global thinking. The original populations, after all, did not invent the Second Wave nation-state. They want to move from the First Wave direct to the Third Wave.

The disintegration of nations will not lead in all cases to guerilla warfare. Some of the fragmentation may be handled in a conflict-resolving way (as Canada is trying to do). But if guerilla warfare does break out in a nation, then it is more likely to be stimulated by a breakaway movement than by any other cause.

THE ERA OF THE TRADE WAR

The Cold War is over. Japan won it.

Throughout the Cold War, the peace movement warned that the US and USSR would bankrupt themselves with their high levels of military expenditure. Less publicised — but no less important — was the role of trade.

The US's strength was economic. But it chose to compete with the USSR on the USSR's terms by having an arms race rather than a trade race.

There are three particular areas of interest in this trade war: the USSR, the US (and its relations with Japan) and Asia.

❑ First, the USSR: from Marx to McDonald's

Soviet consumers conquered the Soviet involvement in the arms race by their thirst for Western goods and services. Mr Gorbachev's *perestroika* and *glasnost* may have enabled his Soviet citizens to have greater freedom and to read previously banned novels (such as *Dr Zhivago*). But what they really wanted were cars, jeans and pop records.

Mr Gorbachev shared his citizens' fascination with the West: the efficiency, economic growth, capacity for quick change and openness to new ideas.

Dynasty and *Dallas* beamed across the Iron Curtain did far more to erode the Cold War than did the official US propaganda. Civilisation arrived in Moscow in May 1989: McDonald's opened the largest hamburger shop in the world in Moscow. Soviet citizens may have been militarily loyal to Moscow, but their hearts were in Hollywood and New York.

❑ **Second, the US: from superpower to Japan's super debtor**
With so much attention focussed on Moscow, the US was slow to recognise the developments in Tokyo. The Japanese imported US ideas, improved them and then sold them back to the US. It now has a US$41 billion trade surplus with the US.

Japan was disarmed after World War II. General MacArthur wrote into the Japanese constitution a renunciation of war as a way of settling disputes — the first nation in history to have this constitutional provision.

Japan had five advantages over the US:

1. *Japan spent far less than the US on the military.*
It spent about one per cent of its GNP on defence compared with the US's seven per cent (the USSR's rate was an even higher percentage of a smaller economy).

In retrospect, this not only benefited civilian economic growth, but also reflected the real state of Soviet military power: the USSR was not as strong as the merchants of fear claimed. The Japanese, then, had few fears of the USSR. They operated on that assumption and have been proved right.

**2. *Japan, unlike the US, concentrated on producing goods for
the civilian market rather than military equipment.***
The US wanted to maintain its policy of controlling defence supplies and so these had to be US companies. Its genius went into military

equipment. Japan, then, had to concentrate on civilian equipment both because of its disarmed status (and therefore a limitation on the Japanese purchase of defence equipment) and in order to meet the requirements unable to be supplied by a US economy concentrating on defence.

3. *Japan, unlike the US, organised its economy for peace.*
The US left the economics of peace to the haphazard nature of the market, but it did not rely on the market for its military activities.

President Eisenhower's warning about the military-industrial complex was based on the damage he could see being done to the US economy by the constant preparation for war.

Defence is the closest the US has come to a nationalised industry. The Pentagon is the greatest single purchaser in the US market. It operates outside the usual accounting procedures. It is a single purchaser buying from a very limited range of suppliers — most of which, as already mentioned, are advised by ex-military officers.

The military-industrial complex has based itself throughout the US electoral districts so that it can apply leverage to any politician who calls for a reduction in military expenditure. Even though the Cold War is over and the USSR has collapsed, there has not been a dramatic reduction in military expenditure. Instead of reducing itself, the complex is looking for new enemies such as Iraq and Libya.

The Japanese, by contrast, put their genius into civilian trade and ·services. Japan's military-industrial complex is a peace-industrial complex — MITI:

The Japanese Ministry of International Trade and Industry — MITI — is a government bureau unlike anything most Westerners know. It is composed of elite bureaucrats (an oxymoron in the West) whose job is to think broadly and deeply about the overall success of Japan's industries. Most especially, MITI's task is to ponder the long view.

For MITI's officials themselves, this function is impelled by two personal circumstances. First, their employment is secure for a lifetime, which frees them to think into the distant future without concern for the vicissitudes of next year's elections or budget cuts that might endanger their job security. Second, each MITI official is regularly rotated among departments in the ministry so that he cultivates friendly personal relationships with the people he will be working with for the rest of his life and gains an understanding of all aspects of MITI's concerns.[1]

The US has no MITI, responsible for gathering information about world market trends and the long-term outlook for particular US industries. The US and Western European flair for the rugged individualistic approach based on domestic competition and confrontation cuts across the creation of a cooperative culture, as Feigenbaum and McCorduck point out:

The secretiveness of both declining and emerging American industries presents difficulties, especially since American firms depend on surprise rather than long-term investment and marketing. Nevertheless, as securities analysts have shown, that information can be gathered. No such group works at the US Department of Commerce. In addition to its information gathering, MITI acts as a forum for special interests to meet and discuss mutual problems and arrive at long-term solutions. Americans end up in court, which is costly and not likely to produce optimal long-range solutions.[2]

4. *Japan, unlike the US, has few natural resources and so has made the most of the one resource it does have: people.*

Its labour force is characterised by a high degree of education, devotion to work and openness to blending tradition with new ideas. With only half of the US's population, Japan's rate of investment equals the US's and its rate of savings is in excess of the US's.

The US, by contrast, squandered its 1945 primacy. The US's share of world trade has dropped from twenty-two per cent at the end of World War II to nine per cent at present. The US is being outclassed in many items of manufacturing which it pioneered, such as cars and machine tools. The US invented video cassette recorders, but all VCRs sold in the US contain Japanese components now.

5. *Japan, unlike the US, was alert to Toffler's Third Wave of economic development: knowledge-based industries.*

This has required Japan to invest heavily in universities, research institutes and research corporations. This has not been copied in the US. The UK, incidentally, is no better: the entire sum of money distributed by the University Grants Committee in the 1982/83 academic year was less than the cost to the UK of the 1982 Falklands conflict.

By the end of the 1980s, then, it became clear to many Americans that as there was less chance of losing their lives in a World War III than of losing their jobs, Japan provided a greater risk than did the USSR. The US's slide in the economic league table was obscured by 'the inflow of foreign money in the 1980s: with no history of nationalisation, the US is a safer place to invest. But that money will need to be repaid eventually.

The US went from being the world's largest creditor to largest debtor in about a decade — it will not be able to reverse that status until well into the next century. Neither Japan nor the European Community is willing to absorb US debt problems over an extended period.

A century ago, when the US was previously a debtor, it borrowed to invest in national development. Now that money has been gobbled up in consumerism. A century ago the US worked itself out of debt; it will not be able to do so this time since it has consumed the debt.

❏ Third, Asia: the region of economic growth

The world is entering a new era. Neither power nor prosperity are now properly measured in acres. Land mass, labour and natural resources are being overshadowed by information, knowledge and wisdom.

The Mediterranean is the ocean of the past; the Atlantic is the ocean of today; the Pacific is the ocean of the future. Japan is obviously the key nation to watch. Most of the other fastest growing economies in the world are also in Asia: Singapore, Malaysia, South Korea and Taiwan.

Economics rather than military power will be the key factor in the Pacific and world affairs generally.

Japan is unlikely to become a major military power to replace the US or USSR for the following reasons:

1. *There is still a great opposition to militarism and the samurai tradition.*

In this respect, then, it is misleading to suggest that the world in the early 1990s is back where it was in the early 1940s. It is not. The samurai and German junker traditions were destroyed in World War II.

2. *There remains a good deal of resentment towards Japan in the Asian region.*

Asians suffered under the Japanese New Order in the 1930s and 1940s and do not want a repeat of it.

3. *There is the hope that Japan may learn from recent history.*

If it were to develop a fighting force beyond the current Japanese Self-Defence Force, then it would trigger a local arms race, especially with China. Additionally, Japan can see how the US and USSR bankrupted themselves over military expenditure.

Perhaps we really have seen the last Cold War. Cold wars were the product of Second Wave nation-states and these are being eroded in the Third Wave fragmentation of power. Additionally Japan, which is due for the next superpower status, is forgoing an equivalent military role.

There is now one global economy. With the disappearance of the USSR and the admission that an isolated, centrally-planned economy could not work, the former USSR and Eastern Europe have now joined the global economy.

China remains a communist nation of sorts, but its impact on the world is due to its population size and not its economic influence. China's GNP in 1987 was about twice the size of Australia's and half the size of the UK's. In per capita terms, China's GNP is even smaller: US$2 470, with Australia at US$14 530 and the UK at US$13 060.

In the early part of this century, there was speculation about China becoming a dominant world power; we are still waiting for that transformation. China remains a nation with a brilliant future somewhere ahead of it.

The world's economy has never been as integrated as it is today.

The global economy has three focal points. No longer can one nation dominate it. The focal points are the US, Japan and the European Community — the mega three.

Japan is the world's largest lender and the leader in key technologies. The European Community will be the world's largest market and largest trader. The Deutsche Mark, along with the Japanese Yen, is becoming more widely used in international finance. The US will remain in the top part of the economic league table by virtue of the sheer size of its economy.

The mega three are entering the new era as political allies with democratic governments. They have developed a pattern of cooperation.

Additionally, the economies of the mega three are being knitted together by transnational corporations. The fragmentation of the production process and the location throughout the world of the various stages of component production and final assembling all mean that a Japanese television sold in the US may have come from Australian raw materials built in Western Europe. These are 'joint ventures'. What nationality, for example, is a car with a Chrysler nameplate, designed jointly by Chrysler and Mitsubishi and built by Americans at a joint Chrysler-Mitsubishi plant in Illinois?

If there were a risk of a massive international war, then it would be a trade one rather than a military one. This risk cannot be overlooked. The world economy during the past century has flourished best when only one strong nation was directing it: the UK (1860–1914) and the US (1945–1970). When power is fragmented (as between 1918 and 1939), there is chaos. The Third Wave's fragmentation means that this era of one economically powerful nation has gone and will not return. Other nations will arise (such as South Korea, India or Brazil). But none will be able to muster the power of a past UK or US. This fact provides an incentive for nations to learn about conflict resolution.

THE ERA OF CONFLICT RESOLUTION

The strongest person in the world is the person who can convert an enemy into a friend. Therefore get rid of your enemies: change them into your friends.

The essence of conflict resolution is to handle conflict creatively. Conflict is a natural part of life. It cannot be avoided — nor should it be. If there were no conflict, our lives would be stagnant. The challenge is to use each conflict for a positive end and to see that it promotes growth. Conflict resolution can be applied within and between families, schools, organisations and nations.

In terms of national security options, there are four ways of organising a nation's way of defending itself against a hostile nation, according to an American book on nuclear war:

By conquest:	Defeat the enemy in war.
By intimidation:	Arm so heavily that the enemy cannot see any gain or advantage in an attack.
By fortification:	Build an impregnable barrier between you and the enemy.
By friendship:	Persuade the enemy that you would both be better off if your competition were friendly and that you might even cooperate in facing other threatening parties.[3]

Conquest is the standard way of dealing with an enemy — and the most dangerous. As the USSR has discovered, it is very difficult to maintain control over people who resent, if not hate you. The Japanese and Germans, by contrast, have flourished partly as a result of forgoing military ambitions.

Deterrence of attack through intimidation — by instilling fear of the consequences — is another old method. The Romans had a phrase for it: 'If you want peace, prepare for war.' As we now know, if you prepare for war, you will get war.

The fortification approach means building fortresses or walls. The only human-made structure visible from the moon is the Great Wall of China. It was built in the fifteenth century to keep out the Mongols. It is now a tourist attraction. Similarly, the Maginot Line between France and Germany has outlived its usefulness. Another monument to a past political priority is the Berlin Wall. In each case, the 'making friends' approach has superseded the defence system's purpose.

The 'making friends' approach to security is as common in human history as those of conquest, intimidation and fortification — but not as nearly well publicised. The UK and France, for example, were enemies for centuries, but have been friends for all of this century. The Cold War is over and the US and Russia are now friends.

The 'making friends' approach (conflict resolution) is based on a deeper understanding of peace. The standard approach to peace is to assume that it is the absence of war. Working for it is based on disarmament: getting rid of the weapons of war. Many peace groups, during the 1980s, for example, focussed too heavily on opposing particular weapons systems.

But disarmament is not enough. Nations will not disarm in a security vacuum. It is necessary to provide an alternative to war.

Peace is not simply the absence of war — it is the presence of justice. There has to be attention to the underlying causes of war: poverty, violation of human rights, depletion of the local environment and so on. Additionally, there has to be an equally active quest for reconciliation. Making friends is not a passive pastime, but a demanding full-time preoccupation in diplomacy.

Peace, then, is not an end in itself, but a process of managing conflicts in a creative way.

❑ Characteristics of conflict resolution

Conflict resolution has the following five characteristics:

1. *Conflict resolution is the avoidance of physical violence.*

Violence does not resolve matters — it often only creates embitterment in the victim and a determination to engage in further violence. One reason that war has been such a common feature in history is the very belief in its inevitability. People and nations which decide that war is inevitable begin to act in ways that make it unavoidable.

There have been changes inside nations to minimise violence. Duelling, for example, is now outlawed in the European nations where it was previously an old tradition. The 'right to bear arms' is now (except for the US) being replaced in most nations by a greater reliance upon the police to maintain law and order. People settle their disputes through the law courts rather than vendettas.

2. *Conflict resolution is a 'win-win' activity.*

Conflict resolution is not peace at any price. It is based on trying to find a solution that is acceptable to all parties. This may be a more complicated process than first meets the eye since the presenting conflict may itself be only the tip of an iceberg and the resolution process will then uncover deeper issues of conflict.

Roger Fisher set this out below in the context of the US/USSR arms race. The US had to accept that its quest for security was making the USSR feel insecure:

> We must make the Soviet Union share the responsibility for our security problem. We should say, 'Look, you Russians have to understand why we build these missiles and how it looks to us when you behave as you do. You must take some responsibility for helping us deal with our security problem.' Similarly, we must

take on responsibility for dealing with their security problem. We cannot make our end of the boat safer by making the Soviet end more likely to capsize. We cannot improve our security by making nuclear war more likely for them. We can't 'win' security from nuclear war unless they win it, too. Any contrary assumption is dangerous.

Here I may point out that we in the peace movement do not always practise what we preach. I am always ready to tell friends at the Pentagon that it does no good to call Soviet officials idiots, but am likely to add, 'Don't you see that, you idiot?' We who are concerned with reducing the risks of war often think that our job is to 'win' the war against hawks. In advancing our interests, we assume that our adversaries have none worth considering.

But our task is not to win a battle. Instead, we have to find out what the other side's legitimate concerns are, and we have to help solve their legitimate problems in order to solve our own. At every level, domestically and internationally, we need to re-examine our working assumptions. We are not seeking to win a war, but to gain a peace.[4]

3. Conflict resolution is a positive and creative activity.

It is not like a fire brigade team racing towards another crisis: 'Here we go again — another problem.' Instead, each conflict holds within it a challenge to resolve that conflict in such a way as to result in an enhanced relationship. It is not so much about putting out fires as creating new buildings.

Europe contains many castles. Some Swiss towns, for example, still have parts of fortifications. They are now tourist attractions. But they were used previously to keep out foreigners. Up until 1847, Swiss cantons were often at war with one another. The so-called 'Sonderbundskrieg' was the last of many such Swiss conflicts. Now a person can travel in safety across Switzerland which prides itself on its law and order.

The Swiss have no magic formula for living in peace with their neighbours — they simply realised that peace is more profitable than civil wars and that a new institution (the Swiss federal nation) was required to maintain law and order.

4. Conflict resolution is not a panacea.

There is no guarantee it will work. But then the use of violence does not necessarily end in a just result. All I am saying is give peace a chance. A world which has devoted so much money to weapons can surely afford to devote some money to avoiding the need for violence.

An example of this successful avoidance of conflict in the face of very difficult odds is the US/UK relationship in North America in the nineteenth century. We take for granted the US/UK 'special relationship'. But it has taken an effort spanning over one and a half centuries. By 1817, the US and UK had fought two wars and tensions were now focussed on the Canadian border. A fragile peace had been reached in 1817, but military leaders in Washington and London wanted to maintain and increase their naval strength on the Great Lakes.

Lord Castlereagh, the British Foreign Secretary, believed any escalation of military strength on the Great Lakes would eventually lead to increased tension and ultimately war. The six-and-a-half thousand kilometre frontier between the United States and Canada was still being drawn up at that time and many areas were disputed. Castlereagh saw that unless agreement was reached which could set the scene for other border agreements, there was going to be trouble.

American and British representatives — Rush and Bagot —

negotiated and signed an agreement in 1817, entirely disarming the Great Lakes except for police and customs vessels. Warships on Lake Erie and Lake Ontario were destroyed and the border between the two North American nations continued to be drawn up in an atmosphere free of tension.

Nevertheless, relations between the United States and Canada have not been free of crises. During most of the years in which this open frontier developed, the UK managed Canada's foreign relations. Viewing Canada as one of the jewels of the empire, the UK defended interests there that were intimately involved with its global policies. Consequently, until Canada assumed complete control of its own foreign affairs in 1931, this area was the meeting place of two major powers.[5]

The most recent war scare between the US and UK came less than a century ago. There had been a boundary dispute for some years between Venezuela and the then British Guiana. Suddenly in December 1895, President Cleveland reasserted the seventy-year-old Monroe Doctrine (by which the US opposed the influence or interference of outside nations in the Americas). He denounced British 'aggression' and implied US support for Venezuela in any conflict with the UK.

This threat passed after a few weeks and it has largely vanished from the history books. But it was very real at the time for Henry James, the US novelist resident in England. His biographer said:

> It came to him as a violent shock to discover how deep trans-atlantic animosities could run. Feelings between the two nations had been on the whole friendly since their differences during the Civil War [1861–1865, in which the UK had some sympathy for the southern states]. Now Cleveland's belligerence, and a huge outcry against England in the American press, shook the foundations of James' security.[6]

5. *Conflict resolution is a continuous and all-embracing activity.*
It should be equated with learning a new language: a person with
that language is best able to use it in a community where that language is widely spoken.

This is likely to be most effectively institutionalised if governments
reorganise their departments of foreign affairs and create ministries for
peace. The essence of the proposal is that it will institutionalise the peace
perspective in government. There is, for example, a distinct treasury
perspective in all government deliberations involving financial considerations (usually to the extent of opposing as much proposed expenditure
as possible). There is a distinct social welfare perspective (usually in
favour of extending the government's mantle of care over its citizens).
There is not, however, a distinct peace perspective. There is no cabinet
minister specifically engaged on peacebuilding activities.

National security is more than just armed forces — the prime
concern of the Department of Defence. National security is more than
just diplomacy and the maintenance of healthy international political
arrangements — the prime concern of the Department of Foreign
Affairs and Trade. We need a new perception of national security.
The new perception of national security cannot come from existing
departments — each looks out on the world and defines 'national
security' according to its own departmental perspective.

For example, such a peace department would provide a unified
approach to disarmament. This has to be done outside of the Department of Foreign Affairs. If disarmament is part of that department,
then all disarmament considerations will be viewed within the context
of wider foreign policy issues — for example, the need not to offend
allies while also missing no opportunity to criticise other less friendly
nations. Instead of disarmament being seen as an important objective
in its own right, it will always be subservient to other considerations,
some of which are accelerating the arms race.[7]

THE PEACEFUL SETTLEMENT OF
INTERNATIONAL DISPUTES

The procedures for the peaceful settlement of disputes are known — but are hardly publicised. These procedures are successful — but are rarely used.

Indeed, there is a neglected history of the peaceful settlement of international disputes. History books are too often written as though they were the biographies of generals and battles.

❏ Two examples of conflicts resolved peacefully

One example of their value may be seen in the US hostages' drama in Teheran, November 1979 to January 1981. The US tried to use force to free the hostages, but the operation failed and some US rescue personnel were killed. The US then tried to settle the dispute peacefully by having the Algerians use their 'good offices' to negotiate an agreement with Iran. This contributed to hostages being freed.

Another example of this is the creation of the nation of Uruguay, a British piece of diplomacy. The South American nation of Uruguay is the result of civil and international conflict resolved by the creation of a buffer state. In the former colonial regions of Spain, independence movements spread widely in the wake of Spain's invasion and defeat by France in the Napoleonic wars. The extensive area of the Viceroyalty of Rio de la Plata, the region known as the *banda oriental* (east shore) was administered from Buenos Aires, even after the area declared its independence in 1810.

The *banda oriental*, however, bordered on its north and east Portugal's enormous New World colony of Brazil. Consequently, the region was involved in the struggles that developed with the wars of independence. In what is now Uruguay, armed insurrection broke out in 1811 which was exploited by Brazil on the one hand and the embryonic Argentine government on the other. First, Buenos Aires, seeing the danger to its security, attempted to quell the uprising and eventually succeeded in 1816. Resenting their defeat, the inhabitants of the region were not wholly averse to cooperation with Brazilian-Portuguese forces but, when the latter moved in during 1817, the *banda* was in effect a conquered region once more.

The condition of the *banda oriental* was that of stalemate from 1811 to 1828. Neither Argentina nor Brazil was strong enough to expel the other and the local population was too weak to oppose either effectively over a long period of time. Had mediation not come, this situation would doubtless have been concluded only with the exhaustion of one of the belligerents.

Instead, the UK came forward in 1826 with an attempt to resolve the dispute. Lord John Ponsonby was sent from London and, after two years of negotiation, was able to bring Argentina and Brazil to the peace table. The Treaty of Rio de Janeiro that they signed in August 1828 provided that both countries would refrain from interfering in the region of the *banda*, which was to be established as the independent nation of Uruguay. Even though the treaty did not clearly define Uruquay's boundaries, that question was settled subsequently without great difficulty.

The UK, whose commercial interests in the region were threatened by the continued hostilities, hardly set itself wholly altruistic goals in working for the creation of Uruguay. Argentina, for its part, needed peace there to settle problems with rebellious provinces elsewhere. Nevertheless, the end result of five years of stalemated warfare was the creation of a state whose existence, guaranteed by Argentina and Brazil, has contributed greatly to the avoidance of major conflict between the largest nations in South America.[8]

This case study is no doubt taught in the schools in Uruguay. But it receives no mention in the main history books used in British schools.

❑ International law and the peaceful resolution of conflict

The international law of the peaceful settlement of disputes has moved quickly during this century. The first international legal effort to limit the right to resort to war was the Covenant of the League of Nations in 1919. This attempted to substitute arbitration for war as a means of settling international disputes, defined an international judicial body for the purpose of such arbitration, attempted to guarantee safety against aggression to members of the League, and provided for sanctions against any nation resorting to war in violation of the provisions of the Covenant.

The 1928 General Treaty for the Renunciation of War, also known as the Pact of Paris and the Kellogg-Briand Pact, went a step beyond the provisions of the Covenant to the absolute renunciation of war. The three articles of this agreement bind its signatories to 'condemn recourse to war for the solution of international controversies, and renounce it as an instrument of international policy in their relations with one another', to seek resolution of disputes among themselves by peaceful means, and to keep the treaty open for additional signatories 'as long as may be necessary for adherence by all the other powers of the world'.

This did not stop the use of force in self-defence. The League's Covenant expired at the end of World War II (when the UN was created). But the Pact of Paris (which was drawn up outside the aegis of the League) remains in force. For example, Australia used it against France in 1974 at the International Court of Justice, when it complained about French nuclear testing in the atmosphere.

The UN's contribution has been continued progress in further limiting the use — or, even now, the threat of the use — of force in international relations. Article 2(4) reads: 'All members shall refrain in their international relations from the threat or use of force against the territorial integrity or political independence of any state, or in any other manner inconsistent with the purpose of the United Nations.' The world has travelled a long distance, in international law terms, since a century ago. As Louis Henkin has observed:

> Unlike the limited restraints in the Covenant of the League and the provisions of the Kellogg-Briand Pact, the Charter's prohibition on unilateral forces was to apply universally: members were bound by it; they were to see to it that non-members also complied. For the first time, nations tried to bring within the realm of law those ultimate political tensions and interests that had long been deemed beyond control by law. They determined that even sincere concern for national 'security' or 'vital interests' should no longer warrant any nation to initiate war.
>
> They agreed, in effect, to forgo the use of external force to change the political status quo. Nations would be assured their fundamental independence, the enjoyment of their territory, their freedom — a kind of right to be let alone. With it, of course, came the corresponding obligation to let others alone, not to use force to resolve disputes, or even to vindicate one's 'rights'. Change — other than internal change through internal forces — would have to be achieved peacefully, by agreement. Henceforth there would be order, and international society could concentrate on meeting better the needs of justice and welfare.[9]

Despite Article 2(4) — one of the most important provisions — there has not been the international peace envisaged by the authors of the UN Charter. Peace cannot be maintained only by forbidding the use of force. There have to be mechanisms for peaceful change. The UN's economic and social work constitute part of those mechanisms. Another part consists of the UN's work for the peaceful settlement of disputes.

The UN Charter's third contribution is based on the Charter's Article 2(3): 'All members shall settle their international disputes by peaceful means in such a manner that international peace and security, and justice, are not endangered.' This immediately precedes the legal regulation of the use of force or threat of use of force (Article 2(4)) and so the provisions constitute two sides of a coin.

Moreover, Article 2(3) is concerned not only with international law and order, but also with the need to pay attention to international justice. It relates to peace with justice and not merely to peace at any price.

F.H. Hinsley has compared this evolution in the Charter with the corresponding developments in the thinking of nation-states:

> No state now has a War Office, but all retain the department and call it the Ministry of Defence. No state now declares war when it uses force in contravention of its pledge; if a state cannot plead self-defence or UN instructions for declaring war, it either resorts to force without admitting that it is doing so or finds some other justification by claiming that it is helping a legitimate government against rebellion or helping rebels to advance an indubitably moral cause. But I believe these subterfuges confirm rather than weaken the argument that in 1945 the states achieved a great advance. They are subterfuges to which states descend in order to remain within the letter of a new rule of international law; and you do not make efforts to appear to obey a rule which you do not accept. . .
>
> When a shift is so fundamental we may be sure of two things. It will have been a long time in preparation. And once it has been made, and if it is consolidated, it will have multiple and far-reaching repercussions.[10]

❑ Forms of peaceful settlement

The main forms of peaceful settlement are as follows:

1. *Good offices, mediation and conciliation*

Good offices, mediation and conciliation techniques, which make use of third parties not directly concerned in the dispute, are intended primarily to compose differences. Intervention by a third party, even if not in the form of a court or arbitral tribunal, usually compels the disputing parties, in order to appeal to the third party, to phrase their demands in terms of rules that could be applied universally to all similar cases.

Good offices, mediation and conciliation are variant forms of a common technique. Technically, good offices are restricted to interceding with the parties to get them to use diplomacy to settle their quarrel; mediation occurs when the mediator aids in the discussion of the substantive issues; and conciliation occurs when the conciliator proposes for the consideration of the parties either the rules that ought to govern the settlement or the actual terms of the settlement.

Despite the seeming distinctions, the lines between good offices, mediation and conciliation are rather difficult to draw. The use of good offices may founder if they are completely unresponsive to the substantive issues that led to the quarrel or if they are unable to achieve agreement on universal rules of justice, for the willingness of the parties to accede to the services of those performing the good offices role depends in part upon the relationship of negotiation to an acceptable settlement of the substantive issues.

2. *International arbitration and international courts*

International arbitration and judicial settlement are virtually identical procedures. In neither procedure may the judge or arbitrator decide the case with a view primarily to the accommodation or compromise of the conflicting interests, although decisions that fail to take such conflicts of interest into account are unlikely to prove effective. In each case, the settlement must be made according to rules that could be applied with equal validity to all other cases involving the same issues of law and of fact.

There is an important difference, however. In arbitration, the arbitration agreement (or special submission to an international court) may specify the issues to be decided and the facts to be taken into account. The contending parties may, if they wish, instruct the tribunal to accept an interpretation of the law to which the parties agree or a special rule to be applied to the particular case. For these reasons, the norm-creating power of the decision is somewhat limited.

To conclude, the peaceful settlement of international disputes has come a long way during the past century or so. The failures of the League, the Pact of Paris and the UN to stop entirely the use of war as an instrument of national policy is not a tale of woe. It is a tale of persistence. What is significant is the way in which people and organisations have maintained their reforming zeal, despite the widespread use of war. They have made valiant efforts — and yet been neglected by the history books.

The 1990/1991 crisis and conflict over the Gulf is a recent reminder of the futility of war. The international community needs to replace the present *ad hoc* system of maintaining international peace and security with a better system for the management of crises and for making international law enforceable. Some hope arises in the way in which the emerging economic giant, Japan, has renounced war as an instrument of national policy.

FUTURE POSSIBLE CAUSES OF WARFARE

'Only the dead have seen the end of war,' according to the Greek philosophers. Over 2 000 years later, war is still a common feature of national and international politics.

But, as this chapter has shown, there are changes to warfare underway. In the future there will be less conventional warfare and increases in guerilla warfare, international economic pressure and conflict resolution.

This chapter ends with two warnings about future causes of warfare: the North/South divide and religion (especially fundamentalist Islam).

❏ The first possible cause: The glass curtain

The Cold War is over. One of its most tangible monuments was the Berlin Wall, erected in 1961 to keep the East Germans from fleeing into West Berlin and West Germany. Chunks of the Wall are now sold as tourist souvenirs.

But I believe that a glass curtain is now being erected — this time by the Western nations.

The iron curtain arose out of the East-West confrontation. The glass curtain is arising out of the North/South division. The 'North' are the developed nations, all but two of which — Australia and New Zealand — are in the northern hemisphere. The 'South' are the vast majority of the rest of the world, most of whom are in the southern hemisphere.

The glass curtain is being erected by northern nations to keep out the people from the southern nations. The curtain is made of glass in that it permits (via television and tourism) southern people to see the northern lifestyles.

Evidence of the existence of the glass curtain may be seen in four ways:

1. *Many refugees leave their countries now for economic and environmental reasons.*

The usual view of a refugee is a person having to flee a nation owing to a well-founded fear of being persecuted for reasons of race, religion, nationality or political opinion. The standard example comes from the Jews fleeing Nazi Germany.

But an increasing number of refugees are on the move not so much to flee persecution, but to obtain a better standard of living. Many boat people from Indo-China, for example, are not now fleeing because the regimes are punishing people for their political views. They are trying to penetrate the glass curtain to have a better lifestyle in, for example, Hong Kong and Australia. These are economic refugees.

There are also environmental refugees: people fleeing their land owing to degradation of the local environment. This is most common in Africa, especially with the spreading Sahara. As people are driven off their own land, they move onto the adjoining land of other people. The increased population may exceed the local environment's carrying capacity and so there may have to be yet another move of the population.

2. *Immigration laws are being tightened up in Western Europe.*

Throughout the Cold War, the US and Western European nations called on Moscow to permit East Europeans the freedom to travel to the West. The end of the Cold War has meant that Eastern Europeans are now free to leave — but Western European nations have, since November 1989, been making migration westwards far more difficult.

Not only are the restrictions themselves becoming tougher, but new regulations have reduced the amount of time refugee claimants may receive social welfare benefits while their claim for refugee status is being assessed.

3. *There has been an increase in racism in Western Europe.*
This is manifested by the growth of far-right political parties. There
has also been an increase in assaults against foreigners. Mainstream
political parties, which publicly oppose overt racism, have nonetheless
responded by advocating tighter immigration laws.

4. *The end of the Cold War means a likely reduction in*
   foreign aid to the South nations.
Instead of benefiting from the peace dividend, these nations may become even worse off.

International development aid was often directed according to the
higher politics of Cold War strategy. A nation might receive aid from
the US because its leadership was anti-Soviet and the US thought it
would be useful to support that regime. Similarly, Cuba received
Soviet foreign aid precisely because it was an anti-US nation in the
Americas.

The USSR is no longer around to supply foreign aid. The US no
longer feels so obliged to provide aid to Third World nations. Additionally, some Western aid is now being siphoned off to help Eastern
Europe. The South is not benefiting from the end of the Cold War.

The late William Clark issued a warning in 1984 about South
backlash, well before the Cold War began to decline. His novel
Cataclysm: The North-South Conflict of 1987[11] talked of a future crisis
over South debt.

The US is, of course, the largest debtor nation — not only in the
world, but also in history. But it is assumed that eventually the US
will be able to repay its debts. The South debt crisis is of a different
nature.

In 1973, the Arab members of the Organisation of Petroleum
Exporting Countries (OPEC) increased dramatically the cost of oil.
They then had a flood of 'petro-dollars' as a result of the higher prices

and these had to be 'recycled' through the global financial system. Private Western banks offered to help the OPEC nations by lending the money to other nations — for a suitable fee, of course.

Some of the money went to Third World nations on the assumption that individuals may go broke, but a nation itself cannot. The banks were irresponsible in how they lent the money; some of it never reached the South, but went back into other banks as deposits by corrupt rulers. The Philippines, for example, is still trying to work out where some of the money lent to it during the Marcos regime actually went.

Additionally, the borrowers are complaining of the unjust terms of borrowing money; more money is being repaid to the North as interest on the debts than the North is supplying the South as foreign aid. In war, arms merchants do well; in peace, the bankers do well.

In 1982, Mexico defaulted on its US$100 billion debt. By the end of that year another nineteen had suspended their debt repayments. In 1983, the number rose to thirty. The debts were not only unrepayable — they were also uncollectable.

It was against this backdrop that Clark (a former employee of the British government and then the World Bank) decided to issue a warning about the debt crisis.

His 'cataclysm' took place in 1987. The North, led by the US, UK and West Germany, was to react to the South's attempt to get easier debt terms by expelling the South from the global banking system. This was to unite the middle income nations of South America with the nations of the Caribbean, Central America and Africa which wanted to pull out of the system anyway. Asia, led by Japan, was to stay in the system.

The novel moves at a cracking pace. There is no 'happy ending' as such — although the Australian foreign minister is able to put together a compromise to bring the nations to the negotiating table. Clark died, unfortunately, before he could write the sequel.

The novel has three points of interest for this book. First, Clark argued that there is only one earth and the combined pressures of population and poverty in the South are destroying the ecology of the whole planet, thereby imperilling both North and South. The North cannot claim that it is the South's end of the boat which is sinking. There is speculation of nuclear terrorism by the South in cities of the North. Nuclear devices do not recognise national boundaries.

Second, there is the recognition that the South is not some far-off nation — it is in the midst of the North. The South lives in the North's ghettoes. They are black and illegal migrants from Central America and the Caribbean. The US rebellions by these trigger a backlash from the extreme right-wing organisations like the Ku Klux Klan.

1 000 people are killed in an urban guerilla battle in Chicago. The frontline now runs through the US cities. Perhaps shades of this could be seen in the Los Angeles riots in May 1992.

The UK is seen in the novel to have similar problems. The blacks and poor Asians in the inner cities side with the South. Sympathisers infiltrate the computer systems and disrupt them, for example, causing chaos at the airports, London Underground and to credit card systems. In Germany, the South is represented by Turkish 'guest workers' who do the low-paid menial work. In France, the problems come from Algerian workers, who also do the low-paid menial work. The dilemma for the North is that if they try to expel the South (a difficult enough task), who will do the menial work? Black immigrants are the South's 'overseas army' — the North feels insecure with them around, but hesitates to expel them.

Third, the novel sees the South as being helped by the latest means of persuasion.

As the US President broadcasts his first message to the nation on the crisis, it is interrupted by an employee loyal to the South with a message of loyalty to the South. The South is able to use the North's television to broadcast directly into homes of the North the plight of the South. The South, following the example of Ayatollah Khomeini living in exile and communicating with his supporters in Iran by audio cassettes, produces its cassettes for use in the North. The South also uses communication satellites to beam television programs directly into North homes.

Eventually, the entire globe slips into chaos. Computer and banking systems are disrupted; the international stock exchange system collapses; exotic South diseases appear in the North; the North tires of the struggle. Australia then proposes a world conference to bring the world back together.

Clark wrote the novel as Lars Svenson, a Swedish academic researching UN history. Svenson begins the novel as though it is August 1988 and he looks back, in the Foreword, to the 1987 conflict. He says that there is ' . . .no conspiracy, only ignorance in the face of abundant information'. Looking to the forthcoming World Conference on Restructuring, Svenson says that 'to prevent conflict information is not enough; understanding is also required'.

The novel ends with an Asian UN Secretary-General saying as he prepares for that conference:

> We have a very short time in which to match consumption with resources; but we cannot succeed unless the urge to acquire is matched by the desire to share, unless the prickly sense of sovereignty is overcome by the neighbourly feeling of community. If we fail it will not need a nuclear war to make the world a desert.

Clark's death has meant we will not find out his specific ideas on how to solve the debt crisis. But at least he issued a clear warning.

❑ The second possible cause: Islamic fundamentalism

The 1990/91 Gulf crisis was seen, in popular terms, as a clash between the Christian West and the Islamic East. US journalist Paul Sheehan commented on the brisk business done by Christian fundamentalists:

> Millions of [fundamentalist] Christians have seen the Gulf war as the possible beginning of the tribulations of the Rapture, the final conflagration between good and evil whose only survivors will be true Christians.
>
> Since the Gulf crisis began last August, more than a million books and religious videotapes about Armageddon and the second coming of Christ have been sold in the US. The most successful book has been *Armageddon, Oil and the Middle East Crisis*, by fundamentalist John Walvoord, but other titles, including *The Last Days Handbook*, *The Rise of Babylon* and *The Coming Antichrist*, have sold briskly.[12]

Ironically, President Hussein's devotion to Islam was flimsy. His real appeal was based on Arab nationalism and encouraging resentment among the vast majority of poor Arabs against the elite lifestyle of the Kuwaitis.

The US and its allies were the real supporters of Islamic fundamentalism: Saudi Arabia has strict prohibitions on all forms of Christian observance. During Operation Desert Shield, foreign troops were forbidden to practise Christianity. Posters advertising religious services read 'Mental Gymnastics — Sunday 8:30 am' and military chaplains, who were not allowed to wear religious insignia, were officially listed as 'welfare counsellors'. All Christmas observances in December 1990 were prohibited — even Christmas trees. By contrast, freedom of Christian worship is permitted in Iraq and Libya.

The crisis engendered various speculations about the Cold War between capitalism and communism being replaced by a fresh struggle between Islam and Christianity. It is too early to assess whether the Islamic/Christian struggle will, in fact, reach the intensity of the Cold War — let alone the violence between both faiths some centuries ago. However, there is certainly an Islamic revival underway.

Relations between Islam and the West have gone through three phases.

The first phase covered the period from AD 622 (the year of Prophet Mohammed's flight from Mecca to Medina and the beginning of the Islamic Era) to 1683 (when the last Muslim invasion of Europe was stopped at Vienna). There was an ebb and flow between the world's two main religions, as American historian Bernard Lewis points out:

> Like every other civilisation known to human history, the Muslim world in its heyday saw itself as the centre of truth and enlightenment, surrounded by infidel barbarians whom it would in due course enlighten and civilise. But between the different groups of barbarians there was a crucial difference. The barbarians to the east and the south were polytheists and idolaters, offering no serious threat and no competition at all to Islam.
>
> In the north and west, in contrast, Muslims from an early date recognised a genuine rival — a competing world religion, a distinctive civilisation inspired by that religion and an empire that, though much smaller than theirs, was no less ambitious in its claims and aspirations. This was the entity known to itself and others as Christendom, a term that was long almost identical with Europe.
>
> The struggle between these rival systems has now lasted for some fourteen centuries. It began with the advent of Islam, in the seventh century, and has continued virtually to the present day. It

has consisted of a long series of attacks and counterattacks, jihads and crusades, conquests and reconquests. For the first thousand years Islam was advancing, Christendom in retreat and under threat. The new faith conquered the old Christian lands of the Levant and North Africa, and invaded Europe, ruling for a while in Sicily, Spain, Portugal and even parts of France. The attempt by the Crusaders to recover the lost lands of Christendom in the east was held and thrown back, and even the Muslims' loss of south-western Europe to the Reconquista was amply compensated by the Islamic advance into southeastern Europe, which twice reached as far as Vienna.[13]

The second phase, which ran between 1683 and about 1945, saw the conquest of Islamic territory and its incorporation into European colonies. The West was able to exploit its Second Wave strength in technology and conventional warfare to achieve a domination over Islamic people it had failed to have during the previous centuries.

The present third phase has seen a resurgence of Islam. The alien domination has been thrown off — at least in the Middle East. Islam has about 950 million followers — about one-fifth of the world's population — and is the fastest growing religion in the world. Muslims make up the majority of the population in forty countries, with their greatest numbers concentrated in Asia and Africa. They constitute about twenty-three per cent of developing countries and sixty-eight per cent of them live in rural areas. Their fertility rates range from a low of 3.3 children per woman in Albania to more than 8 in North Yemen. The Muslim population could nearly double to 1.9 billion by the year 2020. Its main source of growth is via natural increase (the excess of births over deaths) rather than conversion.

About 300 million Muslims live under non-Muslim rule. Indeed, there are more Muslims in Asia and sub-Saharan Africa than in the

Middle East Arab nations where Islam began.

Muslims arrived in Australia centuries before European settlement — they were fishermen from Macassar (in present-day Indonesia) who lived among the Aborigines of Arnhem Land. Muslims in Australia have attracted little hostility from the non-Islamic population. Out of seventeen million people, there are about 210 000 Muslims (compared with 70 000 Jews). It is the nation's second largest religion — and growing at a fast rate.

The UK situation is not, however, so tranquil. The largest congregation in the Western world is at the Central London Mosque. According to a newspaper report, by the year 2005, practising Muslims will outnumber their Anglican counterparts.[14] There are already more Muslims than UK Methodists. Two new mosques are opened each week.

A focal point for the present deterioration in relations has been the *fatwa* — religious decree — issued by the Ayatollah Khomeini on 14 February 1989, calling for Muslims to execute Salman Rushdie because of his novel *The Satanic Verses*. In the *fatwa*'s first year, Penguin Books received 5 000 threatening letters and twenty-five bomb threats. Bookshops refused to stock it in the face of similar threats of violence. Rushdie spent his first year of the death threat living at fifty-six different residences. He remains in seclusion and under guard, virtually a prisoner to Islamic fundamentalism.

The Rushdie affair has three features of interest to the Third Wave. First, the affair is based on the revived strength of Islam: a similar *fatwa* issued, say, a century ago in a non-Muslim nation would have been ineffective. This is an attempt by Muslims to impose their own culture on a majority of people who are non-Islamic.

Second, there is the global dimension: a death sentence was imposed by a religious leader upon a person 4 000 kilometres away in a non-Islamic nation. The death sentence is now reaching beyond the grave — Khomeini died shortly after issuing the *fatwa* and his successors have not wanted to revoke it. Even further away — in Pakistan — six Muslims were shot dead in connection with *The Satanic Verses* even before the *fatwa* was issued. There was a demonstration which police had to quell in Islamabad, where the book was not available, four months before the *fatwa*. Others who have also been killed include the person who translated the book into Japanese and an imam in a Belgian mosque who criticised the *fatwa*.

Third, the responses encouraged by the *fatwa* have been of a Third Wave type: small-scale threats of violence and the threat of Muslim nations to stop the sale of all Penguin publications in their territories.

A far bigger change is underway in the former USSR. The fifty-five million Muslims constitute the fifth largest group of Muslims (after Indonesia, Pakistan, Bangladesh and India). With zero population growth in the European part of the former USSR, the Muslim population by the year 2000 would have represented about a quarter of the total Soviet population because of the rapid population growth.

With the end of the USSR, its central Asian republics — Tajikistan, Turkmenistan, Uzbekistan, Kazakhstan and Kyrgyzstan — are now having to get used to independence. These straddled the great Silk Road (which ran from Lisbon to Peking) and are now having to become again accustomed to dealing directly with other nations, rather than working through Moscow.

In 1917, the USSR had 26 000 mosques. By 1987, the figure was only 1 400. During World War II, Stalin forcibly deported to Siberia entire populations of Muslims who were suspected of disloyalty. No Arabic was taught by the mosques, few Muslims could read the language of the Koran, and no translation of the Koran was available in the modern script of any Soviet nationality.

But Islam survived. More recently it was helped by technology: Soviet Muslims listened to broadcasts from Iran, Pakistan and Saudi

Arabia for religious instruction. Throughout all this bleak period, the concentration and growth of Islam within the five republics enabled them to maintain a local identity, rather than become 'Russified'. It gave the Soviet Muslims a strange sense of security — ultimately vindicated — based on the belief that the future belonged to Islam rather than communism.

Islam is the only faith to have successfully taken on the two superpowers. The US was a consistent supporter of the Shah of Iran, but he was overthrown by Khomeini. Khomeini then took on the US by, for example, supporting the taking of US hostages in Teheran. The US used force to rescue them — and failed.

Immediately to the east around this time, the USSR also misunderstood the extent of Islamic warrior strength. It invaded Afghanistan, secure in the belief that modern conventional weapons could beat a guerilla force. It soon learned otherwise. It also found that the soldiers drawn from the Central Asian republics could not be relied on to kill their Muslim brothers and sisters in Afghanistan. Consequently, the regiments had to come from the European part of the USSR — and for these soldiers Afghanistan was as alien as Vietnam was to US soldiers. And with the same result.

Finally, Islam is making itself felt in the political life of many other nations. In Indonesia, the province of Aceh has an Islamic secessionist movement wanting independence. A similar one is underway in the southern Philippines. In Pakistan, Malaysia and Algeria, Islamic political parties have all drawn wide support.

But it is necessary not to overstate the Islamic situation. Khomeini's rhetoric should not be mistaken for reality.

First, we should learn from the error of the Cold War's merchants of fear. They talked of one monolithic communist bloc running from Berlin to Peking. The merchants of fear were slow to recognise the split in the late 1950s/early 1960s between the USSR and China, and they consistently underestimated the internal forces opposing communism within the bloc.

In a similar way, Islam itself contains divisions. There is not an 'Islamic mind' and there is no more one Islam than there is one Christianity. Indeed, Muslims are often fragmented (especially in non-Islamic nations like Australia and the UK) by being located in separate ethnic enclaves, each with its own imam and its own place of worship.

Second, one factor which helped erode communism will also create problems for Islam: Western materialism and technology. Communications technology helped the Islamic revival in the central Asian republics (via radio broadcasts from outside) and Khomeini (whose supporters distributed cassette tape recordings of his messages, made while he was still in exile in Paris, to his underground supporters in Iran). But that same technology carries the seductive messages of consumerism and the way in which problems can be solved by spending money. Khomeini's fundamentalism was a direct assault on Western materialism. Like any campaign, it made great progress initially. But I remain doubtful if that crusading fervour can continue indefinitely. *Dallas* and *Dynasty*, Coke and McDonald's may yet chalk up another convert to consumerism.

Third, it is necessary to note the secular political agenda which runs under the Islamic veneer. The Middle East's Islamic revival is based on Arab nationalism; this has little relevance to (say) Indonesia. The Islamic banner can become an important rallying call in opposition to current values. It remains to be seen if authoritarian, Koran-based regimes can themselves last.

Even Khomeini's *fatwa* against Rushdie may be viewed as a political gesture. Robin Wright has argued[15] that Khomeini's revolution began to run out of steam by the end of the 1980s, as people became tired of the Iran-Iraq conflict. The *fatwa* was not issued until the book was already controversial. He jumped on the bandwagon, capitalising upon Sunni annoyance (he was a Shi'ite leader) as a demonstration that he represented all Muslims. It was an astute political move. It boosted his standing, diverted the attention of his citizens away from Iran's economic and social problems and revived his international profile. He died before he had to confront a fresh demand that he address Iran's domestic problems. As with communism, Islamic slogans may be more useful in protests than as a basis of public administration.

But Muslims have no monopoly over violence, as Northern Ireland and Sri Lanka demonstrate. As Bernard Lewis has argued, there is a need generally for less religious fundamentalism and a greater effort being made for religious understanding:

> The movement nowadays called fundamentalism is not the only Islamic tradition. There are others, more tolerant, more open, that helped to inspire the great achievements of Islamic civilisation in the past, and we may hope that these other traditions will in time prevail. But before this issue is decided there will be a hard struggle in which we of the West can do little or nothing. Even the attempt might do harm, for these are issues that Muslims must decide among themselves. And in the meantime we must take great care on all sides to avoid the danger of a new era of religious wars, arising from the exacerbation of differences and the revival of ancient prejudices.
>
> To this end we must strive to achieve a better appreciation of other religious and political cultures, through the study of their history, their literature and their achievements. At the same time, we may hope that they will try to achieve a better understanding of ours, and especially that they will understand and respect, even if they do not choose to adopt for themselves, our Western

perception of the proper relationship between religion and politics.[16]

The world is not doomed to conflict over the glass curtain or Islamic fundamentalism. But handling those two challenges will require imagination and conflict resolution — and a fresh way of looking at the globe.

Endnotes:

1. Edward A. Feigenbaum and Pamela McCorduck, *The Fifth Generation: Artificial Intelligence and Japan's Computer Challenge to the World*, Pan, 1983, p.135
2. *Ibid*, p.266
3. Ground Zero, *Nuclear War: What's in it For You?*, Pocket Books, 1982, p.158
4. Roger Fisher, 'Preventing Nuclear War', in *The Final Epidemic: Physicians and Scientists on Nuclear War*, Ruth Adams and Susan Cullen (eds), Educational Foundation for Nuclear Science, 1981, pp.227–228
5. For further on this, see Keith Suter, *Alternative to War: Conflict Resolution and the Peaceful Settlement of International Disputes*, Women's International League for Peace and Freedom, 1986.
6. Leon Edel, *Henry James: A Life*, Collins, 1987, pp.448–449
7. For further on this, see Keith Suter, *Ministry for Peace*, United Nations Association of Australia, 1984.
8. This case study is taken from Ben Brown, 'Uruguay: A Negotiated Resolution of Conflict', in *The Elements of a Network to Educate for World Security* (information kit), World Policy Institute, 1981.
9. Louis Henkin, *How Nations Behave: Law and Foreign Policy*, Columbia University Press, 1979, p.137
10. F.H. Hinsley, *The Fall and Rise of the Modern International System*, Australian National University, 1981, pp.17–18
11. William Clark, *Cataclysm: The North-South Conflict of 1987*, Sphere, 1984
12. Paul Sheehan, 'US Rage', *The Independent Monthly* (Melbourne), March 1991, p.12
13. Bernard Lewis, 'The Roots of Muslim Rage', *The Atlantic Monthly* (Boston), September 1990, p.49
14. 'UK Takes Stock of Muslim Power', *The Australian Financial Review*, 1 August 1989
15. Robin Wright, *In the Name of God: The Khomeini Decade*, Simon & Schuster, 1991
16. Bernard Lewis, *ibid*, p.60

PART D:

The new global agenda

10

GLOBAL CHANGE

How is the journey into the future shaping up?

WILLIAM BLAKE, THE ENGLISH POET AND PAINTER, spanned the UK's change from the First Wave to the Second Wave — he was born in 1757 and died in 1827. The UK led the world into the Industrial Revolution and Blake was there to see it happen.

In his biography of Blake, James King writes:

> As an apprentice, Blake witnessed the onslaught of the new industrial ethic which was sweeping England. Richard Arkwright's 'Waterframe' spinning machine was put into operation in 1769, and Arkwright inaugurated his first factory at Cromford, Derbyshire two years later. Josiah Wedgwood started 'Etruria', his new pottery works, in 1769.[1]

Blake saw the rise of a very different British society. Historian John Beer writes of it:

The growth of industry, the spread of commerce and the establishment of a great empire abroad had produced an unprecedented increase in wealth. [Blake's] indignation, vividly expressed, was directed partly against the dark side of that civilisation: the ignorance, disease and poverty which a society founded on individual enterprise allowed to flourish unchecked.[2]

In 'Jerusalem', for example, he talked of the 'dark Satanic mills', which were built in England. He could feel that England was undergoing a major change, but he had no way of predicting accurately just what form the change would take.

We are in a similar position today. We are living on the hinge of history: the Third Wave is replacing the Second Wave. Like Blake, we can feel the change, but cannot predict accurately how it will evolve.

This book has tried to help people make sense of all the changes now underway. It has identified major trends, but it cannot predict how those trends will work themselves out.

Additionally, it is not a 'to do' book, with a list of specific steps to be carried out. It is focussed more on what I believe is happening, rather than what I would prefer to happen.

Consequently, I do not conclude with a list of proposals on what ought to be done. The range of issues dealt with is so broad that such an action program would in itself constitute a new book.

Instead, this final chapter is concerned with two matters. First, recapping the main themes of the changes now sweeping the world; and second, listing some Christian principles which I believe will be of assistance to individuals thinking about how to respond to all these changes.

THE MAIN CHANGES SWEEPING OUR WORLD

In order to exercise some influence over the world around us, we need to understand the way it is changing. These changes can be placed under three themes: the speed of change, the fragmentation of power and the interdependence of peoples.

❏ The first theme: the speed of change

This book has been about change and so it is unnecessary to labour the point that change is occurring at speed. Two quotations will suffice. The first, from journalist Salah Mandil:

> If the aircraft industry had evolved as spectacularly as the computer industry over the past twenty-five years, a Boeing 767 today would cost US$500 and could circle the globe in twenty minutes on twenty litres of fuel.[3]

The second is from social commentator Adam Osborne:

> One hundred years ago the stagecoach was the principal mode of overland transportation. It moved at approximately twenty-five miles per hour and carried perhaps five passengers. We have come a long way in the last hundred years. Today the Concorde supersonic airliner is the most advanced vehicle of transportation available. It travels at 1 300 miles per hour, which is approximately fifty times as fast as the stagecoach. Concorde carries two hundred passengers, which is forty times the capacity of a stagecoach.
>
> If Concorde has forty times the capacity of a stagecoach and fifty times its speed, then in electronic terms Concorde and the stagecoach are about the same, because in far less time electronics logic capacity has increased by a factor of one hundred thousand, and logic speed of operation has increased by a factor of one

million. If Concorde could carry half a million passengers at twenty million miles per hour, it would then equal the rate at which microelectronics has advanced in the same time frame. And a ticket for a Concorde flight would have to cost less than a penny if it were to compare with the rate at which microelectronics has gotten cheaper.[4]

But the change in computer technology is not necessarily illustrative of the total change around the world. In other words, life is even more complicated because the change is uneven: there is great change in some matters and much less elsewhere.

Communications technology has made the world smaller, but not necessarily closer. People in the North now know that fellow human beings are starving in the South, but they still prefer to provide more money to pets than to foreign aid. This is the point made in this extract from an article entitled 'The Affluent Cat':

How does the life of a Third World citizen stack up against the life of an average British cat? Not well, reports Worldwire. According to Lloyd Timberlake in his book, *Only One Earth*, 'the average British cat eats twice as much animal protein every day as the average African citizen, and a third more than the average [person living in the third World]'.

Further, the estimated cost of maintaining a British cat is $260 per year — a figure that is 'more than the average annual income of the one billion people who live in the world's fifteen poorest nations'.[5]

Similarly, a message can be sent around the world at the speed of light, but it can take years for it to go from the outside of a person's head to the inside.

We can put a man on the moon and take close-up photographs of Venus, but we cannot walk safely on the streets at night — or even during the day. The US created a nuclear missile to fly 4 000 missiles around the world and to land on the Kremlin, but US police are ineffective in protecting American lives and property from criminals, amply demonstrated in the May 1992 riots in Los Angeles.

Finally, here is a piece of nostalgia. It reads initially as though it came from the 1960s and 1970s — and yet, as the quotation proceeds, it is obviously based on an era a century earlier:

> 'Life was very simple when I was a young man,' Sir Henry said
> rather wistfully in old age. 'It was wonderful to be a young
> Liberal in the sixties and seventies. . . I never doubted that we
> were moving rapidly towards a new world in which the problems
> of war and social justice would be solved.' The First World War
> did little to dampen his enthusiasm. He conceived the idea that if
> only the Christian churches were to unite they could somehow
> harness the League of Nations to bring about a lasting peace. He
> travelled round the world to promote this rather nebulous cause,
> addressing meetings, broadcasting, preaching in churches.[6]

In short, the world seems to be decreasing in size and yet increasing in complexity. In some matters, there is great change — and yet in others, life goes on as usual. Human behaviour may change, but human nature does not.

❏ The second theme: the fragmentation of power

We are in an era of globalising power, but also fragmenting politics. The traditional nation-state is now having to share its power with international organisations, transnational corporations and non-governmental organisations. There is an end of hierarchy, with the nation-state at its apex. Now the power structure is more dispersed.

Many national governments preside over ethnically diverse nations. An ethnic minority may form the ruling elite (as in white-controlled South Africa) over a majority who may be ethnically different. This provides the temptation for that minority to run the nation for its own benefit only.

There is no easy way out of this dilemma. A world reorganised on ethnic lines would require nearly every national boundary to be redrawn. People presumably would need to be shifted to new locations so as not to disturb the ethnic balance. But would they want to leave a territory which they themselves regard as 'home'?

Additionally, there is the question of whether people are simply to be defined by their nationality. Nationality is a one-dimensional description of a human being. But it is a powerful one, because it is a dimension into which a person is born — unlike other features (such as employment) in which they make a decision.

The challenge, then, is to reconcile ethnic loyalties with the new global era. This cannot be done by force. The USSR tried to quell ethnic loyalties by mass murder and deportation — and yet still failed. Indeed, not only has the USSR itself now gone, but Russia itself could break up into the old medieval pattern of city-states.

This book has shown that nationalism itself is a recent invention. It comes from the Second Wave. First Wave communities had no sense of nationalism and only a hazy idea of ethnic loyalty — their world was the local tribe or village.

The challenge is to make the world safe for diversity — and to do this in a conflict resolving way. The Swiss example mentioned earlier is a good one in that it does not impose uniformity from the centre and, instead, allows a great deal of local decision-making. The globe is not moving towards one bland, uniform culture; not everyone will want to watch *Dallas* while eating a Big Mac and drinking Coke.

The new global era in all its diversity requires more attention to conflict resolution. The world's people, economy and environment cannot stand too many more armed conflicts. Alternative ways need to be developed to settle disputes; of turning 'them' into 'we'.

❑ **The third theme: the interdependence of peoples**
If the theme of fragmentation represents breakdown, then the third theme of interdependence represents breakthrough.

The mass media focus on the negative stories: conflict, scandal, suspicion and crime. People become accustomed to the breakdown side of life. Good news is not news. The breakthrough side of life is neglected. As people face common problems together, some progress can be made.

American lawyer Dietrich Fischer writes:

Six thousand years ago, the farmers in the Nile and Euphrates valleys faced a problem that they could not solve as individuals, the recurrence of floods and droughts. The construction of a dam to regulate the flow of water required the organised cooperation of thousands of individuals. This led to the formation of the first advanced civilisations in ancient Egypt and Sumer, with the emergence of written language, a flourishing of the arts and sciences, the codification of laws and organised government.

Today we are confronted with a range of problems that cannot be solved by even an entire nation, but only by the global community. It is time to build a global civilisation to deal with these common threats. The first pictures of the earth taken from outer space, showing a fragile floating sphere without any national boundaries, can help us understand that we must cooperate as one common species, or we may perish.[7]

There are three important ways in which there has been an increase in interdependence:

1. *The increasingly transnational character of many of our problems.*
Jessica Tuchman puts it this way:

> Put bluntly, our accepted definition of the limits of national sovereignty as coinciding with national borders is obsolete. The government of Bangladesh, no matter how hard it tries, cannot prevent tragic floods such as it suffered last year. Preventing them requires active cooperation from Nepal and India. The government of Canada cannot protect its water resources from acid rain without collaboration with the United States. Eighteen diverse nations share the heavily polluted Mediterranean Sea. Even the Caribbean Islands, as physically isolated as they are, find themselves affected by others' resource management policies as locusts, inadvertently bred through generations of exposure to pesticides and now strong enough to fly all the way from Africa, infest their shores.[8]

There is nothing new in environmental disasters. But what is novel is the level of interconnectedness in the world.

2. *The new transnational networks of cooperation that are emerging.*
For example, there is international cooperation enabling a person to make an air reservation to fly around the world on a mixture of international and national carriers. The passenger takes for granted the assortment of booking arrangements. But the ticketing represents an

intricate networking system by travel agent computers. Other matters that involve similar transnational networking complexities which are now taken for granted include disease control, weather forecasting, radio and television signals, and banking.

3. The difficulty in telling the difference between foreign policy and domestic policy.

Here are two examples of this. If US economic policy produces a depression in Mexico, then this will trigger a further flood of illegal immigration into the US. If Australia, as a nation of the North, is contributing to the greenhouse effect, Australia may feel obliged to acknowledge its partial responsibility for the Pacific Islanders' plight and face the issue of allowing them to settle in Australia, thus blurring the line between foreign and domestic policies.

*   *   *

The broad sweep of this book has, I hope, shown that there has been a clearly discernible pattern in the affairs of humanity from tribe to nation state to some form of new global order. People have come to lose some of their parochialism and to see themselves as part of a greater whole.

SOME CHRISTIAN PRINCIPLES IN RESPONSE TO GLOBAL CHANGES

We live in a global village, so the changes dealt with in this book affect all of us, whatever our viewpoint. How we respond to them is very much dependent on our undergirding viewpoint. Mine is Christian, so here I seek to bring to bear that viewpoint in responding to the new era. I am sure there will be points of contact with many readers in what I now say.

The principles that are important to me are the need to engage with the world, the need to share, the need to make peace with the planet, and the need to dream and to act.

1. *The need to engage with the world*
Humans are the only inhabitants on earth that have an awareness of history and an anticipation of the future. Animals know how to survive the changes in seasons, of course, but they have no concept of time as has been given to humans.

We need to be concerned about the future of the world because that is where we are going to be spending the rest of our lives.

There are three ways of handling the challenge of change:

(a) There is an enthusiastic acceptance of change. This applies particularly in science and technology, on the assumption that all change is for the better.

This can, of course, result in the heedless pursuit of new technology and the treating of it as a new idol. New machines become new gods of metal. We can then become blind to their disadvantages. The video recorder allows people to view television programs at convenient times — but also creates a new addiction among young people for the excitement of video games. Narrow casting on television (via satellites and cable) provides, in theory, greater choice — but may, in fact, provide less choice as people restrict their viewing to only one kind of program, such as sport. New technology can create a 'new poor', being those people who lack the money or skills to use the new technology to their advantage.

(b) There is an avoidance of change. Some humans cannot bear very much reality. The power of memory is strong. There is a longing for the past: 'We must get back to the time when. . .' Politicians during election campaigns talk of a golden era when there was little crime, everyone could read and write, the economy was flourishing for everyone's benefit, the nation was held in high respect abroad and children were seen but not heard.

Change cannot be ignored. It will not go away. We cannot postpone the future. We cannot stop time by smashing clocks.

(c) *There is the acknowledgement that change is underway and that it has to be scrutinised carefully.* This is my position as a Christian. As the Rev. Geoff Smith said at the UK 1988 Consultation organised by Church Action on Poverty and Christian Action:

> Christians have a responsibility to bring the truths and insights of scripture to bear on aspects of human living. This responsibility is given to us by God. It is part of our duty as stewards of the world's resources. We are required to exercise responsibility for our brothers and sisters, to be our brother's keeper. We are exhorted to love one another, to seek the common good. This is more than a concern with the individual; there is a social and corporate dimension to our responsibilities as stewards.
>
> We are ministers of a created order, groaning and travailing as it seeks to give birth to a new thing, a new kingdom, under the Lordship of Christ. Of course, this responsibility is denied by those who seek to limit Christian influence to the personal and individual, but there is no biblical support for their claim.[9]

2. *The need to share*

I believe each person is of equal dignity and worth in God's sight. Consequently, social systems should be focussed on the needs of the individual.

There is not one set Christian social system; the Bible is not that explicit. But whatever the system, I believe we are expected to look after our neighbours (Matthew 22, verses 36 to 40), particularly those that are hungry, poorly clothed, sick and imprisoned (Matthew 25, verses 31 to 46).

In 1980, at the beginning of yet another United Nations conference to help the South, South writer Varindra Tarzie Vittachi set out the moral arguments for the North to help the South:

> The greatest difficulty facing advocates of an equitable world order may be to answer the Northerners' most fundamental question: why should we give a damn? One approach is to try to make people look beyond the statistics to the individual; [compare] the words of Simone Weil, 'Nobody is of the opinion that a man is innocent if, possessing food himself in abundance and finding someone on his doorstep three parts dead from hunger, he brushes past without giving him anything.'
>
> The Amazonians had a similar answer. They told their children the story of a priest speaking with God about the difference between heaven and hell. 'I will show you hell,' said God. They went into a room where a delicious beef stew sat on a table surrounded by people looking desperately famished. They held spoons with long handles that reached into the pot, but which were too long to get the stew back into their mouths. Their suffering was terrible.
>
> 'Now I will show you heaven,' said God, and they went into a second room. There sat the same savoury stew and people with identical spoons and handles. But they were well-nourished and joyous. The priest was baffled until God explained: 'Quite simple. You see, these people have learned to feed each other.'
>
> It seems to me that there is only one answer to the question of why we should care about another person's hunger, illness or homelessness: we are all human. That has always been the answer and always will be.[10]

Jesus began his public ministry (in Luke's Gospel) by reading in the Nazareth Synagogue an extract from Isaiah:

The Spirit of the Lord is on me, because he has anointed me to
preach good news to the poor.

He has sent me to proclaim freedom for the prisoners
and recovery of sight for the blind,
to release the oppressed
to proclaim the year of the Lord's favour.

Luke 4, verses 18 and 19

The statement is significant for three reasons. First, Jesus told the
amazed congregation that 'today the scripture is fulfilled in your
hearing' (verse 21). Second, he identified himself with the priorities
of Old Testament prophets who had criticised what we would call the
'rich and famous' for their behaviour. Jesus by birth, statements,
temperament, practice and behaviour was clearly not, so to speak, a
graduate of the University of Israel.

Third, his message was one of good news to the people least able
to help him. A politician would have presented a softer message with
more appeal to the rich and would not have antagonised his local
constituents. Jesus was no calculating politician. The next part of the
passage is how the residents 'drove him out of the town' (verse 29).

If Jesus had a message of good news to the poor, why are
Christians often such bad news for the poor?

The Rev. Andrew Williams, a Uniting Church minister, has posed
these questions:

Since the God of the Bible is on the side of the poor, why are we
undisturbed by the fact that we are among the non-poor?

Since the God of the Bible cries out for justice, why are we
such complacent recipients of goods that are gotten unjustly?

Since the God of the Bible yearns for peace, why are we
untroubled by constant preparations for war?

Since the God of the Bible decries worship that is oblivious to the plight of the stranger 'outside the gate', why do we enter our sanctuaries oblivious to the human destruction outside those sanctuaries?

Since the God of the Bible wills that all be fed, how can we feel right knowing we consume a disproportionate amount of the world's resources?[11]

Rich countries of the North (such as Australia) are directly linked to the mounting environment and development crisis in the South through government policies on issues like aid, trade, debt, agriculture and energy, and through Western banks and companies. Instead of concentrating on producing more food and greater economic opportunities for their own people, nations are forced to over-exploit natural resources — forests, farmland, minerals and fisheries — in order to pay their huge debts.

This situation will not change until people demand political action to avert the crisis and set an agenda for a new type of development. The dismal overseas situation also can be seen at home. Writing at Christmas time in 1988, economics journalist David Clark said:

This Christmas, for every man, woman and child in the country, we will spend on average about A$480.

Yet we will donate to charities and voluntary agencies an average of only eighteen cents each — and this is the peak period for such donations.

As anyone who works for the Smith Family, the Salvation Army, St Vincent de Paul or other similar organisations will readily testify, it takes real courage to seek their assistance.

It takes no courage to send such organisations a Christmas cheque.[12]

As a Christian it concerns me that the gap between the North and the South has not been narrowed. It is a denial of the fundamental principle of sharing.

3. *The need to make peace with the planet*
Humankind increases its chances of lasting if it puts the environment first. Such a preoccupation would be in accordance with what I see the Bible as teaching.

Genesis contains two sets of instructions. Genesis 1, verses 27 to 28 states: 'So God created man in his own image, in the image of God, he created him; male and female he created them. God blessed them and said to them, "Be fruitful and increase in number; *fill the earth and subdue it*'" (emphasis added). But Genesis 2, verse 15 says, 'The Lord God took the man and put him in the Garden of Eden to work it and *take care of it*' (emphasis added). So the Bible sees us as both having power over the environment and as caring for it.

Humans have gone back and forth between these responsibilities to the environment — and with a consistent record of perverting those responsibilities and abusing it! The record has been bad from the outset. Humankind forges iron — and then uses it for murder (Genesis 4, verse 23). Humankind cultivates grapes — and then starts getting drunk (Genesis 9, verse 21).

The Rev. Robert Brown, Managing Director of a UK recycling company, has identified five stages of the relationship between humankind and nature:

In the first stage, primitive humanity saw nature as a magic force.
Every wind, rock, tree, river and forest could overwhelm
human beings who felt *they were within nature*, which was alive,
terrifying and full of awe. It was a period of timelessness.
Change was hardly possible.

The second stage came as a result of the growth of cities and the intense social life that developed in them. People *had* moved from the nomadic life into the cities — *apart from nature*— and they became more aware of the problems of society, justice, authority, organisation, work and individuality. The great prophets clarified the issues of moral responsibility before the higher realm of God. Apartness led to boundaries of the mind.

The third stage has come about in the past three hundred years or so. As a result of the confidence imparted by Christian culture, people in the Western world believed in a faithful creator of nature and that his word or reason was within it. As a result, humanity could practice science, exploring, dissecting, understanding and finally *dominating nature*. In this stage we are over nature with all our technological powers. Mastery has abolished mystery — and atheism seems a sensible option.

The fourth stage is a very contemporary one in which something quite negative is happening — *nature is striking back*. Forests die with acid rain, rivers and lakes die from pollution, rain clouds do not form, crops fail and millions starve, the ozone layer is punctured and we tremble at the consequences. At Sevesco, Chernobyl, Flixborough, Bhopal and Three Mile Island, our confidence is called into radical question. Dominant humanity hears doom-laden warnings.

The fifth stage must come — *humanity collaborating with nature*. To get to that stage is going to involve a very profound journey of change within human beings. It will require a death to the way we have hitherto understood ourselves and our relationship with nature.[13]

The concept of the common heritage of humankind — what I have elsewhere called 'the public heritage of humankind' in the case of Antarctica[14]— is an example of bringing together two key principles:

making peace with the planet and sharing. The seabed and outerspace are among the areas so far proclaimed as common heritage and so fulfilling these principles.

The common heritage concept, as it has been refined and elaborated over the past two decades, is now formulated as follows: common heritage resources cannot be owned; they require a system of management; they require active benefit-sharing (not only of financial profits, but of management and decision-making as well); they are reserved for peaceful uses only; and they must be preserved for posterity.

The theological foundations of the common heritage are found in the biblical doctrine of creation. In the biblical view of the natural world, the earth belongs to no individual, group or nation: creation is a gift to which no-one may lay claim. Our common creatureliness is, however, the basis of responsibilities with respect to the use and enjoyment of the physical world.

Our primary responsibility is to care for the lives of other human beings. Accordingly, no-one can claim resources if the exercise of that claim places the lives of others in jeopardy. All have equally received life as a gift. No-one has a warrant to diminish the lives of others or to enforce conditions which degrade them. Following this line of reasoning, the church has always maintained the goods of the earth must be used for the well-being of all before they may be used for the private benefit of any group.

The Christian moral tradition has had to recognise that we live in a world where gratitude for life, a sense of common creatureliness, equity and reverence for the created world are displaced more often than not by collective and private egoism, exploitative domination, inequity and violence. Accordingly, it has reasoned that the authority of governments rests on the need to curb such negative behaviour and promote the common good when private or individual actions disregard it.

The concept of common heritage is just beginning its career. It could be applied, for example, to information gathered by satellites, in fields such as earth resources, pollution and weather patterns and in environmental concerns such as forests, topsoil and the atmosphere. There is scope for Christian action in all these areas.

4. The need to dream and to act

Prophets, in biblical terms, warn and encourage rather than predict. They do not make precise predictions about the future, but call upon people to change their ways. They comfort the disturbed and disturb the comfortable.

A prophet's lot was not a happy one. Jeremiah, for example, was most reluctant to undertake the work and probably died by stoning. Even Jesus had a difficult start to his public ministry. Luke 4, verses 21 to 30 tells how he was rejected at Nazareth and was obliged to begin work again at Capernaum.

The late Richard Hauser of the London-based Institute for Social Research did research on a Responsibility Charter which would be a voluntary social contract in which a person assumes a responsibility towards others as a response to conscience and to others' needs. The responsibility is always voluntary (otherwise it is glorified duty) and taking on increasing burdens of responsibility is a way to grow socially. Unfortunately modern society, with the development of the welfare state (which has so many advantages), has inadvertently discouraged people from assuming responsibilities and instead has given them a reliance upon a paternalistic state.

The Charter challenges its signatories to:

1. respect and care for humanity and the basic dignity of every other person;
2. respect and care for the other living creatures which make up

our world;

3. be the link between those people in the past who have fought for us and the thousands of generations as yet unborn;

4. participate as a significant and effective member of one's own family, peer group, community and society as a leader or co-leader;

5. be fully aware of one's own capacities;

6. participate in creating neo-organic social structures at every level;

7. be aware of conditions throughout the world and to keep oneself constantly informed;

8. take part in humanising conflict at every level;

9. foster identification with others before identity;

10. develop to the full one's inner potential and resources to the cost of no-one or nothing else;

11. strive continually for positive growth in every sense.[15]

There is, then, much that I believe concerned Christians may do to work for justice, peace and the protection of the environment. It is necessary to avoid the frame of mind which tries to show that by being sceptical a person is being wise, and that by being pessimistic such a person is a source of great wisdom.

We are not going to be able to operate our Spaceship Earth successfully unless we see the earth as a whole and our fate as common. It has to be for everybody, or it will be for nobody. Moreover, there are no passengers on Spaceship Earth — everybody is a member of the crew.

There is much work to be done. 'It is not for you to finish the work,' said a rabbi of the second century, 'but neither are you free to desist from it.'[16] The rabbi was martyred by the Romans, but he spoke like a person who knew he would be succeeded by others who will continue to work.

The late Alan Paton, author of *Cry, the Beloved Country*, was invited by *Time* magazine to write an essay on South Africa today. He died just before completing the manuscript. Towards the end of the manuscript he praised a South African leader, J.H. Hofmeyr, who had a great skill in finding apt quotations:

> In 1939, when the threat of Hitler and a second world war hung over the world, [Hofmeyr] spoke to a meeting in Johannesburg on the dangerous times and quoted to them the words on a tablet in an old English church: 'In the year 1652, when throughout England all things sacred were either profaned or neglected, this church was built by Sir Robert Shirley, Bart., whose special praise it is to have done the best things in the worst times and to have hoped them in the most calamitous.'[17]

This is a task to which each generation must pledge itself. Global change is an inevitability; the question is what we do with it.

Endnotes:

1. James King, *William Blake: His Life*, Weidenfeld & Nicholson, 1991, p.27
2. John Beer, *Blake's Visionary Universe*, Manchester University Press, 1969, p.311
3. Salah Mandil, 'Health Informatics', *World Health* (Geneva), August/September 1989, p.2
4. Adam Osborne, *Running Wild: The Next Industrial Revolution*, McGraw–Hill, 1979, pp.162–163
5. 'The Affluent Cat', *World Development Forum* (Washington DC), 15 August 1987, p.1
6. Richard Ingrams, *God's Apology: A Chronicle of Three Friends*, Andre Deutsch, 1977, p.15
7. Dietrich Fischer, 'Peace Through Co-operation', *Peace Review* (Palo Alto, CA), Fall 1989, p.23
8. Jessica Tuchman Mathews, 'Redefining Security', *Foreign Affairs* (New York), Fall 1989, p.174
9. Geoff Smith, 'Fish Head Soup', *Poverty Network* (Manchester), Autumn 1988, p.16
10. Varindra Tarzie Vittachi, 'Is Altruism in Retreat?', *Newsweek*, 25 August 1980, p.36
11. Andrew Williams, 'The Larrikin God: Mission Strategy for the Uniting Church', *Trinity Occasional Papers* (Brisbane), December 1988, pp.48–49
12. David Clark, 'Help to the Needy is the Ultimate Yardstick for Judging a Nation', *Australian Financial Review*, 20 December 1988
13. Robert Brown, 'Resources and Religion', *The New Road*, Gland, April 1988, p.7
14. Keith Suter, *Antarctica: Private Property or Public Heritage?*, Zed, 1991
15. Richard Hauser, *The Last Chance and the Best*, Institute for Social Research, 1984, pp.11–12
16. Rabbi Tarfon, *Pirke Avot (Wisdom of the Fathers)*, II, 21
17. Alan Paton, 'A Literary Remembrance', *Time*, 25 April 1988, p.48

Index

Bold lettering *indicates an index heading with sub-headings;* bold numbering *indicates a major entry in the text.*

Bibliography

ADAMS, Stanley	*Roche versus Adams*, Jonathan Cape, 1984
AMBROSE, Stephen E.	*Eisenhower: The President*, George Allen & Unwin, 1984
ARCHER, Clive	*International Organisations*, George Allen & Unwin, 1983
BARNABY, Frank (ed.)	*The Gaia Peace Atlas: Survival into the Third Millennium*, Pan, 1988
BARNETT, Paul	*Apocalypse Now and Then: Reading Revelation Today*, Anglican Information Office, 1989
BROWN, Lester	*Building a Sustainable Society*, Norton, 1981
BRUCE, Steve	*The Rise and Fall of the New Christian Right: Conservative Protestant Politics in America, 1978–1988*, Oxford University Press, 1988
BRZEZINSKI, Zbigniew	*Power and Principle*, Weidenfeld and Nicholson, 1983
CALLAGHAN, James	*Time and Chance*, Collins, 1987
CHURCHILL, Winston S.	*If I Lived My Life Again*, Allen, 1974
CLARK, William	*Cataclysm: The North–South Conflict of 1987*, Sphere, 1984
COOMBS, H.C.	*Trial Balance*, Macmillan, 1981
COUSINS, Norman	*The Pathology of Power*, Norton, 1987
COUSTEAU, Jacques-Yves	*Attacking Power with Wisdom: The Need for Long-Term Thinking*, Nuclear Age Peace Foundation, 1990
CROSSMAN, Richard	*Inside View*, Jonathan Cape, 1972
CROUGH, Greg & WHEELWRIGHT, Ted	*Australia: A Client State*, Penguin, 1982

DICKER, Gordon S.	*Faith with Understanding*, Unichurch Publishing, 1981
DRUCKER, Peter F.	*The Age of Discontinuity*, Heinemann, 1969
EVANS, Harold	*Good Times, Bad Times*, Coronet, 1984
FEIGENBAUM Edward & McCORDUCK, Pamela	*The Fifth Generation: Artificial Intelligence and Japan's Computer Challenge to the World*, Pan, 1983
FUKUYAMA, Francis	*The End of History and the Last Man*, Hamish Hamilton, 1992
GALBRAITH, John Kenneth	*A Life in our Times*, Corgi, 1983
GALBRAITH, John Kenneth	*The Age of Uncertainty*, BBC, 1977
GALBRAITH, John Kenneth	*The Galbraith Reader*, Penguin, 1981
HAUSER, Richard	*The Last Chance and the Best*, Institute for Social Research, 1984
HAMMER, Armand	*Witness to History*, Simon and Schuster, 1987
HENKIN, Louis	*How Nations Behave: Law and Foreign Policy*, Columbia University Press, 1979
HERSH, Seymour	*The Price of Power — Henry Kissinger in the Nixon White House*, Faber, 1983
HINSLEY, F.A.	*The Fall and Rise of the Modern International System*, Australian National University, 1981
JAMES, Donald	*The Fall of the Russian Empire*, Granada, 1982
JAMES, Michael	*How Much Government?*, Centre for Independent Studies (Sydney), 1987
JONES, Barry	*Sleepers Awake! Technology and the Future of Work*, Oxford University Press, 1982
KAUFMAN, Gerald	*How to be a Minister*, Sidgwick & Jackson, 1980
KINSMAN, Francis	*The New Agenda: Business in Society*, Spencer Stuart Management Consultants, 1983
KRIESBERG, Louis	'Non-Governmental Organisations', in *Peace and the War Industry*, Kenneth Boulding (ed.), Transaction, 1970
KUMAR, Krishan	*Prophecy and Progress: The Sociology of Industrial and Post-Industrial Society*, Penguin, 1978
LEASOR, James	*War at the Top*, Michael Joseph, 1959
LEVINSON, Charles	*Vodka-Cola*, Gordon and Cremonesi, 1981
LINDSEY, Hal	*The 1980s: Countdown to Armageddon,*

	Bantam, 1980
LINDSEY, Hal	*The Late Great Planet Earth*, Bantam, 1970
LINDSEY, Hal	*The Road to Holocaust*, Bantam, 1989
LIVESY, Roy	*Understanding the New Age: Preparation for Antichrist's One World Government*, New Wine Press, 1986
MEADOWS, D. et al	*The Limits to Growth*, Universe, 1972
O'BRIEN, Conor Cruise	*The United Nations: Sacred Drama*, Hutchinson, 1968
OSBORNE, Adam	*Running Wild: The Next Industrial Revolution*, McGraw-Hill, 1979
PETERS, Charles	*How Washington Really Works*, Addison-Wesley, 1980
SAFIRE, William,	*Before the Fall: An Inside View of the Pre-Watergate White House*, Belmont Tower, 1975
SAMPSON, Anthony	*The Money Lenders: Bankers in a Dangerous World*, Hodder & Stoughton, 1982
SCHEER, Robert	*With Enough Shovels: Reagan, Bush and Nuclear War*, Random House, 1982
SCHOENBAUM, Thomas J.	*Waging Peace and War: Dean Rusk in the Truman, Kennedy and Johnson Years*, Simon & Schuster, 1988
SERVAN–SCHREIBER, Jean–Jacques	*The World Challenge*, Collins, 1981
SINE, Tom	*The Mustard Seed Conspiracy*, Word, 1981
SINGER, Andre	*Battle for the Planet*, Pan, 1987
SIVARD, Ruth Leger	*World Military and Social Expenditures 1987–1988*, World Priorities, 1987
STOCKMAN, David	*The Triumph of Politics*, Hodder & Stoughton, 1986
STOKES, Bruce	*Helping Ourselves: Local Solutions to Global Problems*, Norton, 1981
SUTER, Keith	*Ministry for Peace*, United Nations Association of Australia, 1984
SUTER, Keith	*Reshaping the Global Agenda: The United Nations at 40*, United Nations Association of Australia, 1986
THOMAS, George	*Mr Speaker*, Arrow, 1985
TOFFLER, Alvin	*Future Shock*, Random House, 1970

TOFFLER, Alvin	*The Third Wave*, Collins, 1980
TOFFLER, Alvin	*Powershift: Knowledge, Wealth and Violence at the Edge of the 21st Century*, Bantam, 1990
TUCHMAN, Barbara	*A Distant Mirror*, Macmillan, 1979
URQUHART, Brian	*A Life in Peace and War*, Weidenfeld and Nicholson, 1987
WALVOORD, John F. & WALVOORD, John E.	*Armageddon: Oil and the Middle East Crisis*, Zondervan, 1974
WASHINGTON, Haydn	*Ecosolutions: Environmental Solutions for the World and Australia*, Boobook Publications, 1991
WHEELWRIGHT, Ted	*Oil and World Politics*, Left Book Club, 1991
WILDAVSKY, Aaron & PRESSMAN, Jeffrey L.	*Implementation*, University of California Press, 1973
WOOTTON, Graham	*Pressure Groups in Britain 1720–1970*, Allen Lane, 1975
WORLD COMMISSION ON ENVIRONMENT AND DEVELOPMENT	*Our Common Future*, Oxford University Press, 1987
WRIGHT, J. Patrick	*On a Clear Day You Can See General Motors: John de Lorean's Look Inside the Automobile Giant*, Avon, 1979
WRIGHT, Robert	*In the Name of God: The Khomeini Decade*, Simon & Schuster, 1991

About the author:

Keith Suter is currently president of the Centre for Peace and Conflict Studies, University of Sydney, and executive director of the National Goals and Directions Movement, Sydney. Formerly, he was director of the Trinity Peace Research Institute, Perth, and general secretary for the Uniting Church in Australia's Commission on Social Responsibility.

A past national president of the United Nations Association of Australia, he is on the international executive committee of the World Federation of United Nations Associations, Geneva. Among other interests, he has been an international law consultant to Friends of the Earth (NSW), Australian convenor of the Minority Rights Group (London) and a key participant in the drafting of Australia's Antarctic policy. He is one of four Australians elected to the Club of Rome, which has 100 members worldwide.

Keith Suter was born in 1948 in England. He has two doctorates: one on the international law of guerilla warfare (University of Sydney, NSW); the other on the economics of the arms race (Deakin University, Victoria). He is the author of several books and numerous articles, and is in popular demand as a public speaker.